ISIS

ISIS

An Introduction and Guide to
the Islamic State

Brian L. Steed

ABC-CLIO™

An Imprint of ABC-CLIO, LLC
Santa Barbara, California • Denver, Colorado

16-17 Ing

Copyright © 2016 by ABC-CLIO, LLC

Library of Congress Cataloging-in-Publication Data

Names: Steed, Brian L., author.
Title: ISIS: an introduction and guide to the Islamic State / Brian L. Steed.
Description: Santa Barbara : ABC-CLIO, LLC, 2016. | Includes bibliographical references and index.
Identifiers: LCCN 2016005650 | ISBN 9781440849862 (hard copy : alk. paper) | ISBN 9781440849879 (ebook)
Subjects: LCSH: IS (Organization)
Classification: LCC HV6433.I722 I8576 2016 | DDC 363.325—dc23
LC record available at http://lccn.loc.gov/2016005650

ISBN: 978-1-4408-4986-2
EISBN: 978-1-4408-4987-9   16-17

20 19 18 17 16   2 3 4 5

This book is also available on the World Wide Web as an eBook.
Visit www.abc-clio.com for details.

ABC-CLIO
An Imprint of ABC-CLIO, LLC

ABC-CLIO, LLC
130 Cremona Drive, P.O. Box 1911
Santa Barbara, California 93116-1911

This book is printed on acid-free paper ∞

Manufactured in the United States of America

. . . It is for us the living, rather, to be dedicated here to the unfinished work which they who fought here have thus far so nobly advanced. It is rather for us to be here dedicated to the great task remaining before us—that from these honored dead we take increased devotion to that cause for which they gave the last full measure of devotion— that we here highly resolve that these dead shall not have died in vain . . .

Abraham Lincoln (Gettysburg Address, November 19, 1863)

To all those who taught me about the Middle East.

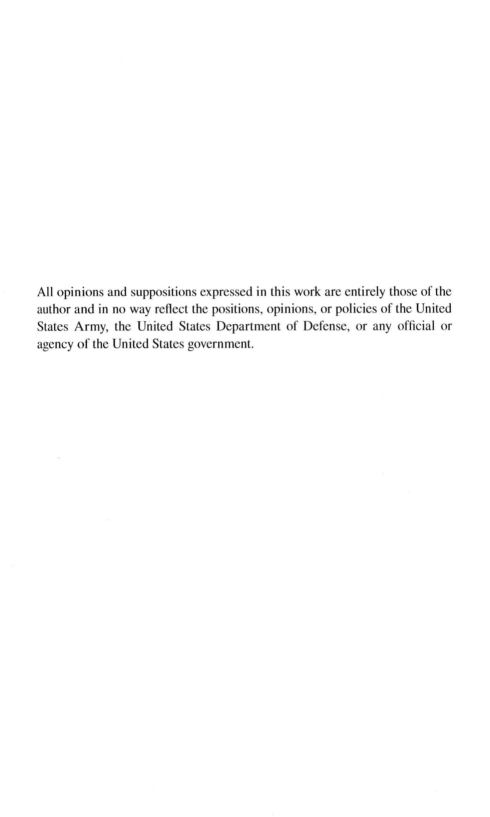

Contents

Preface

The Islamic State represents a generational fight and the most fascinating development in the Middle East to happen in the last 35 years. The reference here is to 1979, the single most significant year in the Middle East in centuries. This was the year that saw a successful Islamic Revolution in Iran—a U.S.-backed ruler was toppled and Islam became the foundation for a modern state, reversing a trend of secularization prevalent in the Middle East since the 1700s. A mob of Iranian students captured the U.S. embassy in Tehran and held embassy personnel hostage for 444 days. A rescue attempt was launched though it failed in a fiery accident in the desert outside the Iranian capital. Of course later in that same year, the Soviet Union entered Afghanistan with military force. Many claim this as an invasion, but the Soviets were invited in by elements of the ruling government in Kabul. These events were broadcast every night on the major network news shows. In the same year, a group of radical Muslims led by a man claiming to be the Mahdi (a Muslim religious leader—see entry on *Mahdi* later in this book) stormed the Grand Mosque in Mecca and held that facility against an armed response from the Saudi security forces for several days. I remember the first two events as I watched them on the television every night like some sort of dark reality television series. I did not understand the implication of the failed hostage rescue attempt, but I remember watching the images of burning helicopters in the desert outside Tehran. I cannot recall seeing or hearing anything about the mosque seizure. I had no understanding that 1979 would set in motion thinkers and doers in the Middle East who would work toward a direct and painful collision and conflict with the United States. For me these events began a fascination with the Middle East that has been fulfilled through a dynamic set of personal experiences in the region.

Like most adult Americans, I know where I was and what I was doing on September 11, 2001, and also like most Americans I had never before heard of al-Qaeda. Within a year of that event, I was considered for promotion to the rank of major in the U.S. Army and I had the opportunity to select a different career specialty. I asked to be a Middle East Foreign Area Officer because I wanted to be a part of fighting those who had directly attacked my country. I understood then that to defeat our opponent we needed to understand them and we did not. I received my request and from 2004 until the present both my personal and professional interests have been focused on all things Middle East.

In my desire to understand the Middle East, I have been able to travel to numerous countries in the region and have lived in four of them. I began my experience in Jordan, where I served as a Jordanian Armed Forces officer for two-and-a-half years. I worked outside the city of Zarqa, Jordan, from which Abu Musab al-Zarqawi came. I regularly traveled into the city to visit with friends and acquaintances from church and work. I became familiar with the poverty and ignorance of most everyday people in Jordan and the ignorance and relative wealth of everyday people in the United States. My wife and I visited a Jordanian prison to see a member of our church congregation who had overstayed her visa. We brought her money because in a Jordanian prison the prisoners needed to purchase anything more than bread and plain yogurt. This was not the prison where al-Zarqawi was kept and indoctrinated, but it was a small insight into that world.

I served in Iraq on three occasions—two trips of about 60 days or less and one for a full year—2005, 2010 to 2011, and 2014 to 2015. In every case, I worked from the U.S. Embassy Annex in Baghdad, across the street from the U.S. Embassy, or in the U.S. Embassy compound itself. Unlike my time in Jordan where I knew the average citizen, was welcomed into their homes, and understood their concerns and thoughts; in Iraq, I was sheltered. I was able to speak with average Iraqis occasionally and I did get some understanding of the complexity of the country and what the U.S. occupation was doing to the society, but I cannot claim to have any similar comprehension of Iraq as I do of Jordan. I was also able to visit Syria several times, all in 2005, and in those brief four or five weeks I came to deeply appreciate the people and culture of one of the oldest civilizations in human history. Similar to Iraq, I was always a little sheltered with respect to the Syrian people and I do not really understand them as well as I would like. I did spend hours speaking with the common people and came to see something of the complexity there as well. I can say that I know what this war has cost the rest of the world and will cost us if Syria is lost to us permanently.

I finally came home to the United States in 2013 after living in the Middle East for eight-and-a-half years. I came back to teach military history at the U.S. Army Command and General Staff College at Fort Leavenworth, Kansas.

When I arrived at the college, we had been at war in the Middle East for more than a decade and the curriculum had no mandatory courses on Middle East history, and only one elective was available on the subject. Since arriving we have added two more electives to communicate a lot of what is being shared in this book. To understand events in the Middle East, one needs to recognize that the roots of all events run deep into history. Nothing is isolated.

In every interaction I have had with Americans, whether military or civilian regardless of rank or position and despite the number of times they may have been to the Middle East, there is a tremendous amount of ignorance with respect to the history that matters—the roots of events and people. For this reason, the electives I teach are titled "Deep Roots of Conflict in the Middle East," "Roots of Conflict in the Middle East," and "What Just Happened? History of the Global War on Terrorism," where I try to help U.S. military officers understand the complexities of what is happening and why.

I know that I do not fully understand everything that is happening and why. I want to understand it, and therefore I wanted to write this book. I want to provide a resource that my high school and college-age children can read and get some concept of what this war is about and why it is currently a failure. War is hard work. It is full of complexity and conflict—not just the kind with bullets—and it involves the most complex of machines ever created—a large human organization—that interacts with a foreign culture. Explaining this complexity and the reasons why mistakes were made and are being made is the driving focus of this book.

ISIS: An Introduction and Guide to the Islamic State is organized in two major parts. The first part is a set of short narrative chapters that seek to answer important questions about the group—who, what, when, where, and why—if you will. The second part is a set of reference entries that provide context by giving more depth to issues, people, organizations, and concepts that should illuminate the thinking of the reader. The fight with ISIS is ongoing and dynamic. As this book was being written, the attacks in Paris, France, occurred on November 13, 2015. Before this book will be published, other events may and probably will happen that will change the course of fighting dramatically. For this reason and others, this book is not intended to be comprehensive and complete. It cannot be. What this book can be is a reference for thinking about this war. Every person filters information through their own experiential lens. What this book should provide is an adjustment to the filter of the reader such that the information one hears or sees can be interpreted more accurately and more beneficially.

I owe a deep expression of gratitude to my wife, Sheri Steed, who has served as my primary editor and research assistant for this book and all previous books I have written. As she lived with me throughout all of my Middle Eastern experiences save those in Iraq, her insights, thoughts, and perspectives are invaluable. I also want to thank the dozens of audiences and thousands of people to whom I have spoken on ISIS since the Fall of 2014. They have helped me refine my message and present the material as you see it here.

A final note about my perspective is important here. What follows in this book is intended to communicate an understanding of the opponent. My personal feelings of the accuracy of their worldview or where they stand with respect to the love and affection of God is irrelevant to the work before you. To defeat an enemy, it is best to have empathy for that enemy. There is no question in my mind that ISIS is an enemy of civilization and the United States. They are also a group that does not have the wherewithal to pose an existential threat to the United States. That said, it is not in our interest to allow them to develop such a wherewithal. The information presented here is done so with the intent of communicating what one needs to begin a journey toward empathy, which, I believe, is also the necessary path for the journey toward victory.

ISIS PRESENCE IN THE MIDDLE EAST (2015)

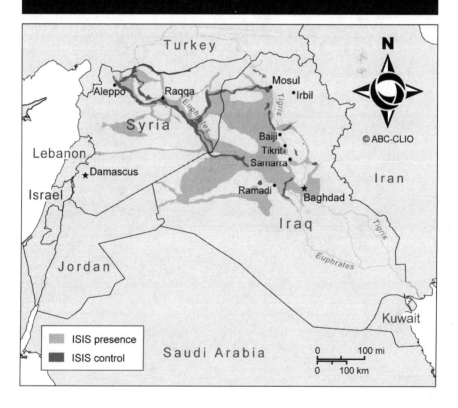

ISIS presence
ISIS control

COUNTRIES WITH ISIS OR AFFILIATE ACTIVITY (2015)

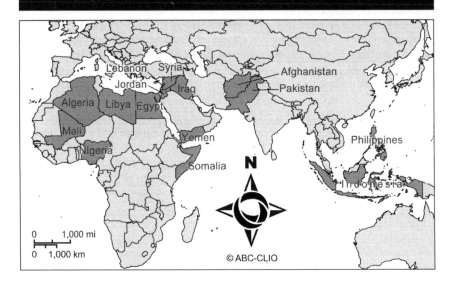

Introduction:
The Significance of ISIS

The Islamic State or the Islamic State of Iraq and al-Sham (ISIS) differs in many ways from its portrayal on talk radio and on the cable news channels. The soaring rhetoric that depicts it as a threat to Western civilization and causes audiences to believe that it is the manifestation of the evil spoken of in religious apocalyptic literature is inaccurate. In many ways, ISIS is at the current end of a long arc of brigands, thieves, robbers, drug cartels, and organized criminals who have sought to weaken and even overthrow civilization. It is the current representation of the apex organization of a robber culture. Some of the talk show participants refer to ISIS as a nonstate actor. It is not a nonstate actor—meaning it operates outside the constraints and statutes of a state—nor is it a substate actor—meaning it operates within a state, but still outside state control and authority—but it is a poststate actor—meaning an organization seeking to be a state using a nontraditional, non-Western model. Currently, it is the only poststate actor in conflict with the global community. What this means is that as a robber culture and a poststate actor ISIS does not need the trappings of civilization—roads, oil refineries, schools, cell phone networks, etc. It will use these things as best it can so long as it has them, but unlike civilization, it does not *need* them. The significance in this statement is that civilization *does* need these things. Civilization does not exist without education, transportation and communication, energy, and law. This is offered to explain why this war matters, or why we should care how this war is fought. If in the process of fighting this war civilized society destroys all of the necessary elements of civilization, then a desert will be created wherein the robber culture can function, but civilization cannot.

ISIS is not the worst incarnation of robber culture that has ever existed, though it is often portrayed as such. Keeping it in perspective is important. It is a serious threat to the survival of countries friendly to the United States within the Middle East, and as such it demands serious consideration and attention. This, however, should not be taken out of context.

The Islamic State is not currently a threat to all of Western civilization. However, it is important to note the speed at which the situation with ISIS has evolved. ISIS was nothing more than one of many nonstate actors conducting operations in Syria in 2013. Maybe it was the most powerful or the largest, but it was not significant enough to be noticed by the Western media. Most of the events people think of in association with ISIS happened since January 2014. In that month, it captured the city of Raqqa in Syria and conducted a parade in Fallujah. These events propelled the group into the public notice. In less than six months, it appeared on the brink of assaulting the city of Baghdad. This, in turn, drew Iran into the conflict in a direct manner.

More than a year later ISIS inspired or directed attacks against a Russian airliner flying from Sharm al-Sheikh resort in the Sinai and attacks on multiple sites in Paris, France. These events drew an already present Russia and a less involved France into direct and increasing intensity of airstrikes against ISIS bases, economic infrastructure, and civilian governance. What will happen in a year or more from the publication of this book?

No one knows. That is important to understand as one reads this book. No one in the West really understands this group. The reasons for this are plentiful. For the most part, ISIS represents a way of thinking that is outside the normal sphere of thought of most Western analysts. Another reason is that the West does not have accurate information regarding what it really is, what it really thinks, and what it really intends. So far it has done what it said it wanted to do so its words as we have them can serve as some guide to what it will do. Even with this information, it is crucial to recognize that its words must be analyzed through the proper lens and perspective. Most of the commentators in writing and speaking are not providing that perspective. Typically ISIS is analyzed as if it were a Western military with Western military objectives and conceptions of combat operations. This is not the same as understanding it as it sees the world and as it interprets events.

This book tries to explain ISIS, as much as possible, as it sees the world and as it interprets events. While it is impossible to fully grasp the world from its perspective, it is useful to understand the influences, events, and narratives that shape that perspective. Understanding that going in may provide a better context for obtaining a fuller picture.

ISIS comes to the world post-September 11, 2001. In this sense, there are things that have been done and seen that cannot be undone or unseen. The idea of terrorist attacks having global reach and significance is now tried and true. ISIS is also functioning in a world that has been exhausted and disillusioned by seeming failures in Iraq (2003–2011) and Afghanistan (2001–present). ISIS tries to draw on the similarities between the exhaustion of modern powers and the exhaustion of two ancient empires in the 600s CE—Persia and Rome—that were conquered by the first Islamic armies to attack out of the Arabian Peninsula. This is part of how it sees itself and how it wants other Muslims to see its organization. As with the initial Islamic conquests, the fighting today is done at just the right time for a miracle to happen. ISIS grew and developed primarily in Iraq and then later in Syria, in direct conflict with the United States and then later the governments of Iraq and Syria. It did not appear out of nowhere, but it did emerge in some force on an unsuspecting world.

It can claim something of miraculous success as well. In this world of success breeding success and the ability to build off a global narrative of Western weakness and Islamic humiliation at the hands of the West, ISIS has grown into a regional player with global reach. That reach may be through inspiration alone, but regardless of how it comes people are attacking in the name of the Islamic State far outside the direct physical influence of that same state. In this world of opportunity and tired opponents, it is surviving. Whether this is a small and limited phenomenon that will flash in its brilliant success and then fade away as rapidly or whether ISIS will expand to its envisioned near global caliphate is yet to be seen. ISIS itself uses the words *remain* and *expand* to inspire and focus followers. It is trying to communicate that it can in fact remain in the world arena and expand to accomplish all that God and His prophet has said is possible. Most (non-ISIS) observers predict that ISIS has only achieved what it has because of the incompetence and disinterest of its primary opponents, and once either the competence or interest increases, ISIS will be swept away. The pages, chapters, and entries that follow will better inform readers to be able to make intelligent contributions to the debates surrounding this iconoclastic organization.

What's in a Name?: IS, ISIS, ISIL, Da'ash

The title of this book uses the term ISIS and that will be the way that the group in question will be referred to throughout this book. This chapter explains the meaning of that acronym and all of the other names used by ISIS in its less than two decades of history. It has used a few names, and the U.S. and Western media have used several others over the years as well. All of this will be explained and clarified over the next couple of pages. This chapter is not the history of ISIS though there will be some history as the various names and explanations are given. The history of the organization will come in the chapter "The History and Operations of ISIS: Iraq to Syria to Iraq Again." The names used will be given in both English and Arabic. This is done to express the importance of language, history, and culture in all things necessary to understand ISIS.

The first name was Jama'at al Tawhid wal Jihad (JTJ) (جماعة التوحيد والجهاد) or Group of Monotheism and Jihad. This name was used from about 1999 to 2004 and applied to the group as it existed in Afghanistan and then early on in Iraq. The significance of this name was to draw people's attention to the importance of the pillars of Islam. (See entry on *Islam, Five Pillars* later in this book.) The first pillar is to acknowledge the importance and oneness of God. He is THE God and THE ONLY GOD, which is what *tawhid* means. The second point of significance was to remind Muslims of the importance of waging holy war against those who are opponents of Islam. This is one meaning of the word *jihad* (جهاد). (See entry on *Jihad* later in this book.) ISIS is and was from the beginning a group dedicated to waging a violent struggle against those who believe differently than it does.

The second name Tanzim Qaedat al Jihad fi Bilad al Rafidayn aka al-Qaeda in Iraq (AQI) (تنظيم قاعدة الجهاد في بلاد الرافدين) or Organization of Jihad's Base in Mesopotamia was taken as the group allied itself with al-Qaeda. At this time, the group did not use the name Iraq, but used the land between the two rivers (Tigris and Euphrates) or Mesopotamia as its location designation. The U.S.-led coalition regularly referred to it as al-Qaeda in Iraq or AQI for short. Note that it maintained the reference to jihad or the struggle of holy war in its title. This name existed from October 2004 to October 2006.

On January 15, 2006, an announcement was made stating the organization of the Mujahedeen Shura Council (مجلس شورى المجاهدين في العراق) that served as an umbrella organization for a variety of salafi-jihadi groups then operating in Iraq. Al-Qaeda in Iraq was the main member of this group.

The third name is Islamic State of Iraq (ISI) (دولة العراق الإسلامية) and it was adopted with an announcement on October 15, 2006. This title provides the first specific reference to Iraq and reference to an Islamic State, which was not the same as the designation of a caliphate, but still important. For the hard core followers, it is this date that it references as the founding of its state. It used this name until April 2013.

The fourth name came as a result of the group moving its leadership to Syria and expanding its area of operations and authority. The name is the Islamic State of Iraq and al Sham (ISIS) (الدولة الاسلامية في العراق والشام). It announced this new name on April 8, 2013. This is when it became ISIS. Note that it uses the Arabic word al-Sham and not Syria or the Levant. Al-Sham is a term used in Arabic that can have multiple meanings: 1) the city of Damascus, Syria; 2) the area of greater Damascus, Syria; 3) the modern state of Syria; or 4) greater Syria that includes all of the modern states of Syria, Lebanon, Israel and portions of Jordan, Turkey, and Egypt. (See entry on *al-Sham (Levant)* later in this book.) This was often mistranslated to be the Islamic State of Iraq and Syria, but ISIS never used the English or Arabic word for Syria in its name. The name, from its perspective, implies much broader influence than Western government and media often gave it credit for.

Shortly after ISIS took this designation, the U.S. government elected to use the term ISIL to refer to the group. ISIL stands for the Islamic State in Iraq and the Levant. Levant is a French word derived from Latin that means rising. Literally, it is the place where the sun rises or the east. The French have long used the term *Levant* to refer to the eastern shore of the Mediterranean Sea or the area currently including the states of Israel, Jordan, Lebanon, Syria, and, at times, parts of Egypt and Turkey. This term is very close in meaning to al-Sham, but it is a European word and not an Arabic one, and as such it has never been used by ISIS to designate its group.

In the Middle East and among Arabic speaking people, the group is typically referred to as Da'ash (داعش). Da'ash is an Arabic acronym for ISIS. It means exactly the same thing. Oftentimes one sees this written as Da'esh or Da'ish. These may be more accurate in the spelling as the "I" stands for Iraq. The problem is that the proper pronunciation is Da'ash and not Da'eesh, which is how most people pronounce it when reading the word written as Da'esh or Da'ish. When used in this book, this name will be spelled "wrong" so that it will be pronounced "right." Over time, the term Da'ash has developed a negative connotation as several different groups have been critical and produced satirical cartoons and videos mocking those who they call Da'ashis for being backward and out of touch with civilization and modernity. If members of ISIS refer to their group as Da'ash, they are subject to harsh discipline. As stated in the next paragraph, it is the State to its followers.

The fifth name the group used is the Islamic State (IS) (الدولة الإسلامية). It took this name with a statement announcing the establishment of the caliphate on June 29, 2014. This is the way members of ISIS refer to their group—Islamic State or the State.

The group being described in this book, though it has had many names, has always maintained a consistent ideological perspective and demonstrated behavior. Because of this consistency in thought and for simplicity's sake this book will consistently use ISIS to designate the group from here on out.

What Is ISIS?

What is ISIS is a complicated question. It is safe to say that ISIS is not what is typically said about it in the nightly news. To understand ISIS at some level of completeness, it will be necessary to read the majority of this book. This chapter introduces the conceptual framework that helps a reader begin to grasp the meaning and objectives of the group. This chapter describes ISIS, but some of these descriptions apply to other groups against which the U.S. government has fought since 2001. ISIS is the only group that puts all of these ingredients together in this same combination and quantity.

The ISIS that is presented on the news as it operates in Iraq or Syria is more than a single group or organization. ISIS is an umbrella organization under which exist numerous other groups that follow the big dog because it is the big dog. In general, the groups that participate with ISIS tend to be former Ba'athists who want to return Iraq to the control of Sunni nationalists. Though they are less extreme in their religious faith than some other groups supporting ISIS, they are still religiously motivated. There are other Sunni nationalist groups—ones who want to return Iraq and Syria to the control of Sunni leadership and encourage Sunni dominance in Mesopotamia and Syria. There are also several different factions that are religiously motivated—salafi-jihadis. These are people and organizations that believe that they need to fight to cleanse Islam from the control of those who are not true believers. They accept a violent approach though they may not ascribe to all of the ideology expressed by ISIS in their most aggressive or extreme opinions. Some of those within ISIS are committed to a lifelong association with the caliphate, and others are committed to something like an adventure vacation of months or years, but with intent to return to their home country to be an old man or woman and enjoy having been a jihadi. The most important point to understand is that ISIS is not a monolithic organization where everyone has the same motivations or the same commitment to service.

As stated previously, ISIS is a Salafist organization. (See entry on *Salafist* later in this book.) By definition, a Salafist is a Sunni and more specifically one who believes that the correct way to practice Islam is as it was practiced by the first generations of Muslims. (See entry on *Sunni* later in this book.) To be Salafist does not equal violent action. There are numerous Salafist groups that are not inclined toward violence. Those who are labeled salafi-jihadis are those who subscribe to an interpretation of Islam that is both driven by a regressive interpretation of the faith and one that is enforced by violence. Violence, from their perspective, grants absolution from sin as well as the opportunity to gain honor in life and the promise of martyrdom if killed in battle.

ISIS is also anti-Shia. (See entry on *Shia* later in this book.) It is unyielding in its virulent hatred for those who subscribe to a variation on their religion. The Shias are the near enemy to ISIS and the most prevalent threat to the faith. The Iraqi soldiers and police, who are predominantly Shia, are often referred to as safawis in the organization's literature and videos. This has reference to the Safavid Empire that espoused an aggressive expansionist Shia message from the 16th to the 18th century. (See entry on *Safavid Empire* later in this book.) Opposition to aggressive Shia expansion and control of the region is one of the primary animating beliefs of the group.

The group's vehement anti-Shia mindset leads to a strict and limited interpretation of the Islamic faith. Associated with this interpretation is the assumption of the power to declare others—Muslims and non-Muslims—apostates and enemies of God. The designation in Arabic is kafr, which is often mistranslated as infidel or unbeliever. The real meaning is stronger and deeper. The word carries with it the association of being an enemy to God: one who is not simply to be avoided, but who must be confronted, returned to the proper path, or destroyed. The verbal noun in Arabic is takfir—meaning to declare one an apostate. ISIS believes that its leaders have the authority to declare others who do not subscribe to their interpretation of Islam as kafr and this is practicing takfir. Once so declared, the apostate needs to be sought out and reconverted or eliminated. Such a declaration leads to many of the atrocities accorded to the group including murder, assassinations, executions, slavery, and rape.

On October 15, 2006, the Islamic State of Iraq was declared, and in the process the group we call ISIS became a ruler of territory, thus distinguishing itself from al-Qaeda and numerous other salafi-jihadist groups. Unlike the Taliban in Afghanistan or the ruler of Sudan, it was declaring itself to be the ruler of a state that it did not control—Iraq. On April 8, 2013, it expanded its fictitious control by stating itself to be the Islamic State of Iraq and al-Sham. Then on June 29, 2014, it further declared itself the Islamic State and designated its leader as Caliph Ibrahim. It was a modern incarnation of the caliphate. (See entry on *Caliphate* later in this book.)

To understand the meaning of caliphate, it is important to understand the meaning of caliph. (See entry on *Caliph* later in this book.) The word caliph means successor, as in one who is the successor in leadership to the Prophet Mohamed. Muslims believe he was the last prophet and any other legitimate leader of Islam in the Sunni tradition is only designated as successor. The caliphate as declared by ISIS is the region that is governed by its version of true Islam. All Muslims are expected to give allegiance to the caliph and to support the caliphate. From the beginning, these declarations have fueled controversy both among the salafi-jihadi community and the broader Muslim community. The primary criticism is that it is not appropriate for a caliph to be self-declared or declared by a small group. The leader should be acclaimed by the ummah or community of believers. (See entry on *Ummah* later in this book.) At the very least, a large number of Muslims should be behind the naming of a caliph. In a faith counting more than a billion and a half people the acclaim of thousands, tens of thousands, or even a hundred thousand or more is not generally viewed as sufficient.

Despite this, ISIS declared the foundation of the modern caliphate and it is functioning as a state entity. It governs territory and seeks to develop and grow the state and the institutions of the state.

In addition to creating a state that it wants to see prosper, ISIS also has an apocalyptic vision. It is preparing for the end of days. In its interpretation of the end-of-days literature, it sees the final state rising in al-Sham (modern Syria) and spreading into Mesopotamia where it will fight many battles. Over time (it is never made clear how long), it may be pushed back into Syria. There it will either be forced into a valley called Dabiq (north of the modern city of Aleppo) or it will send its army to Dabiq to respond to the arrival of the Roman-Crusader army. (See entry on *Dabiq, Battle of* later in this book.) In this valley, Jesus (the Christ to Christians) will return to earth and both save the army from defeat and also lead the army of the righteous to victory in battle against the Dajjal (best interpreted as the anti-Christ) bringing about the final judgment. (See entry on *Dajjal* later in this book.) In these final battles, the army of the righteous will fight a group that is referred to in the modern literature as a Roman-Crusader army. This army includes nonbelieving Muslims—kafrs, Christians, Jews, and many other heathens and infidels. This is the Muslim equivalent of Armageddon.

In understanding the brief details of this chapter, it is important to know that the group referred to as ISIS is a multifaceted group that taps into Quranic and prophetic teachings to create a narrative aura in which it sees itself as the fighter for Islam—the real Islam. It is trying to create and lead pure warriors destined to prepare the world for the final battles in the final days and to face proudly the final judgment. In this belief, it is allowed to make bold, extreme, and exceptional decisions and actions. It can do things that other groups could not have done because it is the army of the righteous doing what no other group has done before. This distinction is crucial to understand what it is and why it behaves in a way that nearly all other Muslims reject.

Leaders of ISIS

There have only been four leaders of ISIS in the entire history of the organization. Two of the four are relatively obscure in terms of what is known of them, but two are well known with a relatively significant documented history. It is the first leader and founder and the current leader (as of the time of writing this book) who will get the majority of space in this chapter. These two characters are bookends for the group—one was a thug and a bully and the other is a scholar. They both were transformed to some degree by a prison experience from which they emerged as charismatic leaders focused on violent promotion of their faith.

Most importantly, we actually know very little of any of these four men. No extensive interviews were conducted with the three who are now deceased and none of them wrote anything like an autobiography to inform readers of their thoughts and what they perceived to be their transformative moments. Thus everything that comes after in this book and in other books is, at best, speculation drawn from interviews of people who claim association with these four men. As Abu Bakr al-Baghdadi is still alive (as of the time of writing), it is uncertain what he may do with respect to writing or interviews later on.

Abu Musab al-Zarqawi

Born October 20, 1966, in Zarqa, Jordan, as Ahmad Fadeel al-Nazal al-Khalayleh. Abu Musab al-Zarqawi is a *nom de guerre* (war name) and has the literal meaning of the father of Musab from Zarqa. Musab means trouble, challenge, difficulty, or problem in Arabic. In this case, his name is both literal and figurative as he does have a son named Musab, but this name is also intended to communicate that he is the father of his enemies' troubles, difficulties, challenges, or problems. This is a poetic war name as so many of them are.

He grew up in a poor family and was known as a local thug and petty criminal. He was a high school dropout in addition to reportedly having drinking problems. In the late 1980s, he traveled to Afghanistan to fight as part of the mujahedeen in driving out the Soviet Union from the country. He arrived as the Soviets were leaving the country so he never fought, but during his time there he reportedly met with Osama bin Laden. He returned to Jordan where he helped start a militant group called *jund al-sham* (جند الشام) (translation: soldiers of al-Sham). For his involvement with this group, he was arrested and imprisoned from 1992 until 1999.

Prison was for al-Zarqawi a period of refinement for his religious beliefs as well as his role as a leader and organizer. One of his prison mates was Abu Muhamed al-Maqdisi, considered to be one of the most influential salafi-jihadi thinkers in recent times. Many writers consider the association of al-Maqdisi and al-Zarqawi in the Jordanian prison a watershed in al-Zarqawi's thinking. Though more is written on al-Maqdisi later in this book, it is important to note that he was the first to declare the Saudi ruling family as kafr or apostate.

It is customary in Islam for leaders to periodically forgive prisoners their sentences and their debts as a way to demonstrate both generosity and mercy. Al-Zarqawi was freed from prison as part of one of these amnesties. He fled Jordan shortly after his release and he traveled to Pakistan and ultimately Afghanistan. He was wanted by the Jordanians for trying to revive *jund al-sham*. Then the Pakistanis revoked his visa. He made it to Afghanistan where he met with al-Qaeda leaders. He received money from Osama bin Laden to start a training camp near Herat, Afghanistan, in the western part of the country. It was in this camp that he began to recruit and train his followers and to develop the intelligence and operations network that he later expanded in Iraq.

The group that was created and developed in this training camp was called jama'at al-tawhid wa al-jihad (جماعة التوحيد والجهاد) (Organization of Monotheism and Jihad). During the U.S. invasion of Afghanistan in 2001, al-Zarqawi was injured either from a collapsed building or in a firefight, and he fled to Iran where he received medical treatment. His movements were fluid in this period; he was reported to have traveled to Iran as stated previously, but then by 2002 he was in Iraq and also in Syria. Jordan requested extradition from Iran, Iraq, and Syria. There are reports that al-Zarqawi or members of his group were responsible for the murder of Laurence Foley, a U.S. Agency for International Development employee who was then working and living in Amman, Jordan, on October 28, 2002. Al-Zarqawi's presence in Iraq was used in a U.S.

government address to the United Nations in 2003 as one of the reasons for U.S. action in Iraq.

By the time U.S. forces invaded Iraq, al-Zarqawi was operating from northwestern Iran and northeastern Iraq. His organization was instrumental in early attacks on the U.S.-led coalition. As will be discussed in a later chapter, the groups created by al-Zarqawi developed over time across a spectrum of activities from assassinations to kidnappings to bombings. The group never developed the organs and administration of a state under al-Zarqawi. There are some who say that al-Zarqawi never really developed as a leader or a manager beyond the street thug that he began as. Regardless of whether or not such a statement is true he did lead an effective insurgency against the U.S.-led coalition in Iraq, and he did plague his home country of Jordan with spectacular attacks that gained significant press. By the time of his death, he was considered the number one single enemy leader of the coalition in Iraq.

Violence was a hallmark of al-Zarqawi's concept of jihad. This is not the violence of combat, but spectacular, staged violence. He directed suicide bombings in Jordan that targeted multiple hotels frequented by westerners in a single night. The biggest group of casualties came from a wedding celebration; all of the victims in that case were Jordanian. The most noteworthy events orchestrated by al-Zarqawi were the staged beheadings in which he had the victims in orange jumpsuits reminiscent of the U.S-held prisoners at Guantanamo Bay, Cuba, and Abu Ghraib, Iraq. The executioners and the soon to be executed often both made statements and then the executioner, sometimes al-Zarqawi himself, sawed off the head of the victim. These videos were posted to the Internet and they gained almost instantaneous notoriety.

Beyond the somewhat typical violence of suicide bombings, al-Zarqawi saw his violence as having a purpose in bringing about the creation of the caliphate. The violence united the Sunnis as they defended themselves from Shia and coalition attacks. It forced his people and cobelievers to band together in resistance, thus creating the nucleus for the eventual establishment of a state.

In this style of thinking, he led and directed attacks against Shia shrines, mosques, and neighborhoods. The most famous of these was the al-Askari mosque in Samarra, Iraq, which was and is considered one of the most holy Shrines for the Shia faith. The shrine was attacked on February 22, 2006. This event is one of the most significant single events leading to the Iraqi civil war that ensued.

Whether al-Zarqawi was the terrorist mastermind behind attacks from Iraq to Morocco and Turkey to Jordan or whether his importance was exaggerated as some purport is something beside the point. He was a galvanizing figure, and he is considered to be the initiator as well as the spiritual and physical father of the Islamic State and ISIS that grew from his organization. His actions and possibly the rumor of them transformed the nature of jihadism in the Middle East to one that uses extreme elements of violence to promote the larger and more important message.

Abu Ayyub al-Masri

Unlike al-Zarqawi or al-Baghdadi, the details on Abu Ayyub al-Masri are vague. He is said to have been born in 1968 in Egypt as denoted by his location name: al-Masri (note: in Arabic the word for Egypt is Mesr). He was born Yusif al-Dardiri or Abdul-Monim al-Badawi. It is unclear of the exact nature of his leadership position though some have him assuming leadership of what was then referred to by Americans as al-Qaeda in Iraq upon the death of Abu Musab al-Zarqawi. He has been known by a variety of other aliases, but this book will simply use Abu Ayyub al-Masri for simplicity.

Like Ayman al-Zawahiri, he was a Muslim Brotherhood member in Egypt as a young man, and he reportedly worked with al-Zawahiri in the organization he started called Egyptian Islamic Jihad. He went to Afghanistan in 1999 and received training in one of the training camps operated by Osama bin Laden where he learned explosives skills. Similar to al-Zarqawi, he fled from Afghanistan following the U.S. invasion and made his way to Iraq where he became a leader of the insurgent fight. He played a role in the 2004 fighting against the U.S. forces in Fallujah. For many of the opposition leaders, the battles in the spring and then later in the fall of 2004 served as a crucible and an identity-building experience. Almost all of the leaders of what would become the Islamic State of Iraq earned their reputations in Fallujah in 2004.

At some point, he was stated to be the leader of the Mujahedeen Shura Council—the same organization that Abu Abdullah al-Rashid al-Baghdadi was claimed to lead.

Abu Abdullah al-Rashid al-Baghdadi

Abu Abdullah al-Rashid al-Baghdadi is the name by which this book will refer to him though he had numerous other aliases and it is believed that his real name was Hamid Dawud Mohamed Khalil al-Zawi. Based on his *nom de guerre*, he is believed to be Iraqi and it is expected that he was a former member of the Iraqi military. With the death of al-Zarqawi, Abu Abdullah became the de facto leader of the primary opposition group to the U.S.-led coalition.

Very little is known of this man. Even the name given as his birth name has no concrete source. He was reported to have been captured by the Iraqi police in 2007, but that proved to be false. What is known is that he was killed on April 18, 2010, by a U.S. missile strike. His death was confirmed both by coalition forensics and by al-Qaeda in Iraq itself. He was killed in the same strike as Abu Ayyub al-Masri.

Regardless of the specifics, both of these men served in positions where they directed activities from 2006 until 2010. They were the bridges between the thug al-Zarqawi and the scholar al-Baghdadi.

Abu Bakr al-Quraishi al-Baghdadi

Ibrahim Awad Ibrahim al-Badri al-Samarrai was born on June 28, 1971, in the city of Samara, north of Baghdad, Iraq. Growing up he was a quiet, pious person who loved soccer. He took to religious scholarship and worked hard on his studies that included graduate studies and eventually a doctorate in Islamic scholarship. His thesis and dissertation both centered on interpreting medieval period Islamic jurisprudence (religious interpretations of law as derived from the Quran, statements of the Prophet Mohamed, and the rulings of other scholars and judges). The stories of his life—early, middle, and recent—are all something of a mystery. There are conflicting reports of nearly every fact already presented in this paragraph. The version stated here is generally considered accurate. It is also the version that fits the narrative ISIS wants followers and others to know and believe—that al-Baghdadi is a religious man who is both a warrior and a scholar of the Quran.

The *nom de guerre* of Islamic jihadists will include the tribal designation of al-Qurayshi whenever it is possible. This is significant because the Prophet Mohamed is reported to have stated that in the final days the leader of the community of believers would be from his own tribe—the Quraysh. Many reports do indicate that al-Baghdadi is actually from the Quraysh tribe, thus making him a feasible fulfillment of the prophetic tradition. (See entry on *Quraysh* later in this book.)

The general story of the life of Abu Bakr al-Baghdadi is that he became a Salafist in 2000 while he was an imam, or religious scholar leader, of the Haji Zeidan mosque in the poor neighborhood of Tobji, Baghdad. He finished his master's degree in 2004 after the U.S. invasion of Iraq. It is unclear whether he participated in the actual opposition to the U.S.-led coalition or he was just a bystander. Different stories exist. By 2015, he had two wives and six children. It is unclear where his family currently is.

U.S. military records indicate he was arrested in 2004 outside of Fallujah, Iraq, and detained in Camp Bucca in the Iraqi desert close to the border with Kuwait. The records show him as a civilian. Thus he was not considered a threat or a prisoner resulting from fighting. Instead he was believed to be one of many rounded up and imprisoned based on association and accusations. These suppositions led to his early release. While he was in Camp Bucca, he was given responsibilities by the Americans and allowed to organize meetings and religious instruction. It is believed that he used this opportunity to develop his network of connections—people who would be loyal to him following his release. The Americans saw him as a calming influence on a camp that was full of malcontents who participated in numerous riots. Anyone who could keep things calm was given leeway. Abu Bakr al-Baghdadi was that kind of person. He was released after 10 months of incarceration though there are conflicting reports that have him serving in Camp Bucca for years.

Following his release, he continued his studies and became more and more a part of the insurgency opposing the U.S.-led coalition in Iraq. He went to Syria in 2006 to study and to become a senior administrator for the Islamic State of Iraq in Syria. His success in working in Syria got him an appointment to the Mujahedeen Shura Council where he was influential in coordinating events and managing personalities.

Abu Bakr al-Baghdadi was announced as the leader of the Islamic State of Iraq on May 16, 2010. He has remained the leader of this organization that grew to become the Islamic State or ISIS. He moved what remained of the leadership into Syria, utilizing the relationships he developed earlier to create a space in the authority vacuum that Arab Spring Eastern Syria had become.

His religious-historical knowledge proved crucial in selecting cities and sites for emphasis for ISIS. ISIS took Raqqa, Syria, in part because it could, but there was also a historical appropriateness to the selection of this particular city. Raqqa was an ancient early capital of the Abbasid Caliphate (796-809 CE). Taking control of Raqqa helped emphasize the narrative developed by ISIS—that it is the manifestation of a modern caliphate. The operational movements of ISIS are discussed in other chapters.

On June 29, 2014, ISIS designated itself the Islamic State and Abu Bakr al-Baghdadi was designated as Caliph Ibrahim. On July 5, 2014, a video was released showing the new caliph in the Great Mosque of al-Nuri in Mosul, Iraq, giving the Friday sermon. He personally called on all Muslims to come to the caliphate and to follow him as the rightful successor of the Prophet Mohamed. As with all the details associated with Abu Bakr al-Baghdadi, there are disputing accounts regarding this sermon with some saying this was not really him, he cannot really be a caliph, etc.

For the remainder of this book, we will use the name of Abu Bakr al-Baghdadi rather than Caliph Ibrahim.

In summary, Abu Bakr al-Baghdadi is someone quite different from Abu Musab al-Zarqawi. He is religiously driven. Unlike al-Zarqawi who chose a *nom de guerre* that emphasized his violent approach to forwarding his message, al-Bagdadi selected a name that reminds Muslims of his connection with the first caliph—Abu Bakr—from the seventh century. He is a scholar. He is an Iraqi. He is also something of a question. It is uncertain whether he is truly the leader of ISIS or a figurehead. Almost every fact known or stated about him is in question. He has taken the violent religious narrative laid down by his predecessors and made it more real. He is someone who seems to fit prophetic statements regarding the leadership of Muslims in the end times, and his organization has succeeded in a way that other jihadi groups have not by creating some semblance of a state.

As the events associated with ISIS are unfolding, it is important to note that this man is quite possibly the most important enigmatic leader in the last millennia of human history.

The History and Operations of ISIS: Iraq to Syria to Iraq Again

The history of ISIS, as already briefly shared when discussing the names and leaders of the organization, is varied. At its beginning, the organization was often characterized as something like a mini–al-Qaeda. Later on the organization was mistakenly characterized by the U.S. government as the al-Qaeda franchise in Iraq. As this chapter demonstrates this was not the case in either instance. ISIS has changed and there were multiple organizations that existed before ISIS became a land-owning poststate in Syria and Iraq. ISIS had also maintained a consistency of ideology and behavior.

Here the history of ISIS is discussed in six phases. The first is the longest in terms of time (from about 1999 to 2006), but it takes place when the group is the smallest in size. The second phase extends from the creation of the Islamic State in Iraq until the expulsion of the organization from Iraq—2006 to 2010. The third phase discusses the events in Syria resulting from the Arab Spring. The fourth phase follows the development of the organization while in Syria pending the opportunity to return to Iraq from 2010 to 2014. The fifth phase is the declaration of the Islamic State and discusses the return of the organization to Iraq. The sixth phase is the protection and governance of the Islamic State as a poststate entity or actor in the Middle East.

Phase One: Operating in al-Qaeda's Shadow

Abu Musab al-Zarqawi started an organization in Jordan predating his travel to Afghanistan in 1999, but this history will start with the creation of the training camp outside Herat and the founding of the group known as Jama'at al-Tawhid wal-Jihad (JTJ) or Group of Monotheism and Jihad. Names have significance and the name for JTJ is important. It emphasized the unity of God and called to the minds of Muslims the *shahada*, or witness statement. (See entry on *Islam, Five Pillars* later in this book.) This is the first pillar of Islam where all Muslims state that there is only one God and that Mohamed is the prophet and messenger of that one God. The other important reminder inherent in this name is the principle of struggle, or jihad. JTJ embraced the concept of a struggle of violence; it focused on the use of violence in order to destroy those who oppose Islam and bring about the foundation of an Islamic State.

From the beginning, al-Zarqawi and bin Laden had a difference of opinion regarding the use of violence in the furtherance of creating a caliphate. This will be discussed in greater detail in the next chapter, but it is important to understand the difference between al-Qaeda and the root organization of ISIS from the very inception of that organization. Al-Zarqawi believed that the caliphate had to be brought into the world in blood and violence. He also felt it should come forward sooner and by force. In comparing the two groups of al-Qaeda and ISIS, many authors and commentators argue that the differences between them are slight and are primarily about leadership. In reality, the difference is about vision. Though this difference existed at the beginning, the two groups were still similar enough in ultimate design that bin Laden gave money to help start the JTJ training camp and al-Zarqawi gave his allegiance to bin Laden later on in Iraq, taking on al-Qaeda's name. Despite those connections—JTJ and all following named groups that became ISIS was never truly al-Qaeda in Iraq. It was always conceptually something else.

JTJ moved from Afghanistan to Iraq following the American invasion of Afghanistan. It operated a training camp in the mountains of northeastern Iraq as the United States prepared to invade Iraq. The existence of the group in Iraq was one of the pretexts used to justify a U.S.-led invasion of Iraq. In the period from about 2002 to 2004, JTJ looked a lot like other nonstate actors in that it recruited, trained personnel, and then conducted terrorist operations regionally and, if possible, globally. JTJ conducted attacks in Jordan, Turkey, and possibly as far away as Morocco. If history stopped in 2003, then JTJ would not make the history books. It was small and it was unspectacular.

The U.S. invasion of Iraq changed that. Most specifically, the Battles of Fallujah and the opportunity to use the U.S. forces as a justification for extreme displays of violence created the mystique and reputation for what became ISIS. In 2003, there were numerous groups in opposition to the U.S. invasion that operated in Iraq. JTJ was simply one of them, and no one at that time imagined it would become the dominate salafi-jihadi group.

In late March 2004, four Blackwater security contractors were killed and hung from an overpass in Fallujah. This generated a U.S.-led operation into

Fallujah that wreaked havoc on the city, which was called off by the interim Iraqi government in relatively short order, giving the impression of U.S. defeat. The insurgents celebrated their victory and continued to demonstrate a complete lack of respect for the Iraqi government. The U.S.-led coalition went back into Fallujah in November. It destroyed numerous buildings and killed a lot of fighters opposing the coalition. The fighting in Fallujah made insurgent leaders. It became the way to demonstrate your prowess as a battlefield commander. Many of the leaders who went on to lead at various levels of the organization gained their street and fighting credibility in Fallujah.

Most of the future leaders of ISIS who fought in Fallujah made it out before the U.S.-led attacks in November 2004. In October 2004, the group formally designated its association to al-Qaeda by taking on yet another name—Tanzim Qaedat al-Jihad fi Bilad al-Rafidayn (Organization of Jihad's Base in Mesopotamia)—or al-Qaeda in Iraq. From this point until the U.S. departure from Iraq, many U.S. military and civilians looked on this group as simply a part of al-Qaeda—just another franchise owned and operated in Iraq. This thinking was wrong. It was its own group with a driving ideology made up of a distinct set of beliefs.

One of the most notorious examples of this ideology was the attack on three hotels in Amman, Jordan, on November 9, 2005. Based off international dating, this was Jordan's 9/11. One of the attacks ended up targeting a wedding celebration where the majority of the casualties were wedding guests. This attack turned Jordan against al-Zarqawi and AQI and caused many others to distance themselves from the group and its tactics. As the group added video beheadings and then attacks on mosques to its repertoire, even Osama bin Laden and Ayman al-Zawahiri cautioned al-Zarqawi to change his tactics. The final voice of reason came from the man who led al-Zarqawi to the path of salafi-jihadism, al-Maqdisi. The strategy to use violence as a means to generate a civil war in Iraq and to force the Sunnis to support the creation of an Islamic State took precedence over all calls for moderation. Al-Zarqawi and subsequent ISIS leaders consistently held true to their conception of the fight regardless of who asked for them to change.

Despite their difference in perspective of the fight, ISIS still made the effort to band together like-minded groups into a common organization of sorts. The idea was to form a council of groups that were opposed to the U.S.-led occupation and also held similar beliefs with respect to jihad against both the foreign occupiers and the perceived puppet government of Shia. So on January 15, 2006, the groups announced the formation of the Mujahideen Shura Council. The leadership of the group was nearly exclusively ISIS supporters. The ISIS of 2014 and 2015, as stated in a previous chapter, was an umbrella organization. That umbrella was being built on the streets of Fallujah in 2004 and again in the formation of this organization in 2006.

A month later on February 22, 2006, the al-Askari mosque in Samarra, Iraq, was partially destroyed with a car bomb. The mosque is considered one of the most holy sites for Shia Muslims and the attack on the site by Sunni extremists sparked a civil war in Iraq as desired by AQI. Al-Zarqawi continued to conduct attacks designed to foment and expand the sectarian violence, tearing the country apart. U.S. forces eventually found al-Zarqawi and killed him with an airstrike on June 7, 2006.

Phase Two: A State Is Declared

On October 15, 2006, the new leader changed the name and declared there to be an Islamic State of Iraq (ISI). This statement received numerous rebuttals from the salafi-jihadi community. Leadership of al-Qaeda and others stated that Iraq was not ready for this declaration. ISIS ignored them and continued to promote the sectarian war that it had effectively initiated.

Despite the declaration of the founding of the Islamic State, there was little change in behavior for ISIS. It continued to act like an insurgency composed of terrorists and street thugs. It conducted kidnappings for ransom and extortion, it facilitated suicide bombings to maintain the sectarian killing, and it manipulated tribal loyalties and relationships. The response to ISIS activities was not typical. Some tribes were fiercely loyal and supportive of the actions and activities of ISIS. Other tribal leaders in al-Anbar province and elsewhere began to oppose the extreme behaviors of ISIS.

Iraq shaded the view of many Americans about Arabs where an Arab is perceived as extreme in belief and behavior. In general, Arabs are moderates. This mindset stems from the nature of their formative life—living in a harsh, potentially life-threatening climate and environment—which inclines one toward moderation and going with conditions as they are. Extreme interpretations violate this natural sense of moderation as well as the majority Muslim perception of their faith as a personal observance that creates the ideal community. One Muslim telling another Muslim how to be acceptably Muslim is not compatible with the general interpretation of the faith.

ISIS also challenged the preexisting power base. In the years between Operation Desert Storm (1991) and the beginning of Operation Iraqi Freedom (2003), Saddam Hussein consolidated his hold on major population centers, but he also allowed local leaders and tribal leaders to act freely so long as they did not disrupt his power centers. This meant that certain families controlled various smuggling routes, specifically the smuggling of certain commodities. ISIS exacted specific rules about what would cross the border and who would receive the benefits of the smuggling. The challenge to culture, religion, tribal economy, and tribal power caused a response that is often referred to as the Awakening (*sahwa*) or, as it is often linked with the increase in U.S. troop levels, the Surge. (See entries on *Sahwa (Sunni Uprising)* and *The Surge* later in this book.)

Sunni tribes, tired of fighting the Iraqi government, and government authorities in what seemed to be an endless sectarian war, grudgingly came together in this Awakening (*sahwa*) to pay Sunni tribal members to provide security. The Sons of Iraq fought alongside U.S. and Iraqi Security Forces against the extremists and foreign fighters including ISIS. This forced ISIS to go to ground and become less significant as a player. It also radically decreased the acts of violence around the country.

It is important to note that the violence did not end.

In specific times and locations, the violence increased. The insurgent community wanted to communicate through its violence—a particular hallmark of ISIS—that the United States and its coalition partners were being driven from Iraq. To send this message it staged attacks, particularly spectacular attacks that garnered significant media attention, immediately preceding the announced withdrawal of U.S. units. So overall attacks reduced across the whole of Iraq, but specific times and specific locations still experienced mass casualty attacks in which dozens of people were killed and wounded. ISIS was concealed and not nearly as active, but it wanted the people of Iraq to know why the coalition member states left Iraq—they were forced out.

Phase Three: Arab Spring

In the Fall and Winter of 2010 and continuing into the Spring of 2011, separate events happened in Tunisia, Egypt, Syria, Bahrain, Jordan, and Yemen. The people in each of these countries rose up in protests—sometimes small and sometimes shockingly large—against their existing governments and the leadership in their states. This was an amazing display of popular will and it featured the use of social media to a degree never before seen. Some called it a Twitter revolution after the name of the social media service. Each of these events needs to be taken as separate and distinct. It is certain that there were inspirational overlaps between the different countries, but the circumstances in each country were unique.

The events in Syria started in the south near the Jordanian border where a young boy painted anti-regime graffiti. For that he was tortured and killed and his body was left in the street. This sparked significant outcry from the people of Deraa. What has come to be called the Syrian Civil War started with this overreaction by the Syrian security apparatus. It rapidly spread to Idlib province in the north of the country. Deraa in the south and Idlib in the north served as centers of opposition to the regime until the time of writing this book—more than five years later.

To understand the Syrian Civil War, it is important to understand Syria and the complexity of the country. Syria has been ruled by an Alawite minority since a military coup in 1978 led by Hafez al-Assad, the father of the current president of Syria. Alawites are typically linked with Shia, but their practices and beliefs, which have common roots, are different enough to be considered heretical by many Shia. Despite this, the first country to recognize the Islamic government in Iran following the 1979 revolution was the government of Syria. From this moment in 1979 until the present, there has been a close relationship between Iran and Syria. With the establishment of Hezbollah in 1983 and the support it received from Iran throughout its opposition to Israel, Syria has served as a conduit of arms and equipment from Iran to Hezbollah. The complexity of the relationships between Iran, Syria, and Hezbollah are worthy of a separate book. It is important for readers to understand this connection in order to understand the dynamics of ISIS and opposition to ISIS within Syria. (See entries on *Alawi* and *Hezbollah* later in this book.)

The Alawites are a minority population in Syria—about 11 to 12 percent. The majority of Syria is Sunni. During the Alawite reign in Syria, the regime has always been supportive of minority groups throughout the country. This is especially true of the Christian population that at one point was more than 10 percent of Syria. Over the decades of rule, the Assad family effectively linked the regime to the Alawite communities, creating an environment wherein survival of the regime equaled survival of Alawite villages and families.

The Assad family was hostile toward Saddam Hussein and the Syrian regime was happy to see the fall of the dictator. They were particularly happy to see the United States suffer in Iraq following their designation as part of the *Axis of Evil* by the U.S. president in a State of the Union address. Syria became a conduit for the flow of foreign fighters into Iraq. This became something of a problem as these foreign fighters eventually took advantage of the vacuum created in eastern Syria by the growing civil war primarily being fought in the western portions of the country. The smuggling lines used to move foreign fighters and material into Iraq were then traced backward into Syria to begin establishing bases of operation within Syria itself.

Since the military success of ISIS became evident in 2014 and 2015, there has been lots of ink spilled and hours of debate over who was responsible for the creation of ISIS. It is clear that the chaos that reigned following the overthrow of Iraq created the first incubation ground for such an organization, but it was in the chaos of Syria that ISIS was truly born as an effective poststate actor and an actual poststate.

Abu Bakr al-Baghdadi traveled to Syria as an operative of ISI and the council to develop the support capacity in Syria during this period. He became the leader of ISI with the death of his predecessor in a U.S. strike in 2010. He used the connections he made in Syria to exploit the opportunities created by growing chaos in the country and the weakening of the Syria security forces.

Phase Four: Building the State

The United States departed Iraq with all forces at the end of 2011 and it seemed, at the time, as if ISI was defeated in Iraq. The Iraqi government had extended its control throughout the country. Nuri al-Maliki (then Prime Minister in Iraq) felt secure enough in his leadership to begin bringing charges against Sunni opponents. He accused multiple individuals serving in senior government positions of corruption. One of the favorite accusations was against the security details of Sunni leaders. The security personnel were often accused of conducting sectarian extrajudicial killings at earlier periods during the occupation. By removing the security detail from the principal, it would both weaken the Sunni leader in the sense of guilt by association and weaken him by making him more vulnerable to personal physical attack. The United States did nothing in this early period to condemn the actions. Al-Maliki believed he had been given a green light to take care of things in Iraq as he saw fit. He then began mass removals of senior Iraqi security force leaders who were nonsectarian or pro-Sunni in their political leanings. Rather than choosing people who were capable, he stacked the military with people who were loyal to him personally.

These actions did more than weaken the Iraqi Security Forces. The actions also angered the Sunni tribes and the Sons of Iraq that had agreed to fight alongside the security forces against the insurgents. The Sunni leaders and fighters felt betrayed and threatened by the government. Even before U.S. forces departed Iraq in 2011, the Iraqi government began to reduce payments to the Sons of Iraq in terms of limiting the number of people who received money. By the time the United States departed, it was almost entirely eliminated and shortly after the departure all funds to Sunni fighters ceased.

In this same period, ISIS continued to develop contacts and operational space in Syria. Though it was yet to possess any Syrian city or area as a dedicated base of operations, it was still operating out of Syria as well as back into Iraq. Even before the United States completely pulled out of Iraq, ISIS was already working the relationships. It focused its engagements on al-Anbar province and on the city of Mosul. ISIS representatives visited their contacts in these areas multiple times—establishing and developing relationships. They conducted the meetings along the standard lines of Arab hospitality—bringing gifts, speaking of family and faith, and eventually speaking of security. They offered a shared vision of Iraq—an Iraq ruled by a Sunni majority.

ISIS conducted a multiyear engagement program designed to turn individuals, influential families, and tribes to its side long before it actually showed up in the country in force. This was aspirational. ISIS offered a positive vision for the country—Sunni-controlled, religiously conservative, and opposed to Iranian and Western influence. This was agreeable to most Sunnis.

It is important to note that many Sunni Iraqis do not believe the demographic statistics of Iraq quoted by Western leaders—60% Shia, 20% Sunni, and 20% Kurd—as they believe these statistics are politicized to favor Shia dominance. Many Sunnis in Iraq will tell you that they are the majority ethnosectarian group (or at least the plurality) in the country and thus they should be the dominant force as they were under the Ba'ath party and Saddam Hussein. Thus the ISIS message that argued for a form of Sunni nationalism appealed to the existing vision of people who believed they should be in charge anyway. The people who received the ISIS emissaries into their homes were inclined to accept the vision presented. As the engagements developed over time (it is important to understand that this process occurred over years), ISIS began to promise future opportunities of leadership positions. For example, if you back us when we come into your area, then you will be the mayor, the governor, etc. Many nonreligious groups began to see the benefit of the message that ISIS was selling. They were inclined toward that vision for Iraq and many believed that the religious extremists could be controlled. Not only did the former Saddam loyalists and other less religiously extreme groups think they could control ISIS and other groups, the secular Sunnis also wanted to harness the dynamism and near fanatic commitment to a cause that these groups demonstrated. In essence, they wanted to control the tornado. So they invited the tornado in.

Their plan backfired; those who thought they could use ISIS were instead used by ISIS.

Many articles and reporters emphasized the development of intelligence and protection rackets in the Sunni communities in Iraq at this time. This did happen. Threats, kidnappings, extortion were and are part of the ISIS playbook. It is crucial to understand that ISIS also presented an aspirational message. The ISIS forces that returned to Iraq in 2014 did not come in as the surprise to Iraqis that the Western media believed them to be. Instead they rolled in on a carpet of engagement and threats that had been years in the making.

This same pattern was also playing out in Syria. ISIS was building a cache of weapons and resources and developing the relationships necessary to facilitate what would be a rapid rise in power that appeared to be a shocking transformation of the Syrian and Iraqi desert maps as they went from a small operating base to controlling large swaths of territory in a matter of months. It was not a matter of months—ISIS built an infrastructure of relationships and intimidation over a period of years that undergirded all of their future success.

Abu Bakr al-Baghdadi sent a group of his ISIS operators into Syria to conduct an assessment of the possibilities to fight against the Assad regime. These operators then developed into an active and powerful fighting force in the western part of Syria. They became so powerful that as al-Baghdadi sought to retain control over them and to continue to direct their actions they grew disgruntled to the point of breaking away. The former ISIS operators used statements from the al-Qaeda leadership as an excuse to separate from ISIS. This group is known as Jabhat al-Nusra or the al-Nusra front. (See entry on *Jabhat al-Nusra* later in this book.) They continue to be an important part of the story of ISIS in Syria until the present time. The clash between Jabhat al-Nusra and ISIS is one of the key stories of actions in Syria throughout 2014 and 2015. What is important to know is that Jabhat al-Nusra was once part of ISIS and they hold the same basic ideology.

Phase Five: Declaring the State

ISIS became a global phenomenon in 2014. In January 2014 in Fallujah, Iraq, there was a parade of ISIS equipment and personnel with flags. This was its coming out party, its announcement to Iraq, the region, and the world that it was a power. Though the Iraqi Security Forces maintained positions within Fallujah, it was no longer truly in full control of the city. ISIS flags and militants appeared in numerous towns and cities in al-Anbar province throughout the winter. When President Obama was interviewed about the events, he referred to ISIS as a JV team. He also quipped that just because someone puts on a Lakers jersey that does not make him Kobe Bryant. These comments were later used as examples of the U.S. administration's lack of touch with the events on the ground. The Iraqi Sunnis were regularly demonstrating against Nuri al-Maliki and the Iraqi government, in general. ISIS was on their side, and it seemed to represent Sunni power.

ISIS went on to launch numerous effective raids against Iraqi Security Force targets. In several attacks, it mounted jailbreaks to free Sunni prisoners. One of the most notable was against the infamous Abu Ghraib prison where it freed hundreds of prisoners and future ISIS fighters. During this same time, ISIS was also acting in Syria to capture entire towns and cities from Syrian forces. It took Raqqa, Syria, which became its *de facto* capital. For the most part, its attacks were focused on towns and cities in the Euphrates River valley. (See entry on *Raqqa, Syria* later in this book.)

One of the main Syrian cities on the Euphrates River is Deir al-Zour. This city still has not fully fallen to ISIS fighters, but it has been hotly contested since early in 2014 until the present among belligerents including ISIS, the Syrian military, and Jabhat al-Nusra. As ISIS began to capture and control cities, fighters from Jabhat al-Nusra, other opposition and extremist organizations began to swear allegiance to ISIS and fight for it.

The Syrian opposition is not a single group. It is not even a hundred groups. It comprises several hundred groups (maybe more than a thousand) that have near-constant shifting allegiances. With success, ISIS gathered other fighters like a large snowball as it rolled downhill.

The big attack happened in June 2014 as a large raid into Mosul, Iraq, originally intended to free prisoners from the jail effectively defeated the Iraqi army operating in and around the city. The fighting occurred over several days. As the Iraqi Security Forces fled or were ambushed and slaughtered, ISIS was able to capture the second largest city in Iraq. As previously indicated, the city had been worked over by ISIS for several years with engagements and intimidation such that numerous municipal, tribal, and civic leaders were already pro-ISIS when it came in. Mosul was a hotbed of pro-Ba'ath opposition to the government in Baghdad for many years. Now it was the crown jewel for ISIS.

On June 29, 2015, the Islamic State was declared to be the caliphate and all Muslims were invited to join the state in its defense and expansion.

Phase Six: Defending the State

At this point in mid-2014, it seemed like the Iraqi Security Forces could no longer protect the country from ISIS and its advances whether in the major river valleys or in the north. The most prominent Shia religious figure in Iraq, Grand Ayatollah Ali al-Sistani, extended a call to all Iraqis (his influence is mostly over Shia Iraqis) to rise up and defend their country and especially the Shia holy sites and the capital. Thousands of young men flocked to what became known as Popular Mobilization Forces (PMF). Many of these groups were backed by Iran in terms of pay, equipment, arms, and ammunition. The Iranian military deployed senior leaders and advisors and later elements of its Iranian Revolutionary Guard Corps and the Quds Force. The senior Iranian leader who helped both in directing the anti-ISIS fight in Iraq and the pro-Assad fight in Syria was Qasem al-Soleimani. (See entry on *Soleimani, Qasem* later in this book.) The PMF became the most successful non-Kurdish fighting force in Iraq by the end of the year.

As ISIS began to expand its operations from Mosul and from the main highway from Syria to Mosul, it captured numerous villages that were populated by ethnic and sectarian minorities. Some of these included Yazidi communities around the Sinjar Mountains. Stories of genocidal atrocities including slavery, massive rape, and kidnapping coming from the attacks on these villages galvanized the west like none of the other reports had. The United States looked at providing humanitarian support to the Yazidis trapped on Sinjar.

Additionally, there was concern for the Kurdish and Christian communities in the areas threatened by ISIS. It looked like ISIS attacks into the Kurdish portions of Iraq might reach the city of Irbil where the U.S. government has a consulate. U.S. airstrikes in support of Kurdish forces and in protection of the U.S. Consulate caused an ISIS backlash. ISIS beheaded two American journalists within a couple of weeks of each other as a way of threatening the United States against the conduct of further military operations. Within days, the United States increased airstrikes and began the deployment of hundreds and ultimately thousands of U.S. trainers and logisticians to support what became known as Operation Inherent Resolve (OIR).

OIR had two components. The first focused on operations in Syria while the second coordinated operations in Iraq. These operations included an international coalition of several dozen countries who provided everything from a couple of staff officers to attack aircraft and special operations forces. The intent of OIR was to train and equip Iraqi and Syrian forces to go in and do the fighting on the ground while the United States and coalition airpower supported their efforts.

In Syria, there was a major fight around the border city of Kobane, Syria, where ISIS first took most of the town, but then was ultimately driven from the city by a combination of Syrian Kurdish fighters on the ground and coalition airpower. The city that was recaptured was little more than a pile of rubble and more than a year later was still a shell of its former self with only a small percentage of its original population having returned.

The year 2014 ended with ISIS fighters operating in some fashion in places along the Euphrates River in both Iraq and Syria. They were also operating in the Tigris River valley in places like Tikrit that is the hometown of Saddam Hussein, and Bayji that houses a key part of Iraqi infrastructure in the form of a large refinery complex. They may not have existed in large numbers, but they were aggressive and committed.

In 2015, the Kurds in Iraq and Syria saw numerous successes as they beat back ISIS from village after village. The Mosul Dam that was in danger of collapse for many years was captured by ISIS in 2014 and regained by Iraqi Kurds in late 2014 with the help of coalition airpower. Fighting expanded from the manmade lake created by the dam as the Kurds regained land contact with Sinjar Mountain and the villages around it to include the retaking of the city of Sinjar itself in late 2015.

In March 2015, the Iraqi Security Forces in combination with tens of thousands of PMF attacked Tikrit. The fighting for Tikrit took more than a month with little gain. Coalition aircraft did not support the attack because of the presence of the Shia militias and Iranian advisors. Finally, after the government of Iraq agreed to withdraw the militias the coalition aircraft began to strike. It still took several more weeks to retake the city and even then it was Shia militiamen who were first into the city. Tikrit was saturated with improvised explosive devices in almost every building. Months after the recovery of the city, very few families had returned.

Tikrit was retaken in May 2015 and within a couple of weeks ISIS attacked to take Ramadi. It captured the city with a combination of more than a dozen powerful truck bombs—each one as strong as the Oklahoma City bombing (April 19, 1995). The rapid response from losing Tikrit to taking Ramadi took the Iraqi forces by surprise and there was seeming confusion about whether or not to defend or to withdraw. A counterattack was begun within a matter of days, but it was poorly resourced and coordinated. Ramadi was reportedly retaken by late December 2015, but despite the reports there were still large sections of the city with ISIS presence and the battle to regain the city destroyed a significant percentage of buildings in the city. By the end of 2015, something like 30 percent of the territory captured by ISIS was retaken, but the major urban areas like Tikrit and Kobane were like ghost towns.

In Syria, the second half of 2015 saw significant success along the border with Turkey as Kurdish forces were able to work in concert with coalition airstrikes to regain village after village. The fighting in the west of Syria was also going against the Syrian regime with numerous opposition groups gaining ground. The U.S.-trained Syrian fighters were a nearly complete failure as only 60 had been trained and almost every single one was either captured or killed within weeks of reentering Syria to fight. The United States abandoned the training program in late September in favor of providing material and air support to groups already demonstrating battlefield success.

As the Assad regime looked like it was on the edge of failure; several key events happened in the summer and early fall to provide new hope. The first event was the signing of a nuclear material agreement between Iran and what became known as the P5+1 countries that included the permanent five countries from the UN Security Council (the United States, the United Kingdom, France, Russia, China) and Germany. This agreement, though not fully approved by all of the participating countries, signaled an end to the arms and economic embargo and sanctions against the Iranian regime, the primary supporter of the Assad regime in Syria. By August 2015, Iran was in a position to provide both more manpower and more financial support to Syria. Additionally, in September Russia deployed attack aircraft, artillery, and armored units to Syria and began attacking Syrian opposition forces. This meant that ISIS only had to contend with the U.S.-led coalition as most Russian air and artillery attacks were directed at non-ISIS opposition forces. That was until October 31, 2015, when a Russian passenger jet was brought down by a reported bomb on board as it traveled from Sharm al-Sheikh. ISIS took credit for the attack through one of its declared provinces. This generated more intense attacks from Russian aircraft against ISIS targets in Syria. Following a multi-location terrorist attack in Paris, France, on November 13, 2015, which killed 130 and galvanized the French people and government against ISIS and spurred on additional attacks against ISIS targets from the air.

As 2015 came to an end, it was uncertain what would be the final result of the Russian participation in the fighting or the added efforts of French aircraft and personnel. It was clear that Russia was in Syria to support the Assad regime as were Iran and Hezbollah. It was uncertain whether or not there would be a resolution such that a combined Shia-led response would be directed from the Syria-Iran-Hezbollah axis to fight ISIS in Syria. The United States was also announcing additional special operations forces deployed to Iraq and Syria to serve as a targeted strike force.

Ideas behind ISIS

ISIS is an organization driven by ideas and ideology—not just ideas alone, but also a system of belief within which many disparate ideas are brought together. These beliefs give the group its power to recruit and to operate. They also drive the way in which ISIS operates within the territory it currently controls as well as regionally and globally. In this chapter, some of the beliefs that are most powerful in driving this action are explained.

Management of Savagery: Violence as a Tool

Management of Savagery: The Most Critical Stage through Which the Islamic Nation Will Pass (إدارة التوحش: أخطر مرحلة ستمر بها الأمة) is the title of a long (more than 200 pages) manifesto written by a salafi-jihadi thinker named Abu Bakr Naji that was published on the Internet in 2004. Based on its publication date, it is clear that this was written for the broader salafi-jihadi community and not specifically for ISIS. That said, the recommendations in the book are significant when viewing the actions of ISIS over time and how it views the violence it performs. In Western media, the violence gets the attention as is intended.

Though the book and its thinking have been described as "al-Qaeda's Play-book," this is probably not true. Naji advocates for numerous small attacks rather than spectacular Hollywood-style or 9/11-style attacks. Al-Qaeda always seemed to be looking for another big attack and ISIS was content with consistent smaller ones as described and advocated for by Naji. That said, this work describes the thinking and behavior regarding how to use violence in the fight between salafi-jihadis and their opponents.

The first doctrinal point identified in the book is that ISIS is fighting a war of attrition or exhaustion where the intent is to drain the resources of the opponent powers such that they no longer have the will to continue the struggle. Second, violence is to be used as a means to generate both energy within the salafi-jihadi community and a sense of urgency within the broader Sunni Muslim community. The author of this work and other salafi-jihadi thinkers acknowledge that the vast majority of Sunni Muslims are not awake to the perils of the West with respect to their belief and their way of life. Thus, the violence will do three things simultaneously. One, it will wake the broader the community to the perils facing them. Two, the violence will bring Western powers into the Muslim world where they will commit their own violence. This will further estrange the Sunnis from the West, causing them to hate the West and struggle against it. Three, the allies of the West within the Muslim world will be discredited. This will come about through the inability of the West to prevent ISIS from targeting Western powers. In addition, the Saudi, Egyptian, Jordanian, and other governments will look weak and wrong because of their reliance on and association with Western powers that would then be responsible for all of the damage in the Muslim world.

The main idea is that violence is not an end to itself. The salafi-jihadis are not killing people and destroying things for a material benefit. They are beheading, burning people alive, and conducting suicide bomb attacks as part of a program to create an environment of Sunni energy and outrage against the West in an attempt to inspire the Sunnis to rise up and support the caliphate. Statistically, ISIS is not killing the most people in the region. It is not comparatively the most violent. What it is, is the most adept at propagandizing that violence into a broader objective.

Salafist Ideology

The Arabic word salaf (سلف) means forefathers. The roots of this idea are derived directly from the words of the Prophet Mohamed when he said:

> The best people are those of my generation, and then those who will come after them (the next generation), and then those who will come after them (i.e. the next generation), and then after them, there will come people whose witness will precede their oaths, and whose oaths will precede their witness. (Sahih Bukhari Volume 8, hadith number 437)

This is in essence, a greatest generation argument. The greatest generation of Muslims was that of Mohamed and Mohamed's companions. The next greatest generation was the following generation and so on. The idea of what is called Salafist thought is to return to the practice of Islam as it was lived by those first Muslims. Note that it is sometimes called Wahhabism because the two ideologies are similar and many groups that are Salafist are also Wahhabis. (See entry on *Wahhabi* later in this book.)

One of the earliest to espouse this idea is a man referred to as Ibn Tamiya (Tāqī al-Dīn Aḥmad ibn Taymiyyah, January 22, 1263–September 26, 1328) who was writing in the aftermath of the Crusading period and in the midst of the Mongol invasion. In an attempt to understand why these bad things were happening to Islam, he postulated that it was because Muslims were not essentially right with God. The solution to the problems of Islam was to get right with God. Who was right with God? Mohamed and those of his generation. This was proven not simply by the statement of the prophet provided previously, but also through the battlefield success of Islam in those earliest generations when Muslims conquered the Persian Empire in total and inflicted numerous defeats on the Roman Empire as well. In the first three generations of Islam, the Muslims united the Arabian Peninsula under Islam, defeated two major empires, and established control that extended from the Iberian Peninsula in the west to the Indus River Valley in India in the east. This was seen as miraculous proof of being in alignment with God. Ibn Tamiya also suggested that killing Muslims who were working with the Mongols was not wrong as they were supporting an evil or, if innocent, then God would grant them martyrdom. This is part of the logic that many salafi-jihadi groups use today in justifying their attacks on what most in the West see as fellow Muslims.

Salafis adhere to the word of God in the Quran and to the traditions of the prophet as provided by his own statements and observed and attested behavior. They do not accept a dialectical approach to reasoning the intent of God by human disputations or human innovation.

This *original intent* interpretation is critical to understanding the mind of ISIS in terms of its governance and the right way to live a Muslim life or even the right way to be Muslim. In their most strict interpretations, ISIS followers view those who do not agree with this original interpretation as not being fully Muslim; they are seen as being either apostate or being wrongly guided. Such people need to repent and return to the basic beliefs of God as outlined in the salafi tradition.

Religious End-of-Days Interpretations

Numerous other groups, to include all those who claim allegiance to al-Qaeda, are salafi-jihadis. Nearly all such groups would accept the reasoning described in the Salafist Ideology section. One of the areas where ISIS is significantly different from other groups is in its views of the end of days and its role in the end of days. As in other religions, end of days' literature in Islam is not widely accepted across the Sunni-Shia divide and not even among the Sunni. The Quran contains little of the details with respect to the end of days. Most of the information comes in the hadith. (See entry on *Hadith* later in this book.) Since those statements are sometimes in dispute, this leads to a wide set of interpretations. Though the details are in variance, the general condition of the earth as a place rife with wickedness and behavior in opposition to the will of God is almost universal for understanding these final days. What follows in this section is an abbreviation of the ISIS interpretation of these events.

According to this interpretation, the fighting in the final days will be between an army of light and an army of darkness. The army of light or army of righteousness will wear black, carry black flags, and it will begin its ascendency from Syria and spread into Mesopotamia (modern-day Iraq). It will fight battles in which it is successful as it expands. Depending on the sources, the battles fought by the army of the righteous may be against the antichrist (Masih al-Dajjal [المسيح الدجّال] or false messiah) or against other forces that are manifesting the behaviors of the end of days. It will lose battles and win many. A Roman-Crusader army will arrive in northern Syria and in this valley northeast of modern Aleppo, Syria they will fight the army of the righteous. The name of the valley and the village that used to be there is Dabiq. In this final battle, Jesus will arrive and he will lead the army of the righteous against the Dajjal and bring about the destruction of the army of darkness and the ushering in of the judgment.

As ISIS interprets these events, it is the army of the righteous. It is currently fighting a Roman-Crusader army aided by the unbelieving Shia. It is currently in the early period of success as it has advanced from Syria and into Mesopotamia. It is not clear if it currently believes that the Dajjal is on the earth leading the fight against it though it is certain that it believes and teaches that it is fighting the forces of evil as foretold in the hadith. It regularly characterizes its opponents as Roman-Crusaders.

Caliphate

The Arabic word for caliph means successor because there is no prophet after Mohamed. He is the last and final word on revelation from God. This means that the establishment of governance is under the direction of those who succeed the prophet. As kingdom is derived from king, caliphate is derived from caliph. The early leaders are referred to as the Rashidun or rightly guided caliphs. They include the first four caliphs following the prophet. Based on the earlier explained salafi ideology, they provide the pattern that ISIS leaders hope to follow. These men were humble and pious. They governed the community of believers, or ummah, according to the direction of God or the sharia, which is primarily based on the Quran; the hadith from the prophet; and the patterns of the prophet's life or sunna (from which is derived the term sunni). Finally, modern sharia also includes Islamic jurisprudence or what could be called legal interpretation or court precedence. ISIS holds to a more strict interpretation of sharia that does not include as much of the jurisprudence which it believes to be corrupted.

The caliphate or kingdom of Islam (as it could be interpreted) once declared, is the gathering place for Muslims. Thus if a Muslim is not seeking to travel to the caliphate, then he or she is not truly a Muslim. Such individuals are either nonbelievers or apostates. Additionally, all believers are expected to obey the commands of the caliph as he is the designated and recognized successor to the prophet.

This should cause readers to question whether or not ISIS's claim to having the caliph and founding a caliphate is legitimate. The simple answer is that most Muslims around the world do not accept Caliph Ibrahim (i.e., Abu Bakr al-Baghdadi) as a legitimate caliph nor do they accept that a caliphate has been established in Syria and Iraq. Despite this statement, there are thousands and even tens of thousands who are motivated by this declaration.

ISIS declared a modern state of Islam on October 15, 2006. This was the first time it named itself the Islamic State of Iraq. This date was not as publicized as the later designation of the caliphate on June 19, 2014. Regardless of the interpretation, it believes that it has a state and it is ruled under the guidance of one who is the successor of the last prophet for God. This state is to be the gathering place for the faithful, and the commands of the caliph are to be adhered to by the faithful. Those who do not obey and gather are thus enemies of that state and its soldiers in one fashion or another.

Slavery

One of the most publicized aspects of ISIS developed after it laid siege to the al-Sinjar mountain area of northwestern Iraq and captured hundreds of Yazidis. The news went out that it made the women slaves. This act garnered significant world attention. This section provides the ISIS justification for this behavior. First, for the women to be considered eligible for slavery they had to be non-Muslims captured in military operations. It is essential for the woman to be an unbeliever for this to be permissible as an apostate woman (for example, Shias or Sunnis who do not agree with the ISIS interpretation) are generally forbidden from being treated as slaves. This last point is debated among the scholars referenced by ISIS. In this matter nonbelieving women are considered as chattel and can be bought and sold and traded as any other property. They are not viewed as equal to a believing Muslim by ISIS.

Many who criticize this practice on humanitarian grounds miss the fact that in a community that does not view all humans as equal, such pleas fall on deaf ears. ISIS does make some concessions to the property as having some humanity in that it does not allow the separation of prepubescent children from a mother by sale or trade. They must be kept together until the child comes of age. There are numerous other rules regarding what is permissible in the relationship. Simply stated, such a person is the property of the captor to be treated as he wishes with some constraints. This is one of the benefits of war and a reminder to the unbelievers and believers of the superiority of ISIS fighters.

Idolatry

In Arabic the word for idolatry is shirk (شرك). The word does not literally translate to idolatry, but rather it is from a verb that means to share and in this context it means to share a place with God or to accept the existence of multiple gods (polytheism). Those who attribute a partner to God are called mushrik (plural is mushrikun) (مشرك or مشركون). It is important to understand that the first pillar of Islam is the declaration that there is no god, but the one God. This testimonial statement implies that the elevation of anyone or anything to being coequal with God is a sin and one of the most serious sins that can be committed. At various times in Islamic history, obedience to this dictum included the defacing of mosaics including human faces and the destruction of statues. Some sects of Islam today still view artwork including humans as inappropriate. This was true to a greater degree 1,400 years ago.

When ISIS goes into a museum and begins to deface or destroy ancient statues, monuments, or relics, it is doing this to destroy evidence of idolatry. All those who honor or value such objects are considered idolaters or polytheists and as such are subject to harsh penalties to include death. Given their interpretation of the faith, these policies are essential to enforce the basic tenets of Islam including a statement that is required to even be considered a Muslim—there is no god, but the God and Mohamed is the messenger (or prophet) of the God. This is all about accepting the one and unified divinity of God or tawhid.

Those who suggest that selling such artifacts can be considered hypocrisy may have something of a point, but it could also be considered a legitimate way to dispose of the items while benefitting the community of believers and those waging the war against unbelievers. If ISIS can earn money from unbelievers, all the better.

Enemies of ISIS

One of the intellectual fathers of ISIS ideology is Abu Muhammad al-Maqdisi, a Palestinian-Jordanian Islamic theorist. Al-Maqdisi was the first to claim that the members of the House of Saud were apostates because of their failure to adhere to the proper Islamic beliefs and their willingness to host unbelievers in their country. From this statement, the intellectual roots of ISIS have grown such that it considers nearly all modern Arab states to be apostate entities. It is opposed, as are all Islamist organizations, to the existence of the state of Israel, and it considers the West, in its broadest sense, to be a source of debauchery, decadence, and evil. From just this simple summary, one can imagine that the list of enemies of ISIS will be large, and it is. This chapter will focus on those currently involved in the fight against ISIS and not include all possible future opponents.

U.S.-Led Coalition (Part of Operation Inherent Resolve)

The United States announced a policy to defeat and ultimately destroy ISIS in September 2014. Even before this date, the United States and other countries that would later join the coalition engaged in hostilities against ISIS. As of December 2014, 65 countries had committed themselves to getting rid of ISIS. The list of countries is included. The countries in this group are participating in very different ways. The coalition has grown and contracted over time and will continue to do so. Some countries provide aircraft, some trainers, others special operations forces, etc. Many provide no military assistance whatsoever; instead they offer assistance monitoring terrorist financing or similar functions. Simply put, do not assume that all of the countries listed are providing something similar. They are not. The variations of support to the coalition are significant and the list continues to change on an almost monthly basis. The largest country in terms of personnel and variety of missions is the United States.

Albania	Iceland	Oman
Arab League	Iraq, Republic of	Panama
Australia	Ireland	Poland
Austria	Italy	Portugal
Bahrain, Kingdom of	Japan	Qatar
Belgium, Kingdom of	Jordan	Romania
Bosnia and Herzegovina	Korea, Republic of	Saudi Arabia
Bulgaria	Kosovo	Serbia
Canada	Kuwait	Singapore
Croatia	Latvia	Slovakia
Cyprus	Lebanon	Slovenia
Czech Republic	Lithuania	Somalia
Denmark	Luxembourg	Spain
Egypt, Arab Republic of	Macedonia	Sweden
Estonia	Malaysia	Taiwan
European Union	Moldova	Tunisia
Finland	Montenegro	Turkey
France	Morocco	Ukraine
Georgia	Netherlands	United Arab Emirates
Germany	New Zealand	United Kingdom
Greece	Nigeria	United States
Hungary	Norway	

Syrian Regime

For the sake of simplicity, this section includes the regime itself as well as those formally allied with it—Russia, Cuba, Hezbollah, etc. As discussed in "The History and Operations of ISIS," the organization as it exists in its current construct was formed in Syria as the regime began losing control of various portions of its territory. ISIS's control of a large portion of the Euphrates River valley and much of Syria's eastern oil wealth poses a serious threat to the Syrian regime's economic stability.

ISIS views members of the regime of Bashar al-Assad as corrupt unbelievers. The Syrian government is a combination of Alawite sectarian families and

Ba'ath Party officials. The Ba'ath Party in Syria and Iraq shares the same roots, but the Syrian arm of the party morphed significantly under the influence of Hafez al-Assad, father of Basher al-Assad. The Ba'athists in Syria are still generally secular in nature. Despite this, Syria was the first state to recognize the government of Ayatollah Ruhollah Khomeini in Iran in 1979. Because of this and its role in funneling weapons from Iran to Hezbollah, it is part of the Iranian hegemony in the Middle East.

Syria has modern capabilities in terms of aircraft, helicopters, tanks, etc. It has been fighting against opposition forces for more than four years and its resources have depleted. It withdrew from locations east of the Euphrates River valley in early 2015 to better position its limited resources. It is no longer trying to hold on to the entire country, but it is focusing on the specifics of the Alawite-controlled west—the coast, the Orontes River valley from Damascus to Aleppo, and Deir al-Zour on the Euphrates River. It has received significant assistance from Hezbollah in fighting against opposition forces along the Lebanese border for several years. Hezbollah has taken numerous casualties in the fighting, but it maintains a force of several thousand in Syria. The Syrian government recently requested and received assistance from Russia in the form of air and ground forces. A smaller contingent of Cuban forces followed the Russian deployment after several months.

The U.S. government is in opposition to the government of Bashar al-Assad for the brutal way in which he has used the organs of state violence to suppress the opposition. These include chemical weapons and barrel bombs (improvised explosive devices dropped from aircraft and helicopters). There has also been bombardment from the land and air against various opposition-controlled neighborhoods inflicting significant casualties on civilians. Hundreds of thousands of Syrians have been killed during the fighting with the majority of casualties probably caused by the Syrian regime.

Syrian Opposition

Few of the groups listed in the following sections fight outside their villages or neighborhoods. Most do not have the resources in weapons, ammunition, or manpower to be expeditionary beyond their local area and almost none have the logistical support to mount anything like a campaign that would include battles in which multiple villages or cities could be captured. Part of the reason for the drawn out nature of this civil war is the limited consolidation of the opposition. This is not the U.S. Civil War where you had the U.S. government fighting the Confederacy. There is no confederation of any size or capability and where alliances do exist in some numbers they only last for a few villages worth of fighting or a few months. Then they break up and reconfigure. Thus any linear projections of Syrian opposition combat success are based off a flawed model. Those groups that are most influential are briefly described in the following sections.

Moderate Syrian Opposition. This is the most fictional group in this chapter. A Russian official made the statement that moderates do not rebel. There is some truth to this. For the most part, this group represents people who are non-Islamist or non-Jihadist. The most publicized group was the Free Syrian Army. This group, as is true with all groups fighting in Syria, is not a single group, but represents numerous small organizations that come together, in a general sense, under an umbrella name. Because of the umbrella nature of both supporters and opponents of both the Syrian and Iraqi governments, there is a mercurial nature to the fight with any small group splintering off to work with another group based off common interests that day, week, or month.

The "moderate" opposition is the groups that the U.S. government was supporting and training through both the Central Intelligence Agency (CIA) and the Department of Defense (DoD). They have received money and arms, and some training from the United States. In some cases, the weapons are significant in terms of firepower. At least one group received heavy antitank guided missiles that are effective against both vehicles and fortified positions at more than two miles. The groups shift from dozens to hundreds in number. There are tens of thousands in armed opposition to the Syrian government, and there may be thousands that can be called moderate. If a reader were to see a group of opposition fighters lined up against a wall, it is unlikely that she or he would be able to distinguish between the moderates and the religious extremists.

Jabhat al-Nusra. (See entry on *Jabhat al-Nusra* later in this book.) As discussed in "The History and Operations of ISIS," this group was formed by members of the Islamic State of Iraq who were sent to Syria to begin establishing a base for the state in the burgeoning civil war. It has grown in power and influence over the years since its initial arrival. It separated from ISIS in a well-publicized disagreement over authority and control, and it swore allegiance to al-Qaeda. It is violent and like all of the other opposition organizations it regularly changes sides depending on who it is fighting. It represents several thousand fighters at the very most. In most areas where it is conducting operations, it has dozens to hundreds of fighters present. They are salafi-jihadis, and they subscribe to most of the same ideology as ISIS with the exception of Abu Bakr al-Baghdadi being the rightful caliph and the Islamic State being the caliphate.

Islamist Opposition. There are numerous (at least several dozen and maybe hundreds) other salafi-jihadi or Islamist organizations participating in the fighting in Syria. As stated previously, they are mercurial and change names, size, and affiliations on an irregular basis. For the most part, groups are defending neighborhoods or villages with which they have lasting relationships and associations. This is common with the "moderate" opposition as well. An analogy that may prove useful is that of gangs that protect their "turf" from interlopers as other gangs attempt to muscle in on the territory.

Iraqi Regime

The relationship between ISIS and the Iraqi government was laid out in "The History and Operations of ISIS." The government of Nuri al-Maliki was forced out of office in September 2014. The new Prime Minister is Hader al-Abadi. He talked about all of the things the U.S. government wanted to hear—creating an inclusive government (Sunni and Shia), controlling corruption, reconciling with the Kurdish Regional Government over oil concessions, etc. Very few of these promises have achieved success. The main complaint against the Iraqi regime is that following the U.S. withdrawal at the end of 2011 the regime became sectarian. In 2014, the Iraqi Army collapsed in the face of ISIS advances. ISIS captured hundreds of vehicles and thousands of weapons plus ammunition. Much of the weapons being used by ISIS have been captured from the Iraqi security forces and some from the Syrian security forces. It is critical to understand that the Iraqi military collapsed in mid-2014, and it still has not been rebuilt at least not in terms of psychological or emotional stability. The army has gotten better with regard to training, but it has not developed into a force that is willing to stand and face ISIS.

As it exists, the Iraqi military mainly organizes in brigades (1,500–3,000 soldiers) though there are divisions. Brigades are assigned to area operations commands. The operational commands are based off provincial governments. Thus the Anbar Operational Command has responsibility for the fight in al-Anbar Province. The regime has received F-16 attack aircraft from the United States and Su-25 attack aircraft from Russia. This gave a significant ground attack capability. Though it has the aircraft, the Iraqis are not sufficiently trained nor do they have the supporting elements to conduct precision strikes from the air.

The main plan for the U.S.-led coalition was to train and equip the Iraqis to fight against and remove ISIS from Iraq while providing close air support from coalition aircraft. Until late 2015, this plan had consistently failed to achieve noteworthy success. The retaking of Ramadi late in December 2015 was the first real success predominately led by the Iraqi military. Early 2016 saw small successes in villages surrounding other ISIS strongholds. Varying reports credited improved Iraqi training received from the U.S. with spurring this additional success. The Iraqi military is dominated by the Popular Mobilization Forces that have more forces in the field and are, generally speaking, better armed.

Popular Mobilization Forces

In mid-2014 as it looked like ISIS was close to attacking into Baghdad the Shia Grand Ayatollah in Iraq, Ali al-Sistani called out to all Iraqis to defend the capital and the country from the attacks of ISIS. This led thousands to take up arms to retain the capital. Numerous groups sprang up, but most people joined one of the three main groups that preceded the existence of ISIS: the Badr Corps, Kitaib al-Hezbollah, and Asaib Ahl al-Haq. In many cases, these groups are referred to in the media as Shia militias. Each of these three groups receives a great deal of its support from Iran. Not all of the Popular Mobilization Forces are linked with Iran, but the largest and most effective are. Since the call for people to rise up there have been efforts in the Iraqi Parliament to make the linkage between the Popular Forces and the Iraqi government semiformal. It is not uncommon for the various groups to receive equipment and pay from the government. This brings up the question of whether these groups are part of the formal Iraqi security forces or separate like gangs.

The nature, size, and delineation of these groups change on a regular basis. To quantify these groups and their supporters is to establish an artificial data point. The city of Tikrit was attacked by the Iraqi security forces and elements of the Popular Mobilization Forces, and the total force was about 30,000 strong. Most of those (more than two-thirds, at least) were from the Popular Mobilization Forces. This should give some idea of the size they have. Almost every town or area regained from ISIS in 2015 (outside of Kurdish territory) had been liberated by these forces or militias with the notable exception of Ramadi in December 2015.

Tribes

Arabs trace their culture back to Bedouin tribes and familial connections. In some parts of the Middle East, there are tribes that still exist in this historical and cultural context—moving from one location to the next with their flocks and tents. Tribes do not have borders or boundaries and they do not have nationalities. Some of the largest Arab tribes are spread across numerous countries. Tribes are not sectarian although there are tribes that are predominantly Sunni or Shia. Despite this when writers or commentators write or speak about tribes in Iraq with respect to ISIS, they are typically referring to Sunni tribes from either the al-Anbar or Ninawa provinces.

The emphasis on tribes in countering ISIS influence goes back to the Sunni Awakening—Sahwa—associated with *the Surge* of 2006 to 2009 during Operation Iraqi Freedom. In 2005 and 2006, several tribal leaders in Anbar became frustrated with the death, destruction, and chaos, and they decided to oppose the foreign fighters (al-Qaeda in Iraq at that time). At first, these were not senior tribal leaders, but typically sons or nephews. They gathered small groups of men, and they cooperated with U.S. forces operating in their areas. By the time the Surge began in 2007, the awakening had been going on for more than a year. Sunni tribes were becoming more and more likely to oppose al-Qaeda and other similar groups. Because the local tribes knew who was an Iraqi tribal member and who was a foreigner, it was much easier for them to identify the enemy. The intelligence provided by the awakening was more important than the combat actions conducted by them. In many ways, this was what changed the combat dynamic in Iraq more so than the extra deployment of U.S. soldiers. That said, extra U.S. forces did make engagement with and exploitation of awakening information much more effective.

The idea by those encouraging greater support to Sunni tribes is to recreate the Awakening. Most Sunnis oppose ISIS and its interpretation of Islam, and many tribes that are opposed to their brand of governance have suffered at the hands of ISIS through intimidation and assassination. As with the Syrian opposition, there is no group or organization that represents all Sunni tribes. Each tribe is a kingdom, and each tribe has internal political dynamics. It represents thousands of possible fighters in opposition to ISIS, but it lacks weapons, equipment, training, and logistical support. The Sunni tribes also do not trust the government in Baghdad or the Popular Mobilization Forces although they will work with them as situations require.

Kurdish Resistance

As previously mentioned in this chapter, this is complicated. Kurds are an ethnic group that is ancient in origin with a rich history, culture, and religion. They are predominantly located in the modern countries of Turkey, Iran, Iraq, and Syria. In each of these countries, they are an ethnic minority and have been historically persecuted. Historically, the Kurds have resided in the mountains of these countries and conducted commerce across the borders without much concern for modern boundaries. Their sense of Kurdishness and the fact that they are a persecuted minority have caused them to bond together and form semiautonomous regions in each of the countries. Despite this statement, there is no monolithic Kurdish identity or singular organization that represents Kurdish interests. At various times to include the recent past, Kurdish groups have fought one another, and there are Kurds who are participants in ISIS.

Kurdish issues are always complicated by the fact that the country with the largest number of Kurds is Turkey. Turkey has been fighting against the Kurdistan Workers Party (PKK) for decades. The PKK is designated as a terrorist organization by Turkey and considered to be one by numerous other countries as well. Its members conduct terrorist attacks against Turkish government targets in Turkey and then often flee across the Syrian or Iraqi border for safety. They regularly use northern Iraq as a staging base for protection from Turkish reprisals. Over the years, Turkey has conducted numerous cross-border incursions to attack the bases in Iraq or Syria. Turkey considers the PKK to be its primary threat.

Regardless of all of the complexity, this section will focus primarily on three Kurdish groups that figure most prominently in the anti-ISIS fighting. Kurdish fighting forces are referred to as Pesh Merga. In Iraq, there is a Kurdish Regional Government (KRG), and three provinces have been given an official level of semiautonomy. Within the KRG, two groups have formed Pesh Merga forces— the Kurdish Democratic Party (KDP) and the Patriotic Union of Kurdistan (PUK). In Syria, there is the Democratic Union Party (PYD) with its designated fighting force the People's Protection Units (YPG).

The Pesh Merga of the KDP has borne the brunt of the fighting and received the bulk of the coalition assistance in Iraq. In many cases, coalition countries have shipped weapons, ammunition, and other supplies directly to the KRG. In the case of the United States, the policy is that all support to Iraq, wherever that support is intended to end up, goes through the central government in Baghdad, which means that the Kurds get less than intended and what they do receive comes to them much slower than it was delivered by the United States to Iraq. The Pesh Merga fighters have been aggressively carrying the battle back against ISIS once ISIS captured Mosul and threatened the KRG capital in Irbil, Iraq. Pesh Merga forces have regained lost villages and territory, and they have captured their ancestrally claimed capital of Kirkuk in Iraq. They also recaptured the Mosul Dam that is dangerously close to collapse and could threaten hundreds of thousands were that to happen. The PUK has also provided soldiers in the fight, but to a lesser degree and with less success. Because it is not the formal leadership of the KRG, it often does not get the same equipment and training that KDP Pesh Merga receives.

In Syria, the PYD is closely aligned with the Turkish PKK. This has proven problematic for the U.S.-led coalition as YPG fighters were the most effective in late 2015 and recaptured numerous villages across northern Syria. U.S. material support of the YPG would be seen by Turkey as support to the PKK. This further complicates what is already a complicated issue. The Russians have also begun supplying YPG personnel with arms and equipment.

With the goal of supporting from the air someone else on the ground, the best fighters on the ground in Iraq and Syria have been members of the Pesh Merga from the previously named organizations. The challenge is how to support their success without exacerbating problems with Turkey.

Iran

The Islamic Republic of Iran is the largest country in the Mesopotamian area of the Middle East in both geography and demography. It is a power that will not be going away as it lives in the region. In 1979, the country experienced a coup d'état by an Islamist group. The nature of the revolt and the new government put in place immediately created a problem between Iran and the United States that has not dissipated despite recent agreements regarding nuclear weapons. The animosity between the two states became more intense once the United States invaded Iraq, and Iranian funds, weapons, and fighters were used to kill American soldiers in Iraq.

Iran has serious and lasting interests in Iraq. It wants a stable and preferably friendly neighbor. Iran and Iraq fought an eight-year brutal war from 1980 to 1988 that included the killing of thousands of civilians and the use of chemical weapons. Iran will not stand for a belligerent Iraq. Thus the instability resulting from the U.S. invasion created an opening for Iranian infiltration and meddling.

Beginning years before the U.S. departure from Iraq, the Iranians began to progress well beyond meddling and have become the most dominating influence on the Iraqi government.

The rise of ISIS gave Iran yet another opportunity to expand its influence in Iraq as it was the first country to offer military and monetary support to fight ISIS. Iran sent equipment, advisors, and ultimately fighting units. One of the most broadcast foreign faces in Iraqi media in 2015 was Qasem Soleimani. He is a major general in the Iranian Revolutionary Guards Corps and the commander of the Quds Forces since 1998. This is the force responsible for actions outside Iran. He has directed much of the counter-ISIS strategy in both Iraq and Syria.

As previously stated under the Syrian Regime section, Iran has maintained a close relationship with the regime in Syria since the revolution in 1979. Iran wants the regime to remain stable and friendly to Iran. Many opponents of Iranian influence point to a "Shia Crescent" that spreads from Iran to Iraq to Syria to Southern Lebanon and sometimes to Gaza. This is part of designating Iranian hegemony through support of cosectarian or like-minded regimes or actors in the area. In the case of Southern Lebanon, it is Hezbollah and in Gaza it is Hamas (not Shia, but they do receive funding and support from Iran).

Iran's participation in the anti-ISIS fight is significant. It has committed ground forces, money, and support to both Iraq and Syria. It is diametrically opposed to the ISIS ideology. Iran's presence in the fight confirms the ISIS narrative of a war against the unbelieving Shia and helps ISIS recruit Sunnis from across the globe. Whether or not Iran's participation is beneficial or good depends largely on perspective. It is certain that Iran's participation is intended to expand its influence throughout the countries in the fight and across the region. As Iran is very much opposed to U.S. influence, this may be construed as negative.

The Attraction of ISIS

Why do people want to fight for ISIS? Why do women want to go to the caliphate and participate in a marriage to an ISIS fighter? These questions have been asked by pundits, journalists, and commentators a great deal in 2014 and 2015 without anyone ever providing an acceptable answer. This is partly because ISIS is portrayed in the media as a bunch of irrational nihilistic barbarians bent on destroying the world. Who would want to live in such a world? It is like a post-apocalyptic dystopian movie where no civilization exists. As stated at the beginning, this book does not seek to place judgment. The following is the ISIS narrative and why it attracts followers and fighters.

There are reasons why ISIS inspires others. For one thing, it provides people with a vision of a world in which it believes it wants to live. This vision provides a purpose to young people who are looking for purpose in their lives. As stated in previous chapters, this vision portrays ISIS preparing the world for the end of days, and by so doing, it is also creating the kingdom of God's people. This is what ISIS invited people to come and join.

This chapter will lay out the manner in which this positive, aspirational message is delivered. It will specifically address the attraction to women. Finally, this chapter explains the financing used to support this vision.

Recruiting

The recruiting process for ISIS is rich and complex yet simple. First, the part that is rich. ISIS uses both specific and general media to encourage participation. There are Web pages, video indoctrination, and chat rooms. The group has individuals designated to recruit who move virtually throughout the chat rooms to pick up people who are interested. In some of the cases where women were specifically recruited, the recruiters were fighters themselves. People are specifically groomed to come to the caliphate through the one-on-one communication. The recruiters take their time and use the tremendous volume of material to portray the cause in its most positive light. They express what the caliphate offers—an opportunity to do something more, to defend Islam, to fight unbelievers and oppressors of the faithful. The messages use Quranic verses, statements from the prophet, and application to what potential recruits are seeing on the news. The desperate plight of Muslim refugees and those who are suffering from despotic leaders further strengthen the message.

The complexity is directly linked to the simplicity in that a lot of the recruiters are not part of the organization through some bureaucratic hierarchy. ISIS does recruiting both collectively and individually. The collective recruitment often comes with the assistance of media broadcasts of the suffering of Muslims in Syria or elsewhere around the world. This is supported with messages that come from conservative mosques and religious leaders. The desire to help may also be enhanced and developed by small groups of like-minded people who may meet with a potential recruit personally or in cyberspace. To call this recruiting is both accurate and inaccurate as nowhere in what is described above is there an ISIS recruiting office or someone wearing a badge that says "ask me about ISIS." ISIS does have people with the responsibility to recruit and bring in immigrants, but it also uses the mass media and what could be called freelance recruiters—fellow Muslims who simply want people to go to the caliphate, but they are not so inclined themselves. It is similar to what often gets labeled as lone wolf attacks. In this case, they are people who, on their own, recruit and indoctrinate people into what is generally called extremist viewpoints. The fact that not all of these types of recruited people will end up with ISIS further adds to the complexity. They might join another group. The simplicity is that there are voices independent of the organization which are helping build the organization.

Once convinced of the rightness of the need to join the caliphate, the recruits travel to the region where they meet up with facilitation networks in major cities in Turkey, Syria, or elsewhere. These networks then provide the information or the transportation to get the recruits into the caliphate. People who come with little or no previous connection tend to be given menial tasks. They, in general, are not trusted with complicated operations. They may be considered for suicide operations if so inclined. Unless the recruit arrives with demonstrable experience and skills, they will probably not be a frontline fighter or leader. Many of the fighters, who are prominent in the fight, were brought in by networks of acquaintances already in ISIS. This is why there are groups of

Chechens or Iraqis or Syrians from specific tribes or villages which fight together.

Women in ISIS

Why would a young, educated, middle-class woman from London want to leave her home, her education, family, and friends to go to the caliphate to become a bride to a young fighter from a different country and different culture? This question puzzles many people in the West. Many of the women who travel to ISIS are not stupid; they are not impoverished. They have options. They tend to be educated. Many are from middle-class families in terms of economic prospects and possibilities. They go because they see in ISIS an opportunity to do something that matters: a chance to participate in something bigger than themselves, something that furthers the will and plans of God. These are powerful motivations. It is true that some (we do not have an accurate understanding of the complete numbers who have gone so any statistics are estimates) women return explaining how disillusioned they were and recount the difficulties and lack of freedom in the caliphate. Despite this, women are still going and seeking to become a part of the caliphate.

The Salafist ideology has strict interpretations of what women can and cannot do in society. That said, women do serve as recruiters for ISIS. It recruits both men and women. Women also serve in all the same roles that women do in any other conservative society. For ISIS, the primary role for women is as wives and mothers as the caliphate takes seriously the importance of the next generation. Additionally, many of those who enforce the strict rules of behavior within the caliphate are women. Meaning that it is typically women who enforce dress code standards on other women.

Early on in the ISIS advance some women traveled to Syria to join ISIS with the intent of fighting alongside others. Some women have been suicide bombers. The number of women who have served as fighters is very low. This is not a new role for women in the salafi-jihadi or even the broader nonstate actor communities.

Financing ISIS

How does ISIS survive financially? War is expensive and it is fighting war on every front of its caliphate. ISIS gets money from a variety of sources. The single largest source is the taxation of residents of the caliphate. Taxes are collected from all residents within the territory it controls as well as additional taxes on nonbelievers living under the authority of ISIS. The two most publicized sources of income are oil and the Iraqi government. In addition to these two, which will be explained next, there are other sources such as the sale of antiquities, extortions, kidnapping and ransom, fees and tolls, and other similar means of deriving wealth.

Oil sales probably make up one of the largest portion of income. These are sales both internal and external to the caliphate. ISIS controls the oil rich eastern desert of Syria. It continues to pump oil from the fields located there and other fields in Syria and Iraq. It also has access to preexisting and then later developed refining capacities. Thus it is pumping crude oil, refining it into sellable product, and then distributing this product to buyers. The buyers include people living in the Islamic State and many who could be considered enemies or who are living in land controlled by enemies of the Islamic State. This is simply one oddity of many when discussing this topic. People need fuel to cook, to run their vehicles and machinery, and especially to run generators. Because this is a need, people do not care so much from where they get the resource. So truck drivers will wait for weeks to get their trucks filled with heavy oil for generators. Destruction of the oil infrastructure has moved up the priority list for those opposing ISIS. The problems with doing this include what people will think when the oil is no longer available. Who will they blame? Also, how will the infrastructure be rebuilt if the fighting ever stops?

As stated previously, a lot of the money used to operate the Islamic State came from the Iraqi government. The government in Baghdad continued to pay employees for months after ISIS took over areas. People living in Mosul continued to receive money from Baghdad for more than a year. The government believed that the land would be retaken soon and the leadership did not want its employees to be destitute and in opposition when it returned. Regardless of the reasoning, the reality is that a significant portion of the money used to pay ISIS fighters came from the very entity they were fighting. The irony of this situation is another case of the oddity of this conflict. Most of these payments ended in November and December 2015.

During the early Islamic conquests, there were Quranic protections for those designated as "people of the book." This phrase has been interpreted to mean those who believed in the Bible and other sacred texts accepted as precursors of the faith by Muslims—Christians, Jews, Zoroastrians, etc. These people were not viewed as opponents of the faith, but as ignorant of the newer revelation received by Mohamed. So long as they agreed to be protected people they would be allowed to remain in Muslim lands as worshipers of their original religion. There were several caveats. One was that they needed to pay a special tax to fund their protection. The Muslims would protect them because they could not have weapons or be trained in their use. ISIS reinstated this tax that is over and above any other taxes levied on all people living within the Islamic State.

Much has been made of the destruction of antiquities. Some of the destruction has been done to communicate the unacceptability of idols, as previously discussed. Many of the antiquities have been sold off as well. This is a much more limited resource, and though it has garnered a great deal of publicity, these sales do not really produce a significant or a continuous amount of wealth for the caliphate. Antiquities sales are sporadic and supportive of the other, more consistent wealth streams.

Allegiance to ISIS: The Loyal Following

It seems that everyone hates ISIS and that everyone wants to defeat ISIS. If that is so, then why ISIS is still around more than two years after it began its most publicized advances? How is a group of tens of thousands of fighters with stolen weapons able to withstand the military onslaught of dozens upon dozens of nations that include the most advanced militaries in the world? Part of the answer lies in the attraction of the message that ISIS communicates. Part of its continuing success comes from the fact that ISIS is not alone in its message. What follows is a brief discussion of who else is fighting alongside ISIS and who supports ISIS. This is not a comprehensive list. As previously and continuously stated, what is known of this organization is less than most people admit and so what appears here is an educated guess regarding its support and following.

Often the discussion of ISIS focuses on the negative aspects of the organization, making it unbelievable that anyone would want to be a part of its state or wish to support it. This book does not make judgments about ISIS as to whether it is evil or good. That is true about a great many of the people who are without choice governed by it or those who are inclined to be governed by it. For the vast majority of these people, the choice is not between benign governance and evil governance. The governance for Sunni Arabs in Iraq or Syria is not positive. Most feel that the governments are opposed to their existence and, at best, want from them their taxes or their performance of tasks necessary for the survival of the state. The average Sunni mother or father did not imagine in 2013 or 2014 that their children could grow up to be whatever they wanted to be. Instead, most were concerned with securing for their children the most basic of human needs to include subsistence, education, respect, and dignity. Theirs was not a choice between self-actualized accomplishment and barbaric abuse. In many cases, the life under ISIS is no worse than under the state regimes and, in some cases, it is better. ISIS provides stability and security. There are no death squads running around the streets of cities controlled by ISIS as there were under the Iraqi government. Though there is a greater level of religious oppression, people can walk the streets in a greater degree of certainty.

As previously stated, the organization of ISIS was like a snowball; as it continued to operate, it attracted more and more followers of various groups, slowly adding to its mass as it moved along. The following sections explain the types of groups and people who became associated with the organization or the movement.

Conservative Sunni Muslims

The largest collection of people within the sphere of ISIS is not necessarily inclined toward the most radical interpretations of the group nor are they inclined toward spreading the beliefs through violence. They believe in sacrifice to advance the faith and in a strict interpretation of the faith. There are many conservative people among the various tribes in Iraq. They want to return to a purer interpretation of life and they want to maintain the old ways of behavior, worship, and social interaction. While they may not be personally inclined toward the same salafist interpretations of the faith which ISIS endorses, many respect those who do subscribe to and live by such interpretations. Most of these people are not inclined toward violence though they believe in protecting their family and property. They believe they have been discounted and disrespected. They have been treated as a minority in their own country, which they (as a people) used to rule. In this disrespect, they have been threatened, their families harmed, and their property destroyed. They want stability and respect.

Former Ba'athists and Former Iraqi Regime Members

In May 2003, when the Coalition Provisional Authority (CPA), then ruling Iraq, issued its Order #2, it put hundreds of thousands of Iraqi soldiers out of work. The CPA believed it was easier to rebuild an army from the ground up than to restructure a standing army. As the new Iraqi Army was being recruited and trained, some of the former soldiers joined, but most did not. Most of the officers were prevented from joining. Their pay ended and their retirements were voided; they needed employment and they wanted honor and dignity.

Many joined the opposition, and as that opposition coalesced around what would become ISIS, they were incorporated into that group. The professional officers, especially those with specific skills like intelligence, explosives, engineer, etc., gained positions of authority and respect as they helped organize the less-trained though highly motivated members of the group.

Sunni Nationalists

Some conservative Sunni Muslims and former Ba'athist Iraqi Regime members may fall into the category of Sunni nationalists as well. These are people who believe in supporting and promoting the Sunni cause especially in opposition to a growing Shia influence. They may come from anywhere in the Muslim world.

Salafi-Jihadis

The center or core of ISIS is composed of like-minded people who believe in the stated goals and ideology of the organization. These like-minded people believe in sacrifice to advance the faith and they believe in a strict interpretation of the faith. They have a belief that it may be necessary and is acceptable to both sacrifice oneself and inflict harm on the enemy to advance the faith. Those who share these ideals can come from anywhere in the world. They can be recent converts or lifelong Muslims.

Foreign Fighters

The groups in this list overlap. This group comes from outside Iraq and Syria. They may have been inspired by the suffering of Muslims in the Middle East, in general, or by the suffering in Syria or Iraq as afflicted on the local inhabitants by corrupt regimes. Regardless, they were inspired and they traveled to the region, typically at personal expense, to participate in this struggle. They are believers. It may be a false belief and they may leave shortly after arriving, if they can, but they are a belief-driven group. Unlike the case of al-Qaeda affiliated groups, those who join ISIS are making a semipermanent or permanent decision. They are coming to the Islamic State to build the state rather than coming for some jihadi tourism. This is not universally true, but it is generally true.

Foreign Supporters

Not everyone who supports ISIS does so with force of arms. ISIS made a choice not to accept support in the form of foreign donations, which left it free to chart its own course without fear of outside direction. There are people who have not and will not travel to the caliphate but want to support the state. Some do this through social media and some do it through recruiting, either online, in mosques, or by other means. Some provide money for the caliphate or for those who desire to travel to the caliphate.

Allies and Franchises

The success of ISIS has inspired numerous other groups to want to enjoy the notoriety and success of association. These groups have declared allegiance to ISIS and to Caliph Ibrahim as their legitimate ruler. To this point, this allegiance has had little real-world impact in terms of shaping the struggle and behavior of ISIS yet the groups are growing and some are achieving notoriety and success on their own. This gives ISIS multiregional reach and the ability to claim that it is an everywhere force. The various groups are termed *wilayah* that is an Arabic word sometimes translated as state or province. (See entry on *Wilayah* later in the book.) These groups are in Afghanistan-Pakistan, Yemen, Saudi Arabia, Sinai Peninsula Egypt, Libya, Algeria, and Nigeria. The most newsworthy group before declaring allegiance was Boko Haram in Nigeria. Another successful group in launching attacks is in Sinai as it most notably downed a Russian airliner on October 31, 2015.

Though a very small percentage of Muslims agree with everything ISIS teaches, there are more who agree with some of what it represents. The idea of Muslims defending their beliefs and standing up against the spread of ideologically opposing groups, peoples, nations, and states appeals to many in the Muslim world. From this group of Muslims, ISIS will draw a tacit level of acceptance, which may be the most important benefit. Though they may be disagreeable, there are many who do not feel they cross the line or that they should be destroyed.

ISIS and the Media

If there is one thing that sets ISIS apart from all other similar groups, it is its mastery of media. It understands how to dominate the news cycle and how to communicate its message. It is a relatively small group in comparison to most nations or states and yet it has the attention of the entirety of the developed world and most of the developing world. As stated in the preceding chapter, it has garnered the loyalty of groups from Pakistan to Nigeria. It operates in Turkey and Europe and inspires attacks in North America. This is both enhanced by and enhances the media perception of the group.

Twitter

The most publicized media success for ISIS is probably Twitter. There are thousands of people who post on Twitter both in opposition to and in support of ISIS. ISIS has people in the state itself and abroad who post and repost both by order and organically. Twitter provides the ability for ISIS to get a message out to the majority of the world within a matter of minutes through using #hashtags. Twitter is credited with bringing about the downfall of President Hosni Mubarak of Egypt in 2011. Whether this is true or not is irrelevant. What is important is that it taught the world what was possible with Twitter. ISIS has now demonstrated to every current and future substate, nonstate, or poststate actor what can be accomplished through the use of a simple phone application. Again, this is both an intentional part of its plan and an organic and supportive nonaffiliated process that benefits ISIS in its messaging.

Web Sites

ISIS has no official Web site because of official controls and sanctions that would have any such Web site shut down by government authority. Despite these restrictions, there are still plenty of images and information available through third-party sites. Many of the sites behave in similar ways as do the recruiters. Some are semiofficials and others are simply individuals broadcasting their own thoughts or trying to be rebels by supporting something they perceive to be on the edge.

Video

There are numerous sites that publish ISIS videos. Some of the videos are ISIS productions. One of the best known and best produced is titled "Clanging of the Swords" and is more than an hour long. Another video published in November 2015 is titled "And No Respite," which targets the U.S. market with English language and well-crafted imagery and special effects. There are numerous other videos in a variety of languages. Each is sending a message. Some of them communicate the power of ISIS to destroy the old borders or to reach out and kill its enemies. Many of the ISIS videos are snuff films as they show the taking of human life in various ways—explosions, executions, shootings, etc. One should only watch these videos with a serious purpose in mind; as a combat veteran said, somethings you cannot unsee.

The jihadi community produces music videos that feature its fighters either dancing or chanting the lyrics themselves. Others feature the fighters with music playing over the events depicted. Music can be instrumental or it can be a nasheed (or chant). These are particularly popular with salafi-jihadis since they believe there is a prohibition against instrumental music. The chants convey a great deal of information about the intent and objectives of the group. They are also catchy tunes that act as advertising jingles to consistently communicate the goals of the group long after the listener no longer has the music playing.

Magazine—*Dabiq*

Al-Qaeda in the Arabian Peninsula began the concept of publishing a magazine as a vehicle to get information out. ISIS has taken that original concept and expanded it. It publishes magazines in different languages. Its English-language magazine is called *Dabiq*. The magazine is named after the Muslim equivalent of the battle of Armageddon where, at the end of days, the army of the righteous will be led by Jesus to defeat the Dajjal or anti-Christ. The magazine is well produced with imagery, articles, and propaganda. It began after the declaration of the caliphate, and by the end of 2015, there were 12 issues published. Though written in English, the tone of the writing is Arabic as many of the articles use poetic imagery and make statements that seem poetically extreme. Reading the magazine is the single best way to understand the ISIS perspective. To fully understand the content requires a grasp of Islamic history and culture as many of the words and references may be easily missed by one who lacks the proper context.

Taking Credit

It took al-Qaeda years to admit to being behind the attacks on September 11, 2001. The intent of the organization was to let the attacks speak for themselves. It was content to conduct its business behind the scenes in the shadows because it wanted the Muslim people to rise up and declare a caliphate organically. ISIS is very different. It is a state. It has the agenda of being in the forefront of people's minds because it is the one that created and declared the caliphate. Thus ISIS takes credit almost immediately upon the commission of an act. In some cases, it seems to take responsibility almost too quickly as if it is trying to beat some other organization to the credit. Receiving credit for attacks is a part of its media effort; it communicates that it is everywhere doing all of the fighting in the name of Islam. The initial credit is typically communicated by Twitter and then may be followed up by video uploaded to a Web site. This, of course, depends on what ISIS is taking credit for. In the case of assassinations and executions, the first word may be through an uploaded video. When the events (like a bomb blast) are covered by international media, Twitter is the common vehicle.

Violence for Media's Sake

As stated earlier, ISIS conducts its violence with the intent of getting media attention. This is why it is extreme in terms of violence and in the staging of events. Like a reality television star, it has to continually increase the spectacle or it will lose viewers. It started with beheadings because that received massive international coverage. These then escalated in number and in variety. It also understands that the nationality of the person being executed matters because certain nationalities get more media coverage than others. The executioner also matters in terms of the coverage. Simply stated, its staged violence is intended as a reality program with staging, script, and schedule for release in order to maximize coverage.

Life in the Islamic State

Understanding ISIS is not about comparing life in the Islamic State with life in the United States or Canada. In that comparison, it does not fare well. That said, for those who travel to join ISIS from abroad the comparison has some value. There are people who have left the United States, Canada, or European countries to live in the Islamic State. The reasons for this have been given elsewhere in this book. The point here is that these people represent a small percentage of those living under the authority of ISIS. For the vast majority of ISIS recruits, the comparison is to life under the Iraqi government or the regime of Bashar al-Assad in Syria.

Life anywhere outside of an immediate combat zone is roughly the same. Even when combat is happening only a few miles away, humans adjust rather quickly to establish some level of normalization—children play, people get food, they eat, they work. Because of this, a detailed account of a day in the life of an ISIS resident will not be provided. Information on this daily life is rather widespread. There are a few bloggers who regularly post about life in the Islamic State and there are people who have left the Islamic State and described life there. Then there are the official and semiofficial versions of life in the Islamic State. They vary wildly in their descriptions. In this chapter, the intent is to communicate a best guess of life for the average person.

ISIS makes a great deal of effort to communicate that it has created a better existence for its community. To determine the validity of this claim, it is necessary to consider what life is like outside the community of ISIS.

If you lived in Iraq in 2014 or in Syria under regime authority, then you would have experienced some of the following challenges regardless of your religious beliefs or ethnicity. Power outages would be common. Depending on where you lived, you may have only had power a couple of hours a day. You probably did not have a refrigerator in your home because it is expensive and requires a consistent flow of electricity. This would force you to prepare your food every day and then eat it all or, if it is perishable, it will spoil. The bread you buy does not have a lot of preservatives so it will go stale or mold within a couple of days so you have to get it every day. You are not safe. There are regular attacks. People get kidnapped. Bombs go off. People are shot. Children are not allowed to play outside most days and many schools are closed because teachers are primary targets. Delivery of cooking gas is spotty; therefore, you may not have a hot meal for some days at a time. Your parents may be out of work, forcing you to live off the generosity of family and friends. This is a bleak image, but by no means the bleakest that can be drawn. Life is hard in both countries. Some of this was true prior to the overthrow of Saddam Hussein in Iraq and the outbreak of the civil war in Syria. The security situation was much better and the frequency of resources was more reliable, but the average Syrian or Iraqi lived a life of significant poverty by North American standards. There are wealthy families in both countries that live much like the rich do anywhere, but average people were much worse off then and are suffering significantly more now.

Without taking these considerations into account, it can be difficult to understand why someone might put up with the lifestyle described in the next paragraphs. Most people will tolerate a lot to have stability of resources and security. Life in the Islamic State is proof of this.

Mosul is the second largest city in Iraq and the largest city under ISIS control. Those living in Mosul currently have spotty electricity because ISIS has not been able to get the main power generators to function at a normal capacity. So people in the city usually get two hours of electricity during the day and two hours at night. ISIS recently restarted schools in Mosul with textbooks and a semistandard curriculum. The textbooks emphasize a strict Islamic interpretation and regularly discuss the glories of jihad in physical education, math, and history. Many parents are choosing not to send their kids to school because they do not agree with the curriculum and the Iraqi government has stated that it will not recognize any educational certificate—diploma—coming from the Islamic State. This may mean a lost generation of children reaching adulthood without an education. In the Middle East, there is no tradition of home schooling. Teaching the children at home is difficult and unlikely.

When a person leaves the home, appearance is important. Women need to not have any flesh showing except maybe their hands. Men must have a beard—preferably a long one. A goatee is not acceptable. Men and women can be punished by being beaten immediately by the morality police or if they continue to violate the standards they can be punished more severely. That said, this tends to be a simple issue of social and immediate correction. No one is being executed for improper dress standards. Women cannot leave the house alone or be unescorted. They must always have a male relative with them. Social interactions are not allowed between Muslim men and women who are not married or properly escorted and chaperoned.

ISIS also forbids smoking, the consumption of alcohol and pork, or the violation of any other Muslim dietary laws. During the month of Ramadan when all Muslims fast from sun up to sun down, all restaurants are closed and eating or drinking in public is a crime.

Many items available in modern societies are in short supply or not available. ISIS can import most things into the caliphate, but it is difficult so they are expensive and typically limited to fighters. Fighters get paid by the state so they have a steady income, and it is a decent income by the local standards—$300 to $500 a month. Regular workers make much less so there is an incentive to be a fighter. In late 2015 and early 2016, U.S. bombers targeted buildings holding large quantities of cash that has affected the amount paid to fighters and other employees of ISIS. Some salaries have been cut by as much as 50 percent.

Minorities and non-Muslims can be treated well though they must maintain their status as protected people. In the United States, we would call this being a second-class citizen. Most, non-Muslims, who have spoken of their life in the Islamic State, say that as long as they keep their head down and live quietly they are not bothered.

In general, life is secure and stable. There are no night raids into people's homes. Respect is shown to heads of households and to families and women so long as standards are followed. Despite the apparent lack of rights and basic services, even the persecuted tend to prefer the predictable security of ISIS over a return to chaos.

Is ISIS a State?

This question is one of the most significant in this book. What does ISIS represent? The president of the United States along with many other noted scholars has stated that ISIS is neither Islamic nor a state. When such notables make these statements what are they trying to say? If they are saying that it is not a state like "us," then they are correct. ISIS rejects Western models of statehood. It rejects the notions of the treaty of Westphalia (1648 CE) from which Europe, North America, and most other modern states derive their concept of statehood. It rejects the United Nations Charter and the claims and rights asserted in that document. It rejects the colonial efforts of Western powers preceding and following the dissolution of the Ottoman Empire (circa 1919) to create Western-style states in the Middle East, North Africa, and elsewhere in the Muslim world. Western notions of democracy, social justice, and government separated from religious guidance are not what they stand for. Islam provided all of those things long before the 1648 Treaty of Westphalia, or so ISIS would argue.

What is a state? This is a complex question; the German sociologist and thinker, Max Weber, posited that a state was a political organization that maintains a monopoly on the use of violence in a given territory. If this is the sole definition of state, then ISIS is definitely a state. It maintains a monopoly on the organized use of violence within the territory it governs. In this regard, it is more of a state than Iraq or Syria since there is less internal violence under ISIS rule than is true for either of those regimes.

ISIS developed a currency—gold coin. There is a proscription in the strictest sense of Islam that eschews the use of paper money. Abandoning paper money has been an objective of ISIS for a while and certainly since the announcement of a caliphate in 2014. This is starting to come to fruition as the coins are minted in some quantity. Since they are supposedly made from gold (what level of purity is uncertain), there is inherent value in the coin itself. Does currency give credibility to being a state? If so, then ISIS gets another mark in the statehood column. That said, there is little evidence by early 2016 that such currency is being produced in quantity or used in average transactions.

Some definitions of a state include the ability to negotiate treaties and other binding agreements with other states. This one is a little difficult to assess as ISIS considers most other states (certainly most Muslim states) as morally corrupt. It therefore has no interest in doing business with them. No country or state has recognized ISIS as a state, thus it is completely excluded from the international community. Such a condition is a blow to being considered a state. Of course, this category implies that there is a club called the international community and if one is not invited in, then one cannot be a state. ISIS may argue that the numerous other *wilayas* that have pledged its allegiance and support constitute a new international community—a community of believers—the only community worth belonging to from its perspective.

Because of the problems associated with being locked out of the international community, there is nothing that ISIS can do to interact with that community. It cannot issue passports or travel documents recognized anywhere in the world. ISIS cannot participate in the international banking infrastructure. From its perspective, this is not a bad thing as it views the globally accepted commerce system as a violation of Islamic law.

The question of whether or not ISIS can be considered a state is dependent on definition and perspective. If by being a state one means that ISIS can participate in the global community, then ISIS is not a state. If the definition of a state is one that includes the monopoly of violence and the ability to make laws to govern people within a given territory, then it certainly is a state.

Certain Iraqi leaders have expressed concern over the potential evolution of ISIS within the minds of people around the world. The following analogy was used to convey the concerns of those leaders. Originally the state of Israel was simply a Zionist entity. Early Zionists bought land and petitioned the international community for rights as a state. The United Nations saw the growth of the Zionist community and proposed the division of lands to include land for a Zionist state. The Zionists fought for the land and took much of it by force, driving off the Arabs who lived there. The world came to recognize this entity as a state, and it is now treated as equal with other states. Iraqi leaders fear that such a thing could happen to ISIS. While its current position is transitory, eventually it may be accepted within the international community. While this argument may make sense to some, others have dismissed it as impossible and unacceptable. Only time will tell the ultimate classification (and eventual fate) of the Islamic State.

Reference Entries

Abbasid Caliphate

Dates: 750–1258 CE (sometimes extended from 1261–1517 CE as ruled under the Mameluke Sultanate of Cairo)

What is important? The Abbassid Caliphate was the second dynastic caliphate in Islamic history following the Umayyad dynasty. The Umayya ruled from Damascus, Syria. The Abbasids ruled mostly from Iraq with the first capital in Kufa (750–762). The Abbasid rulers constructed the city of Baghdad to be their capital. At one point, the empire was ruled from Raqqa, Syria. The Abbasids claimed their lineage back to Abbas ibn Abd al-Muttalib who was an uncle of the Prophet Mohamed. Their claims in opposition to the Umayya included that the Umayya clan usurped the authority of the family of the prophet and that they also ruled impiously.

The dynasty did not rule a consolidated empire for long. Initially the fragmentation was due to distance, the challenge of communication, and the ability for local rulers to withhold resources from a distant central authority. Even when the empire was centrally controlled, it was a loose form of control. In the 10th century, Turkic tribes swept into the imperial lands and began to exert local authority. Many of the Turcoman sultans gave, at least, verbal obedience to the Abbasid caliph in Baghdad (or other capitals) though they typically governed in a semiautonomous fashion. The end date given previously coincides with the Mongol sack of Baghdad, which was a deep scar on Muslim and Arab consciousness. Support of the Abbasid caliphs continued under the Mameluke Sultans as they ruled from Cairo until the conquest of the Ottoman Turks and the movement of the caliphate from Cairo to Constantinople.

Many consider the Golden Age of Islam to be during the Abbasid Caliphate and especially in the 9th and 10th centuries. During this time, much of ancient Greek thought was preserved through translation from Greek to Arabic. In addition, there were numerous mathematical and scientific theoretical and practical developments.

Why does it matter to ISIS? Every culture refers back to its Golden Age. The use of Raqqa, Syria, and the focus on attacks toward Baghdad are attempts on the part of ISIS to control the physical territory from which the greatest Islamic caliphate ruled.

al-Amiri, Hadi (هادي العامري)

Dates: 1954–Present

Key Events in His Life: Current Iraqi political leader. He was opposed to Saddam Hussein and he fought with the Iranian Army against the Iraqi military in the Iran-Iraq War (1980–1988) as part of the Badr Brigade. He later became the commander of the Badr Corps that was then the military wing of the Supreme Islamic Iraqi Council, a party closely aligned with Iran. His organization received training from the Iranian Revolution Guards Corps and the Quds force. He was opposed to the U.S. occupation of Iraq and was a staunch opponent of U.S. interests and long-term influence through the occupation. He was elected to the Iraqi Parliament in 2009 and designated as the minister of transportation in 2010.

Why does it matter? He works closely with Qasem Soleimani of the Iranian Quds Force and he is one of the most prominent Iraqi figures in the anti-ISIS campaign. He leads the Badr Corps as one of the largest elements in the Popular Mobilization Forces.

al-Assad, Bashar Hafez (بشار حافظ الأسد)

Dates: September 11, 1965–Present

Key Events in His Life: He assumed office as the President of Syria following the death of his father in 2000. He is a graduate of Damascus University

Medical School and later he completed postgraduate studies at the Western Eye Hospital in London where he specialized in ophthalmology. His wife is a UK citizen and he has three children. He was not expected to succeed to the leadership of Syria, but his older brother died in a car accident in 1994. His father ruled Syria for 30 years and established a powerful control of Alawite and secular leadership in the country. This organization and manner of government passed to Bashar.

Why does it matter? Leadership in Syria is a corporate form of rule. It is unclear just how much authority Bashar has and whether or not he can make unilateral decisions. His father was a dominating personality and many suggest that Bashar did not fill his father's shoes as much as he inherited the position along with others close beside him. He is the international lightening rod for all of the problems in Syria and many call for his departure. It is unclear if he can simply depart or what his departure would do to the Syrian government establishment. Regardless of his personal position a collapse of the regime would certainly spell increased chaos as the Alawite communities have been tightly linked by the Assad family to the government. They will have to continue to fight as this is an existential struggle for them.

al-Baghdadi, Abu Abdullah al-Rashid (ابو عبدالله الراشد البغدادي)

Dates: Unknown–April 18, 2010

Names:
Abu Omar al-Qurashi al-Baghdadi
Hamid Dawud Mohamed Khalil al Zawi
Abu Hamza al-Baghdadi

Key Events in His Life: See "Leaders of ISIS" chapter.

Why does it matter? See "Leaders of ISIS" chapter.

al-Baghdadi, Abu Bakr

Dates: June 28, 1971 (near Samarra)–Present

Names:
  Abu Du'a (أبو دعاء)
  Abu Bakr al-Baghdadi al-Husseini al-Qurashi (أبو بكر البغدادي الحسيني الهاشمي (القرشي
  Amir al-Mu'minin or Caliph Ibrahim (خَلِيفَةُ إِبْرَاهِيم)
  Ibrahim Awad Ibrahim al-Badri al-Samarrai (إبراهيم عواض إبراهيم علي محمد (البدري السامرائي

Key Events in His Life: See "Leaders of ISIS" chapter.

Why does it matter? See "Leaders of ISIS" chapter.

al-Maqdisi, Abu Muhammad

Dates: 1959 (Nablus, West Bank)–Present

Name: Aasim Muhammad Tahir al-Barqawi (عصام محمد طاهر البرقاوي)

Key Events in His Life: Leading Islamist thinker and writer. His family immigrated to Kuwait when he was a young boy and he later studied at the University of Mosul, Iraq. He traveled a great deal speaking with various religious leaders in the Arab-Muslim world as he developed his ideology. He developed a following after returning to Jordan in 1992; he was eventually arrested and imprisoned for his radical views. He was released and then arrested for planning attacks against American targets in Jordan. He was, however, acquitted because the Jordanian government had said there were no American forces in Jordan at the time he was to have allegedly planned the attacks. He was again arrested for his extreme views. He was released from prison most recently in June 2014. He advocated for the release of a British hostage from ISIS control on September 21, 2014.

Why does it matter? He is one of the most influential Islamist writers and speakers currently living. He shared part of his prison experience with Abu Musab al-Zarqawi. It is presumed that it was his thinking that shaped the thinking of al-Zarqawi into the man who would form the parent organization and ideology for ISIS. Al-Maqdisi was one of the first people to accuse the Saud family and regime of being apostate. This opened the door for others to so criticize most of the Arab-Muslim regimes.

al-Masri, Abu Ayyub

Dates: 1968–April 18, 2010

Name: Abu Hamza al-Muhajir (أبو حمزة المهاجر)

Key Events in His Life: See "Leaders of ISIS" chapter.

Why does it matter? See "Leaders of ISIS" chapter.

al-Qaeda

Dates: 1988–Present

What is important? Al-Qaeda (القاعدة) means the base as in a base camp, a foundation, or a base as in baseball. The group that adopted this name was led by Osama bin Laden and also Abdullah Azzam. Abdullah provided the inspirational ideology and Osama provided the money and charisma. The group began in Pakistan/Afghanistan with the intent of fighting against the Soviet invaders of the country. Following the Soviet withdrawal from Afghanistan, the group ceased to function for some time. The Iraqi invasion of Kuwait and the invitation made by the Kingdom of Saudi Arabia for western soldiers, primarily American, to enter the kingdom and defend it from possible attack from Iraq served as an irritant that grew over time when the Americans did not leave as promised. Al-Qaeda then became active with statements in 1996 and 1998 declaring war on the United States and its possessions and interests abroad. In short, the organization wanted to draw the United States into the Middle East by use of violence in order to weaken it economically and discredit it in the eyes of Muslims and the Muslim governments that look to the United States as a protector.

The attacks against the United States and Western interests began in 1998 with the bombings of two U.S. embassies in Africa. In 2000, a U.S. warship was attacked while docked in Aden, Yemen. The attacks on the World Trade Centers and the Pentagon on September 11, 2001, were continuations of this intent to draw the United States into the region and then fatally weaken it. Al-Qaeda became a prime target for U.S. intelligence collection and targeting. This resulted in serious damage to the senior leadership and its ability to continue to mount spectacular attacks against major U.S. facilities and interests. As this was happening, al-Qaeda began to become a franchise operation with other groups taking on the mantle of al-Qaeda with designations for their location—in Morocco, the Arabian Peninsula, and Iraq.

In 2011, Osama bin Laden was found and killed by U.S. special operations forces. He was succeeded by Ayman al-Zawahiri as the leader of the organization.

Al-Qaeda has funded itself primarily through the personal wealth of Osama bin Laden and donations and thus it has always been beholden to the outside source of income for conducting operations. Since the death of bin Laden and really since the attacks against al-Qaeda in late 2001 the organization has struggled to control the global salafi-jihad in the manner it envisioned. It existed in Afghanistan because the Taliban protected it. It seems to continue to exist and provides some level of guidance to a variety of affiliates or franchises throughout the region and, to some degree, around the world. Otherwise it is not a major player in the fight—primarily because it has been effectively targeted and killed.

Why does it matter to ISIS? Al-Qaeda provided the ideological inspiration for ISIS. The idea of having a jihad that could succeed against the United States came through Abdullah Azzam, Osama bin Laden, and Ayman al-Zawahiri. Without Osama bin Laden and al-Qaeda, there would probably not have been ISIS.

al-Sham (Levant)

What is important? Al-Sham is a word that has multiple meanings. It can mean the specific city of Damascus, the greater Damascus area, the modern country and boundaries of Syria, or something called Greater Syria. This last area includes the modern states of Syria, Lebanon, Israel, most of Jordan, and portions of Turkey and Egypt. This is an Arabic phrase that dates back centuries.

Levant is derived from Latin and French words that mean rising. Literally, it is the place where the sun rises or the east. In Western academic circles, the Levant includes the same general region as given in the explanation of al-Sham previously. It is important to note that few Arabs use this phrase and if they do they typically only do so in an academic setting.

Both al-Sham and Levant are conceptual terms. There is no fixed border for either of the geographic designations and they do not represent a historic kingdom or geographic division. It is an area like referring to "the south" in the United States or "the West" in terms of culture.

Why does it matter to ISIS? ISIS uses the phrase al-Sham. It has never used Levant in its name. Few Arabs have ever used ISIL as a designation because it is not reflective of the Arabic acronym for the organization here referred to as ISIS.

al-Zarqawi, Abu Musab

Dates: October 20, 1966–June 7, 2006

Name: Ahmad Fadeel al-Nazal al-Khalayleh (أحمد فضيل النزال الخلايله)

Key Events in His Life: See "Leaders of ISIS" chapter.

Why does it matter? See "Leaders of ISIS" chapter.

al-Zawahiri, Ayman

Dates: June 15, 1951–Present

Name: Ayman Mohammed Rabie al-Zawahiri (أيمن محمد ربيع الظواهري)

Key Events in His Life: Current leader of al-Qaeda. Born in Cairo, Egypt, to a prosperous and well-educated family. He grew up as a studious youth who became a surgeon. He was also an Islamist and he joined the Muslim Brotherhood at age 14. He was one of the founding members of al-Jihad or Egyptian Islamic Jihad. He was arrested with hundreds of others in 1981 following the assassination of Egyptian president Anwar Sadat. He was an active member of the organization inside Egypt and then abroad after fleeing the country. He is considered to be the instigator and maybe the mind behind the first Sunni suicide bombing. He met Osama bin Laden and Abdullah Azzam in Pakistan when they were part of a group called Maktab al-Khadamat (MAK) or Office of Services that was providing material support to the mujahidin in Afghanistan. It is suspected that Ayman al-Zawahiri was responsible for the assassination of Abdullah Azzam in 1989. Al-Zawahiri went on to develop a close coordinating relationship with Osama bin Laden, and in 1998, he merged the Egyptian Islamic Jihad into al-Qaeda. He became the second in command and was responsible for much of the group's operational and strategic thought. He took over as the emir of al-Qaeda following the death of Osama bin Laden. He has continued that leadership to the present. He and Abu Musab al-Zarqawi and each subsequent leader of the groups that became ISIS have had public disagreements over the direction and nature of the global Salafist jihad. He does not command the respect nor the military might to force compliance with his vision or directions. One of his lifelong goals was to place the Muslim Brotherhood in the leadership of Egypt. This was realized for a short time under the presidency of Mohamed Morsi (June 30, 2012–July 3, 2013).

Why does it matter? He is the leader of the originating group for global jihad against a superpower. He is in opposition to Abu Bakr al-Baghdadi as caliph and he is presenting a different view of salafist-jihadi ideology that is currently seen as more amenable than ISIS with its harsh tone. His origins and background are important to remember. Although he may seem more reasonable than ISIS, he was an advocate for violent overthrow of Egyptian leaders and the use of suicide bombs to create an environment wherein political change becomes feasible.

Alawi (Alawite[s])

What is important? The Assad family in Syria is Alawite. This is a religious subdivision of Islam. Alawites are a form of Shia Islam breaking away from the major sects in the ninth century. They have beliefs and practices adopted from Christianity and Judaism; these beliefs are labeled syncretistic because of the way in which they pull in these elements and add them to the previous Islamic tenets and practices. Alawites tend to be protective of their beliefs. For this reason, little has been known of them until the last decade or so. They are called Alawites because they are followers of Ali (Ali ibn Abi Talib), the first imam of Shia Islam and the son-in-law of the Prophet Mohamed. Because of the hidden nature of their beliefs and the perception of them as different, they were often viewed as heretics within Islam.

Alawites comprise about 12 percent of the population of Syria. The French occupation of Syria following the end of World War I brought an opportunity for Alawites to enter government service and created a short-lived Alawite state along the western coast and mountains of Syria. Although the state did not last long, this did bring the Alawites into the Syrian military where they continued to gain positions of authority until the coup de-tat that brought Hafez al-Assad to power in 1970. He then increased Alawite participation and power in the government, and both he and his son effectively linked Alawite survival with regime survival.

Why does it matter to ISIS? The linkages between Alawites serving in the Syrian military and government positions and the close ties between the regime and the Alawite community means that any collapse of the Syrian Assad regime will threaten the survival of the Alawites as people, thus opening up the possibility of genocide. As a result, 12 percent of the population is fighting the Syrian civil war to protect their right to exist.

Amir al-Mu'minin (Prince of the Faithful)

What is important? The title *amir al-mu'minin* is one that carries a lot of symbolic value. It is often translated as prince of the faithful because amir (or emir) is typically translated as prince. The word is derived from a root that means to command. Thus an amir is one who commands. In many cases, this phrase is translated commander of the faithful. This is a designation that has been used by nearly all of the caliphs throughout history, but it is also a title that has been used to designate particularly respected Islamic military or governing leaders. The leader of the Taliban, Mohamed Omar, used the title amir al-mu'minin though he never claimed to be, nor was he ever designated a caliph. That said, the designation is significant and means that the person holding the title is to be listened to and followed by the faithful.

Why does it matter to ISIS? Abu Bakr al-Baghdadi is referred to as the amir al-mu'minin and he was also designated the caliph of Islam.

Arab

What is important? What is an Arab? There is no simple answer to this question. The term has a variety of meanings: one who speaks Arabic; one who lives in the Middle East; one from the Arabian Peninsula; one who is a Muslim; one who has a common "Arab" culture. There are other possibilities as well, but these capture the sense of difficulty in answering this question. In thinking about what makes a person of a particular group, a lot of preconceived notions and prejudices exist. For each one of these five answers to the question of "what is an Arab?" there are exceptions as well as significant issues. Language alone does not grant the full identity as there are many people in the Middle East who speak Arabic and do not consider themselves Arabs. The historic and most limited definition is that Arabs did come from the Arabian Peninsula, but that is no longer accurate as many other ethnicities live there. Muslims live across the globe and most Muslims are not Arabs. The largest Muslim countries by population—Indonesia, Pakistan, and India—are all non-Arab. The last response—one who has a common "Arab" culture—is probably the most accurate. In essence, Arabs are those people who speak like Arabs, act like Arabs, and think they are Arabs. This includes many peoples in the Middle East and North Africa. It includes Muslims and Christians. It includes people in a shifting set as there are those who will say in some circumstances that they are Arabs but in other times and places will identify themselves more with their nation, religion, etc. For the most part, this final answer is the one that this book applies when using the word "Arab."

Why does it matter to ISIS? Despite the fact that many westerners equate Islamic jihadism with Arabs, ISIS does not sell itself by ethnicity. They are not Arabs though Arabs make up a significant portion of their leadership. They regularly advertise the international and broad ethnic sweep of their community of believers.

Arab Spring

Dates: December 18, 2010–October 26, 2013

What is important? In the late fall of 2010, a green grocer in Tunis, Tunisia, was fed up with the oppression he felt from government officials and set himself ablaze in the street. This single act of self-immolation lit a fire that is still burning throughout the Middle East. Riots began in the capital and spread throughout Tunisia. The government leadership resigned and the president fled the country. News of the uprising in Tunisia sparked similar responses in other parts of the Middle East. By the spring of 2011, several countries were dealing with revolts and subsequent power shifts. Riots similarly overthrew the

President of Egypt (January—February 11, 2011). As a result, open elections were established that brought the Muslim Brotherhood to power. Then there was a military coup followed by the establishment of a military dictator.

In Libya (February 15–October 23, 2011), riots led to violent suppression of the rioters, which in turn led to NATO and Arab League sanctions. A military adventure ensued that removed the Libyan President from power and ultimately led to his murder.

Bahrain (February 14–March 18, 2011) had riots as well. These led to a brutal government crackdown along with some minor government concessions and liberalization of some laws.

Likewise, Jordan made some minor political concessions in the face of mobs and riots.

Yemen also experienced a popular overthrow of the ruling president, which was then followed by an ongoing civil war.

For the purposes of this book, the most significant place affected by the so-called Arab Spring was Syria. The events in 2011 sparked a violent response from the government that escalated into a multiyear ongoing civil war with hundreds of thousands killed and millions displaced either internally or externally.

It is called the Arab Spring because it looked so positive in the spring of 2011. It looked like despotic rule was ending in the Middle East and that a peaceful and pleasant transition was set to happen. That changed and much of what came of the events in that spring have been negative for the residents of those countries, the region, and the world.

Why does it matter to ISIS? ISIS has risen to its current dimensions because of the Arab Spring in Syria and the chaos that followed. As ISIS has grown around the Middle East and North Africa, it is possible to see the Arab Spring as an opening door. ISIS is most powerful in Syria, but it also has powerful elements in Yemen, Egypt, and Libya, and some of the most significant reasons can be traced back to the Arab Spring.

Baghdad, Iraq

Dates: established by Abu Jafar al-Mansur in 762 CE

What is important? Located along the Tigris River in modern-day Iraq, Baghdad, was founded with the intent of becoming the capital city of the Abbasid Caliphate. Within a short time of its founding, it became a center for governance, arts, science, and culture. Baghdad was considered to be the heart of the Arab Golden Age when it was a center of learning. The city was brutally sacked by the Mongols in 1258 CE. Stories say that the Tigris River ran black from the ink of the books thrown into it by the Mongols. In many ways, the city never fully recovered its former glory as one of the great cultural centers in the world.

Baghdad is the capital and largest city of Iraq and boasts a population of more than seven million people, making it the second most populous capital in the Arab world behind Cairo, Egypt. It is the single most important city in Iraq, and it dominates Mesopotamia in terms of political, cultural, and economic influence.

Why does it matter to ISIS? As a historic capital for the most respected ancient caliphate, Baghdad holds a position of significance. It is also a city important to the Shia. Thus taking the city would establish ISIS as a true power, making it worthy of its self-proclaimed title.

Bay'ah (Oath of Allegiance) (بَيْعَة)

What is important? The word comes from the same root as the words sale, commerce, seller, etc. The meaning implies a transaction or some sort of contractual relationship between two persons. With respect to ISIS, this word references the contractual relationships between supporters and the organization with regard to loyalty, fidelity, allegiance, and support. Within Islamic jurisprudence, there are different types of such contracts. For the sake of ISIS, these contracts can be either temporary or permanent, literal or conceptual.

This will be explained using the Prophet Mohamed and early Muslims. When the prophet united the Arabian Peninsula, each tribe made an oath of allegiance to him. Following the prophet's death about four years after all of the peninsula was united, many of the tribes claimed that their oath was to the Prophet Mohamed and therefore they owed no allegiance to Abu Bakr who had then been declared the caliph or successor of the prophet. Abu Bakr ordered Muslim armies to go out and compel the tribes to make another oath of allegiance to him and essentially to the faith. In this historical reference, there were those who saw their oath as being to the man and therefore that oath ended upon the death of the man (literal as used previously) and those who saw the oath as being to the representative of the new faith (conceptual) and therefore it held regardless of who was the leader of that faith.

Why does it matter to ISIS? This legalistic issue comes into play with respect to groups that have sworn allegiance to al-Qaeda or the Taliban. ISIS is now seeking to get them to swear loyalty to it. Was their previous oath of the temporary or literal variety or was it permanent and conceptual? These things matter when trying to sway entire groups. Jabhat al-Nusra will argue that its original oath was to al-Qaeda and even though it was subordinate to the Islamic State in Iraq (ISIS forerunner) it owed loyalty to al-Qaeda when al-Qaeda and ISIS disagreed.

Bayji, Battle of

Dates: June 11, 2014–October 23, 2015?

What is important? The Battle of Bayji began as many ISIS operations have—as a prison break. The group moved into the area to free prisoners from the local prison. From that point forward, there have been various degrees of combat. This has included everything from sporadic gunfire to mortar attacks to platoon and company-sized assaults to clear the refinery and control it for ISIS use. The most important thing about Bayji is the fact that it is the largest refinery in Iraq. Whoever holds the facility and can control the output has the ability to process crude oil into refined and sellable product.

The Iraqi Army attacked to regain the town and facility in October 2014. The town and refinery have passed from one side to the other multiple times. In October 23, 2015, there were reports that the Iraqi Army accompanied by Shia militia had captured the town and facility once and for all. By October 25, there were additional and conflicting reports of continued fighting and the need to clear more of the facility. As of the time of writing, the final status of the facility is uncertain though the facility generally seemed to be under Iraqi government control.

The participants in the fighting were initially in the dozens and hundreds. By the end, the Iraqi Army and militias brought thousands to the fight. Casualties were high for both sides given the challenging nature of the facility and urban fighting.

Why does it matter to ISIS? The refinery is important both to ISIS and to the Iraqi government. The town controls a critical crossroads for major highways one of which runs from the Tigris to the Euphrates River valley. Controlling this terrain and the refinery or denying either to the opponent has value to both sides, making it unlikely that October 2015 will be the end of the battle of Bayji.

bin Laden, Osama

Dates: March 10, 1957–May 2, 2011

Name: Osama bin Mohammed bin Awad bin Laden (أسامة بن محمد بن عوض بن لادن)

Key Events in His Life: Osama bin Laden was the son of a wealthy and successful construction company owner. His father died in 1969 in a helicopter crash. The bin Laden Group built some of the most important structures contracted by the Saudi government to include the renovations and expansion of the Grand Mosque in Mecca. The money this business connection provided allowed Osama to travel to Afghanistan in 1984 to begin the organization called the Services Office that would later transform into al-Qaeda in 1988.

Osama bin Laden was married five or six times. Separated from the first wife after 27 years of marriage and divorced his second wife in the 1990s after about 10 years of marriage. He reportedly divorced the sixth wife (though there are conflicting reports of this wedding even happening) shortly after the marriage. Thus, he was in a polygamous relationship from the early 1980s until his death. He had between 20 and 26 children.

In 1992, bin Laden returned to Saudi Arabia and then he was later expelled. He opposed the invitation of United States and other Western forces into the Kingdom of Saudi Arabia in support of Operation Desert Storm and he agitated for the removal of all Western forces, making him less and less welcomed by the Saudi government. He later traveled to Sudan. It was while he was in Sudan that the majority of early al-Qaeda operations began: 1993 World Trade Center bombing (not directly linked to al-Qaeda, but those who conducted the attacks were ideologically connected), 1996 Khobar Towers bombing that killed 19 U.S. service members in Saudi Arabia, 1998 Embassy bombings in Nairobi and Dar-es-Salaam that killed more than 200, and the 2000 attack on USS Cole in the port of Aden killing 17. In 1999, bin Laden was placed on the FBI "10 most wanted" list.

The most spectacular and obviously al-Qaeda led event was the attacks on the Pentagon and the World Trade Center on September 11, 2001. This attack was funded and coordinated by Osama bin Laden and those he recruited and retained in al-Qaeda. They followed him from Sudan to Afghanistan where he was welcomed by the Taliban. Following the attacks against the United States, he was the most hunted man in the world and he was variously reported to be in Afghanistan, Iran, Pakistan—or dead. In 2003, he released a series of statements confirming that he was still alive. In 2004, he was quoted as offering a peace initiative to the West by saying, "I present a reconciliation initiative . . . to stop operations against all (European) countries if they promise not to be aggressive towards Muslims." (Al-Arabiya audiotape) Later he warned Europe of a "reckoning" after controversial cartoons of Prophet Mohammed published in 2008. He later claimed responsibility for the botched Christmas Day bombing of US airliner and threatened more strikes on U.S. targets. He was killed by a U.S. special operations raid in Abbottabad, Pakistan, in 2011.

Why does it matter? He was influenced by the 1979 seizure of the grand Mosque in Mecca, the teachings of Sayyid Qutb, Abdullah Yusuf Azzam, and other Salafist and Jihadist thinkers, and the establishment of Islamist governments in Sudan (1979), Iran (1979), and Afghanistan (1996).

He is the face for turning terrorism into global jihad. He also conceived of the use of violence as a means to generate interest and effort on the part of Sunni Islam to organically create a new manifestation of the caliphate.

He used financing, education, and purpose to generate the single most effective terrorist organization until his time. In the process, he took terrorism from single acts to generate public attention to massive attacks designed to generate a sense of purpose and possibility.

He took the ideas of deeper thinkers and better educated salafi-jihadis and he combined those ideas with money to create an organization that executed the single largest nonstate terrorist attack in human history.

He created, funded, and exported the idea of franchise terrorism.

Boko Haram

What is important? Boko Haram is a salafi-jihadi group that operates primarily in Nigeria, but also in small portions of Niger, Chad, and Cameroon. In March 2015, it officially pledged its allegiance to ISIS and accepted Abu Bakr al-Baghdadi as its caliph. When it did so, it accepted the new name Wilāyat Gharb Ifrīqīyyah or the West African State (or Province) (الولاية الإسلامية غرب)

أفريقيا). The group began in the late 2000s as an Islamist group with strict religious interpretations. It evolved into a salafi-jihadi group that used violence to achieve its ends. Its aspiration was to achieve an independent Muslim majority and Islamic governed state in western Africa. The group did not solely focus on one modern defined state though it primarily operated in Nigeria. Like ISIS, Boko Haram used violence and crime to generate the funds for its military actions, including kidnapping large groups. A kidnapping of nearly 300 school girls in 2014 garnered global attention. The Nigerian government has claimed to be successful in the fight against Boko Haram. In September 2015, it went so far as to state that it had effectively defeated the group. In this statement, the Nigerian military official acknowledged that Boko Haram still exists in small numbers and that it was trying to adapt. The Nigerian government, it was reported, is also adapting vis-à-vis its fight with Boko Haram.

Boko Haram may in fact has been removed from the global competition regarding violent extremism. Regardless it represented a significant amount of frustration and angst of the Muslim populations in the geographic area in which it operated. Despite the optimistic comments from the Nigerian government, the group known as Boko Haram or the West African State was still claiming to be conducting attacks in West Africa that resulted in the deaths of dozens at the end of 2015 and the beginning of 2016.

Why does it matter to ISIS? As a province of ISIS, Boko Haram represented the near global reach of the influence of ISIS. If Boko Haram is ever actually destroyed, then this might play against ISIS. It undermines its narrative of being everywhere and expanding throughout the Islamic world. Regardless, Boko Haram represented a non-Arab, non-Middle Eastern group willing to ally itself with ISIS. This was an important endorsement for the ISIS brand. It is unlikely that it is truly defeated as the group continues to conduct attacks in various places within its former area of operations. It will continue to conduct deadly attacks for some time to come.

Caliph (pronounced in Arabic khalifa) (خَلِيفة)

What is important? The caliph is the ruler of the community of the faithful and the polity called a caliphate (see Caliphate). The word means successor in Arabic and it denotes a worthy person who serves as the rightful successor of the Prophet Mohamed who is believed and accepted to be the last legitimate prophet. Caliph is really a Sunni Muslim term. The Shias refer to their legitimate leaders as Imams. Within Sunni Islam, a caliph should be identified and selected by the community of the faithful.

Historically, this has not been the case. Each of the caliphates designated its leader and caliph as it designated and demonstrated its power. These caliphates existed in preindustrial periods when there was no way to vote or even to inform all of the various tribal leaders in a relatively short period of time. After the first four rightly guided caliphs, the empire of Islam was spread from India to Spain and the reach of communication required weeks to travel to the various parts of the caliphate.

In some circles of Sunni Islam, the caliph should come from the Quraysh tribe. Among the Shia, the imam is to come from the family of the prophet.

Prior to Abu Bakr al-Baghdadi and the declaration by ISIS that he is now Caliph Ibrahim, the most recent generally accepted caliph was the ruler of the Ottoman Empire—Abdülmecid II (عبد المجيد الثاني) [May 29, 1868–August 23, 1944]) who was removed from the title by the Turkish National Assembly in 1924 with the formal dissolution of the Ottoman Empire. For a brief time, Hussein ibn Ali al-Hashimi (الحسين بن علي الهاشمي) [1853/1854–June 4, 1931]), the Sharif and Emir of Mecca, took the title until he was removed from Mecca by the al-Saud dynasty in 1925. Since that time, there has been no caliph recognized by Muslims.

Why does it matter to ISIS? Abu Bakr al-Baghdadi claims now to be the one and only holder of the title of successor of the prophet. This title is disputed by most Muslims. One of the primary criticisms of the title by scholars and lay people alike is that so few of the community of believers accept this title. By that argument, he cannot be a caliph. Obviously, ISIS disagrees and claims that he does have authority because the only community that matters—the truly faithful community—has bestowed him with that authority.

Caliph, Rashidun (الخلفاء الراشدون)

What is important? Within Sunni Islam, the first four successors of the Prophet Mohamed are referred to as *rashidun* or rightly guided. The use of this word is meant to dispel any controversy regarding their leadership. They are to be seen as those who ruled all of the community of the faithful without opposition. That is a little more positive than the reality. Regardless, they were generally uncontested in their leadership, they were all pious, they lived in accordance with the teachings of the prophet and the Quran, and they were nondynastic. Each of the other major caliphates that followed established some level of dynastic succession. As a result, they were seen as less than ideally pious. Brief entries on each of the *rashidun* caliphs are given in the following sections.

Abu Bakr

He lived from October 573 to August 22, 634, and served as the first successor to the Prophet Mohamed from June 8, 632, until his death. He was a merchant and one of the earliest converts to Islam. He was almost always with Mohamed. He was the father-in-law of the prophet. He had the responsibility of reuniting the Arab tribes that departed the community of believers following the death of the prophet. Then he oversaw the invasion of the Sassanid Persian Empire and the Roman Empire and initiated the expansion of the caliphate beyond traditionally Arab lands. Islam was to be a global religion and Abu Bakr instituted its spread.

The primary criticism of Abu Bakr from those who later became Shia was that Ali should have been the successor. Additionally, there was some criticism from the family of the prophet that Abu Bakr did not provide the inheritance that was their due. There are explanations and arguments on both sides. What is important is that he was universally respected as a pious and worthy man and Muslim.

Umar ibn al-Khattab

He lived from October 583 to November 3, 644, and served as the second successor to the Prophet Mohamed from August 23, 634, to his death. He was selected to be caliph by Abu Bakr. He was another pious and faithful man. He was a respected scholar and jurist and one of the most knowledgeable about what would come to be called *sharia* or Muslim law and jurisprudence. Unlike other Islamic leaders, Umar never killed a man in battle. He was not a warrior. Despite this, he oversaw the invasion of the Sassanid Persian Empire and its incorporation into the Islamic Caliphate. He also oversaw the conquest of much of the Roman Empire in what is referred to as the Levant. The caliphate grew more under his rule than under any other single person in history.

He did not use money from the conquest for himself or his family, rather he provided pensions for the companions of the prophet and their families. This allowed the companions to study the faith and created a culture of religious scholarship as a respected and honored way of life. He established the Islamic lunar-based calendar with the first year beginning with the immigration or *hijra* of the prophet from Mecca to Medina (622 CE). Umar was stabbed to death during morning prayers.

Uthman ibn Affan

He lived from October 576 to June 17, 656, and served as the third successor to the Prophet Mohamed beginning on November 11, 644. After being stabbed and before he died, Umar appointed a committee of six men to select the next caliph. Ali, the son-in-law of the prophet and Uthman, were both on the committee. The committee chose Uthman to serve. Uthman was from the powerful Umayyad family who had a ruler in Syria at that time. Early in his reign, he was considered one of the most popular, if not the most popular, of the rashidun caliphs. He continued to extend the caliphate geographically to the Indus River in the east and the Iberian Peninsula in the west. Under his reign, the Quran was finally compiled and published.

Late in his leadership, he began to appoint family members to senior positions around the caliphate. This generated concern about dynastic succession and the preeminence of certain tribes over others—always a sensitive subject among tribal cultures. The concern evolved into protests and ultimately led to a siege of the caliph's home. The siege turned violent and a group broke into the home and killed Uthman.

Ali ibn Abi Talib

He lived from September 20, 601, to January 27, 661, and served as the fourth successor to the Prophet Mohamed from 656 to 661. He married the only surviving daughter of Mohamed—Fatima—and he produced the only direct line successors of the prophet's line. He was the favored option for the successor to the prophet from the beginning in the eyes of Shia and he was always in consideration at each and every change in leadership. He was in the committee designated by Umar to choose his successor and politically outmaneuvered by Uthman. After Uthman's murder, he became the caliph. This began a tumultuous period of Islamic history.

By this point, in world history the caliphate was massive—the largest geographic empire then on the planet. Governing such territory with preindustrial means was problematic, and as demonstrated by Uthman, there was a propensity for leaders to select subordinates whom they could trust. Uthman did this and Ali followed suit by replacing key rulers appointed by Uthman with those he trusted. In addition to this, he moved the governing capital from Mecca to Kufa in present-day Iraq.

Ali was hounded and criticized by the Umayyads for not pursuing the murderers of Uthman. This, and the removal of Umayya rulers, certainly played a part in the increasing tensions that eventually led to an Islamic civil war. He was ultimately killed by a member of the Kharajite group, his former supporters. The Kharajites hoped to end the civil war and the associated chaos within Islam by removing key figures in the dispute.

Why does it matter to ISIS? Even this cursory look at the lives of these important men conveys something of the challenges within the early period of the Islamic faith. Three of the first four—rightly guided—leaders of Islam were murdered. These men and the time period in which they ruled are seen by ISIS as its desired ideal age.

Caliphate (خلافة)

What is important? A caliphate is a form of Islamic government ruled over by a caliph. In this sense, a caliphate is to a caliph what a kingdom is to a king. This simple definition was all that existed in the early decades of Islam. Later on, the definition of a caliphate grew more complex as the geography governed by the caliph expanded to continental size. The early period of the caliphate was called the Rashidun Caliphate or the rightly guided caliphate (see Caliph, Rashidun) and there was no hereditary or dynastic succession. This period lasted from 632 to 661.

The last Rashidun caliph, Ali ibn Abi Talib, was assassinated in 661 and the Umayya tribe established the first dynastic caliphate governed from Damascus, Syria, from 661 to 750. The Umayya were, in turn, replaced by the Abbasid Caliphate (see Abbasid Caliphate), which was governed from Baghdad, Iraq (and a few other places). It is during the Abbasid rule that the history gets complicated as the role of the caliph as the final word in governance, faith, and life gradually changed. At times, the Abbasid and later caliphs were little more than figureheads who lived in splendid isolation from their people, the community of believers. In some fashion, the Abbasids held the caliphate until 1517 when it passed out of Arab hands for the first time and into the Turkish hands of the Ottoman Sultans until 1924.

During World War I the British Empire was deeply concerned about the impact of going to war against the Ottoman Empire. The British Empire ruled over the largest number of Muslims in the entire world—the modern countries of Bangladesh, India, and Pakistan—under the Government of India. The British demonstrated a lack of understanding of the role of the caliph in this period and of the influence he had over Muslims, in general. Because of this ignorance, they sought to elevate others over the Ottoman caliph in search of a religious alternative. This affected the relationship between the British Empire and the Hashemite family of the Sharif of Mecca. The reality was that the caliph had ceased to be the powerful unifying voice of Islam. Non-Muslim meddling in the position of the caliph created tremendous animosity.

Why does it matter to ISIS? The role of Abu Bakr al-Baghdadi as the self-proclaimed caliph of Islam is questionable in terms of what this means to modern Muslims. A caliphate does not have the draw that it did centuries ago. ISIS claims that all Muslims are expected to come to the caliphate and support it to the greatest extent possible.

CENTCOM

What is important? The proper name is the U.S. Central Command. The abbreviated acronym is USCENTCOM or simply CENTCOM. CENTCOM is one of many U.S. geographic combatant commands used to organize and administer military relations and activities around the globe. In this organization, each command has responsibility for a specified area. CENTCOM has responsibility for the Middle East, Central Asia, and a portion of Africa. The area of responsibility for the command has changed several times since CENTCOM was established in 1983. The command currently coordinates actions within the following 20 countries under the direction of the U.S. Department of Defense: Afghanistan, Bahrain, Egypt, Iran, Iraq, Jordan, Kazakhstan, Kuwait, Kyrgyzstan, Lebanon, Oman, Pakistan, Qatar, Saudi Arabia, Syria, Tajikistan, Turkmenistan, United Arab Emirates, Uzbekistan, and Yemen.

The command headquarters is located at MacDill Air Force Base, Tampa, Florida, with a forward headquarters outside Doha, Qatar. CENTCOM is commanded by a four-star general who typically serves in the position for three years. The commander is responsible to the Secretary of Defense, the Chairman of the Joint Chiefs of Staff, and the President of the United States for operations and policies conducted in the countries within his area of responsibility.

Why does it matter to ISIS? CENTCOM is the senior headquarters responsible for conducting the combat operations in Afghanistan since 2001 and in Iraq from 2003 to 2011 and from 2014 until the present. The CENTCOM commander is responsible for the primary combat operations directed against ISIS though some of the supporting bases and some ISIS affiliates are outside the area of responsibility: Turkey and Libya are not included in CENTCOM.

Crusades

Dates: 1095–1291 CE

What is important? The crusading period began with the preaching of the First Crusade by Pope Urban II in 1095 and continued through the end of the Crusader States established in the eastern Mediterranean in 1291. Elements of this period—particularly the military orders—continued for a couple of centuries beyond these dates. This entry focuses primarily on the military ventures associated with the capture of Jerusalem by the First Crusade and ending with the loss of the last Crusader stronghold—Acre—on the Levantine coast in 1291.

The preaching of the First Crusade in 1095 generated a greater response than anticipated by Urban II. More than 100,000 people participated in the armed pilgrimage. The effort to conquer Jerusalem is one of the great military adventures in human history with all of the intrigue and salacious details fit for a movie or television series. Suffice it to say that although only a few thousand warriors actually made it to the city, this crusade was successful in capturing Jerusalem in 1099. The city was taken by means of a brutal and ferocious sack of the city that was emphasized by the Muslim forces for rallying support in freeing the land of the Franks of the Coast or the Crusaders. On the way to capturing the city, several other territories were also conquered and controlled. Overall four Crusader States were established in addition to Jerusalem. The four states were the Kingdom of Jerusalem, the County of Tripoli, the County of Edessa, and the Principality of Antioch. Over time the other three would owe fealty to the King of Jerusalem.

The timing of the Crusades worked in favor of the Christians. Much of their success can be attributed to the divided nature of Muslim leadership at the time. The Fatimid Caliphate (Shia) who ruled from Cairo also controlled Jerusalem. At the same time, the Abbasid caliph, who was little more than a figurehead, ruled from Baghdad. The caliphate, however, was subdivided into numerous locally controlled sultanates that operated under mostly Turkish leadership. This division allowed the Crusaders to take on one local lord at a time rather than facing the power of an empire in full force.

Along with the crusader efforts were efforts made by the Roman (Byzantine) Emperor fighting against Turkish rulers in the Anatolian Peninsula. Islam was divided and under attack from multiple forces only sometimes working in concert, but certainly presenting multiple directions of attack.

The loss of the County of Edessa to a Muslim Turkish force in 1044 was the impetus for the preaching of the Second Crusade. Despite being led by the powerful kings of Europe, this crusade did not regain the County of Edessa, so the Crusader States were reduced by one. In 1187, the Kurdish Sultan Salah al Din (Saladin) defeated the King of Jerusalem and over several months he captured most of the fortresses in the kingdom to include Jerusalem. This loss initiated the Third Crusade that included several kings. Among these was Richard I of England (Richard Lionheart). Although several major cities and fortresses were retaken, Jerusalem was not. The Kingdom of Jerusalem continued to exist as a coastal kingdom with some fortresses in the highlands of modern Israel and Lebanon and without the city of Jerusalem, its namesake, itself.

It was the rise of the Mameluke Sultanate in Cairo, which was brought on by the Fifth and Sixth Crusades and their attacks against Egypt, which brought about the ultimate demise of the Crusader states and their various strongholds. The Mamelukes who had been the slave soldiers of the sultan finally took over the sultanate themselves and they were able to generate the force and the impetus and drive to complete the destruction of all crusader fortresses in the former Crusader States. The last city to fall was Acre in what is now northern Israel. By the fall of the city in 1291, there was no further interest by European kings or nobles to mount major military operations to support existing lords or regain lost lands. The Crusader States ended.

Viewing the Crusades as a series of numbered adventures misrepresents what this period was about for many European nobles—an armed pilgrimage. Even before the designated beginning of the Crusader period, it was common for European nobility to travel with medium to large entourages to Jerusalem for religious reasons. Throughout the existence of the Crusader States, there was a near constant flow of European Christians to the states to conduct their armed pilgrimage. The numbers were not large enough to constitute a numbered crusade, but often a lord would arrive with dozens of fighters in train and support one of the local nobility in defending or expanding their lands. This created an odd relationship between the transient crusader and the permanent local nobility that passed their holdings from one generation to the next. The first group wanted to fight and make a name for itself in order to earn its penance. The second group often wanted stability to develop its lands. One group wanted friction with the Muslims—it was what it came for—and the other group wanted peace and stability.

Why does it matter to ISIS? It is common in jihadi literature and speeches to refer to the modern state of Israel as a crusader state. Such jihadi statements claim Israel was an entity thrust on the region by European powers as were the medieval crusader states. In this vein, ISIS refers to its enemies as

Roman-Crusaders. As noted previously, the Roman Empire (many refer to it in the West as the Byzantine Empire though no one at the time referred to it in this manner) was also fighting the Muslims simultaneously to the crusaders. The idea of Europeans imposing their will on the Middle East is consistently characterized as crusader like. The imagery and rhetoric used emphasize these ancient conflicts as a way of encouraging local inhabitants to recall the mythology and history of the suffering inflicted on Islam by the crusaders.

Dabiq, Battle of

Dates: Just before the end of days and/or 1516 CE

What is important? Dabiq (دابق) is a village about 25 miles north-northeast of Aleppo, Syria. It currently has slightly more than 3,000 inhabitants. In 1516, the Ottoman Empire fought and defeated the Mameluke Sultanate in the area. According to some interpretations of Islamic end-of-days beliefs, this is to be the site of the battle where Jesus will return to earth and lead the Army of the Righteous in victory against the armies led by Gog and Magog and the Dajjal (see Dajjal) ushering in the end of days and the final judgment. In this way, Dabiq is similar to the Christian concept of the battle of Armageddon (to happen about 300 miles to the south). In the hadith given by the Prophet Mohamed it is the Romans who will come to this battle (in either Dabiq or al-A'maq) and be defeated (see Crusades).

The town used to include a shrine to Caliph Suleiman bin Abd al-Malik (سليمان بن عبد الملك), an Umayyad caliph who led an army against Constantinople. In August 2014, ISIS captured the town of Dabiq and destroyed the shrine.

Why does it matter to ISIS? ISIS has named its magazine after this town and this battle (see *Dabiq* Magazine) to remind its followers of the significance of this battle. It is a group focused on preparing for the Battle of Dabiq. It believes it will play an important role in preparing the world for the end of days and the triumphant events, which will be set in motion at Dabiq. According to prophecies regarding the end of days, the Army of the Righteous (which ISIS believes itself to be) will not be doing well immediately prior to the arrival of Jesus. It will need his supernatural assistance to win the battle and defeat the Dajjal's army.

Dabiq Magazine

What is important? ISIS publishes *Dabiq* as a near monthly periodical with the purpose of promoting unity, truth-seeking, migration to the caliphate, holy war, and community. The magazine is published in English and has a very professional and modern look. The writing is in English though it has an Arabic poetic style that people sometimes misinterpret. In the magazine, ISIS explains its perception of the principles behind the organization, the actions of the organization, and vision for the future of the organization. Brief summaries of each issue available at the time of writing are as follows:

1. **The Return of the Khalifah (July 5, 2014).** In this issue, ISIS describes the declaration of the caliphate and what that means for the faithful. The issue explains the name of the magazine and discusses the recent victories achieved.
2. **The Flood (July 27, 2014).** ISIS uses the metaphor of the flood of Noah to communicate two different things: one, that ISIS is a flood that will sweep the earth and two, that ISIS is the ark and the only protection for the faithful from the flood of filth that is the non-Muslim world.
3. **A Call to Hijrah (September 10, 2014).** This issue discusses the responsibility of the faithful to immigrate or make *hijrah* (the Arabic word for immigration) to the caliphate. This has a religious link to when Mohamed made his *hijrah* from Mecca to Medina in 622, the date from which the Islamic calendar begins to reckon time.
4. **The Failed Crusade (October 11, 2014).** This is a mockery of the U.S.-led coalition's attempts to fight against ISIS. The cover is a picture of St. Peter's Square in Rome with the ISIS flag placed on the obelisk in the center of the plaza. The idea is to communicate that the U.S.-led crusade will ultimately fail as all of the other crusades did and the ISIS vision will conquer the world as prophesied.
5. **Remaining and Expanding (November 21, 2014).** The ISIS motto is "Remaining and Expanding." This issue discusses the expansion of the state into new areas—the Sinai, Libya, Yemen, etc. It also explains the new currency of gold dinars and silver dirham, which communicate the staying power of the state.
6. **Al Qa'idah of Waziristan: A Testimony from Within (December 29, 2014).** In this issue ISIS takes responsibility for an attack in Australia. The remainder of the issue addresses disputes within the jihadi community.

7. **From Hypocrisy to Apostasy: The Extinction of the Grayzone (February 12, 2015).** The emphasis of this issue is on the division of the world into two camps—true Islam and those opposed to true Islam. ISIS boasts of the murder of the Jordanian pilot, declares war on Japan, and promotes successes in other parts of the caliphate.

8. **Shari'ah Alone Will Rule Africa (March 30, 2015).** Boko Haram's pledge of allegiance and successes in Tunisia and Libya are the main focus of this issue. It also promotes the child-soldier training program to further communicate the long-term vision of the group.

9. **They Plot and Allah Plots (May 21, 2015).** The title of this issue refers to the plots of the world intended to defeat ISIS. The magazine seeks to strengthen supporters by reminding them that God knows all and will conquer all. There is a lengthy segment on sex slavery that explains the justification of the practice.

10. **The Law of Allah or the Laws of Men (July 13, 2015).** The first article praises the near simultaneous attacks in Tunisia, Kuwait, and France and the significant casualties that resulted. As the Ramadan issue, it reminds readers of the historic victories of Muslim armies during the month of Ramadan. It calls on children and wives to obey ISIS and flee their families or husbands who oppose ISIS.

11. **From the Battles of Al-Ahzāb to the War of Coalitions (August 9, 2015).** The Battle of al-Ahzab was a battle between the early Muslims and the idolatrous Meccan tribes. This issue calls out al-Qaeda and the Taliban for lying about Mullah Omar's death and opposing ISIS. An article also states that the Mahdi of the Shia is the Dajjal and in league with the Jews.

12. **Just Terror (November 18, 2015).** This issue boasts of the downing of a Russian airliner and the terror attacks in Beirut, Lebanon, and Paris, France. In this issue "terrorists" are likened to knights in a fairy tale like story. Essentially they are owning their global label as terrorists.

13. **The Rafidah: From Ibn Saba' to the Dajjal (January 19, 2016).** This is the first issue published after the destruction of large amounts of ISIS-controlled cash and increased coalition air strikes. The magazine is shorter and less polished than its predecessors and therefore may reflect degradation of the ISIS publishing ability. The magazine emphasizes the continued struggle against those who oppose or refuse to accept the message of the Islamic State.

14. **The Murtadd Brotherhood (April 13, 2016).** This issue attacks the of the Muslim Brotherhood as apostates. ISIS also attacks several Muslim leaders in the West who call for peaceful co-existence between Islam and the West.

Why does it matter to ISIS? This is the flagship magazine for ISIS. It has made this the primary means of communicating to the West—both to enemies and to possible recruits.

Dajjal

Dates: Before the Day of Resurrection

What is important? The Dajjal is properly labeled al-Masih al-Dajjal (المسيح الدجّال) or "the false messiah." It could also be thought of as the anti-Christ from a Christian perspective. The linguistic root means to lie, thus communicating the idea of deception or falsehood. Both Mohamed and his son-in-law Ali spoke about the Dajjal. They indicated that he would be blind in the right eye. He is to appear with the pretense of being the messiah at some future date in advance of the Day of Resurrection. The Dajjal is not referenced in the Quran though he is mentioned in several of the hadith. As with Christian Biblical references of the end of days, there are signs that describe the state of the world when he will come. These signs discuss the wickedness of the world and the abandonment of God and these teachings.

Jesus is to arrive and lead the Army of the Righteous against the Dajjal. The very breath of Jesus will destroy those who follow the Dajjal. The Dajjal will be defeated and all his followers rooted out and Jesus shall rule in an age of peace. Other versions include the presence of Gog and Magog along with the Dajjal.

Why does it matter to ISIS? ISIS regularly uses the imagery of the Dajjal to motivate its followers and to focus them on the opponents of Islam. The 13th issue of *Dabiq* magazine includes the Dajjal in the subtitle to again make clear that those who oppose ISIS are in league with the most important opponent of God—the Dajjal. Most followers of ISIS are not religious scholars and they do not understand all of the details. Because of this, ISIS and its followers are able to play fast and loose with the details of the end of days.

Deir al-Zour, Battle of

Dates: September 21, 2014–Present

What is important? Deir al-Zour sits on the Euphrates River. It is one of the only remaining Syrian government holds in Eastern Syria. This city is critical across history as it sits at a crucial river crossing on an important trade route from the Mediterranean Coast to Mesopotamia and beyond. The city and its environs have been the scene of fighting and the movement of armies for millennia.

In September 2014, ISIS began attacks on Syrian government facilities in the city. The town has seen clashes between ISIS and Jabhat al-Nusra, Jabhat al-Nusra and the Syrian Army, and the Syrian Army and ISIS. It has a complicated history in this current struggle. As of writing the city is still held by the Syrian Government.

On May 15, 2015, the U.S. military conducted a raid to kill or capture a senior ISIS leader in Deir al-Zour. It ended up killing Abu Sayyaf who was identified as a senior financier for the group.

Why does it matter to ISIS? Deir al-Zour represents a critical movement corridor for any force operating in or through Eastern Syria. It is crucial at some point that ISIS controls this river crossing in order to fully dominate the Euphrates River valley. Readers should expect to hear more of this city in the future.

Fallujah, Iraq

What is important? Fallujah is the second largest city in al-Anbar province, Iraq with a population of more than 300,000 people. It sits on the Euphrates River about 40 miles from Baghdad and 30 miles from Ramadi. The city is a major hub for commerce and opposition to the Shia government in Baghdad. During the U.S. occupation of Iraq, it was the site of two major battles, both in 2004.

The first battle began April 4, 2004. The second began October 31, 2004. They both happened in the same locations and for many of the same reasons, but they were conducted in different ways and with significantly different outcomes. Fallujah had a reputation of being something like the wild west of Iraq, even during the reign of Saddam Hussein. During the Iraq War (2003–2011), it was part of the Sunni Triangle—an area of violence and difficulty for U.S.

and coalition forces that extended from Baqubah in the east to Ramadi in the west to Bayji in the north. Fallujah sits in the middle of the east-west axis. Throughout the entire eight years of the U.S. occupation, Fallujah was a consistent problem for both coalition and Iraqi leadership. Following the disbanding of the Iraqi Army, there were approximately 70,000 unemployed young men in the city. The city is heavily influenced by tribal structures and the religion tends to be more conservative.

The attack launched in April 2004 was smaller than and not as well prepared as the one later in the year. In March 2004, the first Marine Expeditionary Force (MEF) replaced the 82nd Airborne Division of the U.S. Army. The Marines took a different approach to their duties—they sought to win the hearts and minds of the local populace. Despite these efforts, the populace remained in violent opposition to the U.S. occupation. The biggest catalyst event to the battle that followed was the March 31, 2004, ambush of Blackwater Security Contractors. Four were killed and their charred bodies were hung from a prominent overpass entering the city. At about this time, Shia militias under Muqtada al-Sadr rose up and began protests around the country. The coalition faced its hardest challenge to date. On April 4, the coalition launched Operation Vigilant Resolve to capture or kill those responsible for the murders and to restore control of the city to coalition forces and the Iraqi Governing Council. The Marine leadership wanted to take a softer approach, but the CPA and leaders in Washington, DC, felt strong action needed to be taken. Four Marine battalions assaulted positions in the city following aerial and artillery precision strikes. The fighting went on for five days. Several key members of the Iraq Governing Council threatened to desert the coalition if the attacks did not stop. The CPA suspended offensive operations. In early May, the Marines withdrew from the city and handed security over to an ad hoc organization raised from local former military personnel called the Fallujah Brigade.

Things did not get better over the summer. The Fallujah Brigade was ineffective in restoring order and by October the coalition, now under the direction of Iraqi transition leaders, ordered another attack on the city. This time leaflets were dropped and people were warned to leave the city. On October 31, the artillery and aerial bombardment began.

Between 75 and 90 percent of the population of the city fled before the battle took place. That is something like 150,000 to 200,000 people. A total of 38 U.S. personnel were killed in the battle as well as six Iraqi soldiers serving alongside coalition forces. It is estimated that between 1,200 and 2,000 Iraqi opposition fighters or insurgents were killed in the fighting with another 1,000 to 1,500 captured. Over 60 percent of the buildings in the city were damaged and 20 percent destroyed including 60 of the more than 200 mosques. The destruction of the city enraged the Sunni population and led to an increase of insurgent activity. It was in this period that al-Qaeda in Iraq began to grow (it was designated by this name in October 2004).

Once the fighting was done, the coalition went to work to rebuild Fallujah. Additionally, a new civil government and a new security force were created. Residents did not begin returning until mid-December. They were warned that they could be displaced for 75 to 90 days at the conflict's beginning. Some reports indicated that Operation al-Fajr destroyed the insurgent's grip on the city. Only sporadic insurgent attacks continued throughout the rest of the U.S. occupation in Iraq. Although this may be technically accurate, it is important to note that when the Islamic State in Iraq and al-Sham entered Fallujah in January 2014 it was greeted with popular acclaim. The reason for this welcome goes back to the social structure of Fallujah and the opposition to the U.S.-led occupation and the Shia-led government in Baghdad.

Why does it matter to ISIS? As stated previously in January 2014, ISIS drove into Fallujah to acclaim. It conducted a parade down some of the major streets of the city with banners and flags flying high. ISIS spent years developing and building relationships in the city. Some of the relationships date back to 2004 and the fighting done there as many leaders of ISIS gained their credibility in that fighting. Other relationships were built over the years through meetings, gift exchanges, basic rules of hospitality, and other cultural overtures. Promises were made of a better life for Sunnis. Offers of support and offers of positions of responsibility were exchanged. This is elaborated on for Fallujah as an example of how ISIS conducted business in building relationships with all of the cities into which it would enter. Fallujah did not fall fully under ISIS control though there is a significant pro-ISIS sentiment in the city. It is still contested space.

Hadith (حديث)

What is important? The hadith is the collection of the sayings of the Prophet Mohamed. This is an Arabic word that means saying, report, account, etc. The hadith is considered second only to the Quran and co-equal to the sunna in terms of the importance for the faithful in living and governing their lives. The collections of the hadith are slightly problematic as there is no one universally accepted collection. Any given statement is open for dispute. That said, some statements are more widely accepted than others and some specific statements enjoy near universal acceptance as they appear in multiple collections.

A hadith is a statement of the prophet. However, it is not a direct statement. Each one of the hadith was quoted by people of respect within the Muslim community. Typically, the people who are most often quoted are referred to as the companions of the prophet or the sahaba. Typically the hadith is preceded by the chain of custody of the statement. This chain traces from person to person the record of the quote back through each person who heard the statement until it reaches the prophet himself. Assuming each person in the chain is deemed to be trustworthy, the hadith is accurate. It is the debate over the trustworthiness of any given chain that creates the differing of opinions regarding which is authentic and which is not.

The two most respected collections are the Sahih al-Bukhari (compiled around 846 CE) and the Sahih Muslim (compiled between 840 and 870 CE). The Arabic word sahih means true. There are other collections accepted by Sunni, but these two are the most universally accepted. The Sunni often refers to the six books as they tend to accept six different collections. That, however, is not universally true. The Shias have different collections altogether. To provide some context of scale, the Sahih al-Bukhari contains about 7,275 hadith including repetitions and about 4,000 unique hadith.

Why does it matter to ISIS? Islamic law (see Sharia) is based, in large part, on the hadith. Thus the interpretations of the hadith are critical to ISIS in justifying its actions. It uses whatever hadith it needs, though it does tend to stick with the most accepted collections as a general rule.

Hijrah (هِجْرَة)

What is important? The Islamic calendar is lunar and it begins from the year 622 CE when the Prophet Mohamed journeyed from Mecca to Yathrib (later renamed Medina). Mohamed was warned of a plot to kill him in Mecca so he and Abu Bakr escaped the city and traveled to Yathrib where the prophet had previously been invited to come and resolve some disputes in the city.

The term hijrah can often mean simply immigration or emigration. In a modern context, it is typically viewed as traveling to a Muslim country. In this common use, one can see the influence of the prophet. His journey to Medina created the opportunity for the faithful to grow as a community and for the faith to actually be created as an entity. The chapters of the Quran are divided between those received in Mecca and those received in Medina with the hijrah serving as the dividing line.

Why does it matter to ISIS? ISIS only uses the Islamic calendar in recording dates of events. Thus the hijrah shapes its perspective on time. In addition, it regularly calls for the faithful to come to the caliphate, which is, by definition, making hijrah.

Hezbollah (حزب الله)

What is important? The argument can be made that the birth of Hezbollah (or party of God) can be traced back to the Ashura festival celebration in the southern Lebanese village of Nabatiya on October 16, 1983. During the festival, an Israeli patrol tried to move through the town. In the process, it disrupted the marching celebrants. A riot broke out. Soldiers fired into the crowd, killing several people. From this spark, the flames grew that created Hezbollah. Hezbollah is a Shia sectarian group that grew in Southern Lebanon as an opponent of the Israeli occupation. It takes credit for driving the Israeli military out of Southern Lebanon in 2000 because of its regular attacks on the Israeli military within Southern Lebanon and Israeli civilians living close to the border. Over the nearly two decades of occupation, there were thousands of mortar and rocket attacks.

From the withdrawal of Israel from the Southern Lebanon buffer zone in 2000 until 2006 there were sporadic engagements across the border between Hezbollah (and other smaller groups) and the Israeli military. Rocket attacks and other forms of indirect fire against Israeli civilian villages were common throughout the period. Hezbollah claimed that it would resist the Israeli occupation of Lebanon continuously. Israel claimed that it had withdrawn entirely from Lebanon in 2000, but Hezbollah used the continued presence of Israeli soldiers on a small plot of land called Sheba Farms as a reason for the resistance to continue.

In 2006, Hezbollah launched an attack directed against an Israeli border patrol. Several soldiers were killed at the site of the attack and two soldiers were abducted. While this was happening, a rocket attack engaged the higher headquarters of the patrol, confusing any sort of immediate response and rescue. The two abducted soldiers were assumed dead. The amount of blood at the scene of the engagement was too much for any other explanation. Despite this assessment Israel launched what would be called the Second Lebanon War that lasted for 38 days, the longest ground war in Israel's short history to that time. The fighting was intense. Hezbollah continued to launch rockets into northern Israel throughout the campaign. It even hit the city of Haifa—a major metropolitan area in the north, but one that had been outside rocket range until this conflict. The Israeli ground offensive failed to stop the rockets and it performed less than optimal by Israeli standards. The aerial bombardment of Lebanon was intense and this forced a negotiated settlement.

The 2006 fighting was viewed throughout the Middle East as an Israeli defeat (at the very least it was not an outright Israeli victory). In Israel, there was intense criticism of the military and civilian leadership, which led to significant reforms in training and operational doctrine. Hezbollah was now twice the hero—it drove the Israelis out of Lebanon in 2000 and in 2006 it successfully defended the country from attack. Despite this rosy picture, the leader of Hezbollah still stated after the war that if he had been aware of the damage Israel would inflict he would never have ordered the capture of the soldiers on the patrol. The soldiers were dead and their bodies returned as part of a prisoner swap in the negotiated settlement.

From these two periods of fighting, Hezbollah was viewed as Israel's primary opponent as it was the only force to successfully (depending on perspective) fight Israel since its founding. Hezbollah fought and fired from tunnels and hidden locations. It used rockets and antitank missiles and fought small unit engagements. This is what Hezbollah was trained to do—fight Israel in this asymmetric manner.

In 2014, Hezbollah sent fighters to Syria to support the Syrian government in its fighting against the various opposition fighters. At first, Hezbollah did not perform as well as expected. It was now the ones fighting through villages and towns and clearing buildings. This was the reverse of what it had always done against the Israelis. It lost significant casualties in the early months of fighting. Despite this, it remained one of the most well-trained and semiprofessional forces augmenting the Syrian government. For the most part, its operations have been in villages close to the Lebanese border.

Why does it matter to ISIS? Hezbollah is one of the best fighting groups defending the Syrian regime. If ISIS actually wants to take all of Syria, then Hezbollah will be a significant obstacle to accomplishing that objective.

Islam (الإسلام)

What is important? In Arabic, the word Islam means submission or more specifically submission to the will of God. A Muslim is linguistically and literally one who has made this submission. The faith of Islam extends back in time to the seventh century and the Prophet Mohamed who received directly the Quran from the Angel Gabriel when he was told to recite (see Quran). Mohamed was the prophet of the faith, called by God, to correct errors that had crept into the Jewish and Christian religions. Islam accepts most of the Biblical prophets, to include Jesus, as prophets. Mohamed was the last and final prophet. He cleansed the divine faith, which began with Adam. The belief is that the faith had become corrupted with incorrect doctrines and practices that drew people away from God. Mohamed brought it back on the correct course.

Islam is built on several key practices referred often to as the five pillars of Islam (see Islam, Five Pillars). The most important belief in Islam is the unity of God or in Arabic the *tawhid*. God is one and indivisible. The faith is explained in the Quran—the perfect word of God—received directly as God's words and not the interpretations or explanations of man.

Islam is a religion that can lay claim to more than 1.5 billion adherents. The faith tends to be divided into two major divisions—Sunni and Shia. Understanding Islam can be complex due to the many divisions and subdivisions, but the practices and principles are generally simple and easy to understand. The articles of faith begin as noted previously with the unity and monotheistic nature of God—the one and only, eternal, and absolute. The word Allah is simply the Arabic version of "the God." As Arabic does not have upper- or lower-case letters, the way to distinguish proper nouns is to provide the definite article. This is what creates the word Allah or, in English, God.

Muslims believe in Angels. The Quran was given from an angel to a man. Angels are the perfect obedient servants of God. In Islam, they typically serve as messengers of God (as in the case of the angel Gabriel), though they believe in a destroying angel as well. Revelation and prophets are critical to the faith though it is believed that such things ended with Mohamed and the complete revelation of the Quran. Finally, there is a powerful belief in judgment and the resurrection. The last day is often referred to as the Day of Resurrection rather than the Day of Judgment though both events will happen on that day. Based on this, there clearly is a concept of repentance and cleansing one's life from sin to stand clean at the judgment. Islam believes in a merciful God who forgives the sins of those who repent.

There are men and women who have devoted their lives to becoming Islamic scholars. It is impossible to capture all of the faith in such a short entry as this. This is a large faith with more than a billion adherents who believe in peace, living according to the teachings of God and his prophets, and being ready to stand and be judged at the end of times. This should not sound radical or unusual to most readers. Islam is a faith that requires commitment in order to live it. It is not a faith that accepts divisions of life and parts of a life that does not include Islam—it is a holistic faith wherein all aspects of life are part of the submission to the will of God. Therefore, a Muslim will dress modestly, will arise early for prayers, will eat food determined as clean and properly slaughtered, will conduct business honestly, and will strive to live cleanly each and every day.

Why does it matter to ISIS? ISIS is a very small fraction of a percentage of Muslims. It is not indicative of the faith though its beliefs are rooted in scripture, hadith, and sunna. It believes its members are the true Muslims and all those who disagree with them are either deceived or apostate. Consider the group psychology of being less than a fraction of a percent and thinking the more than 99 percent are all wrong. This is ISIS.

Islam, Five Pillars

What is important? Sunni Islam has five main practices so important to the faith that they are referred to as the five pillars of Islam. They are the declaration of faith, daily prayer, charitable giving, fasting, and pilgrimage. Each is described in brief as follows:

Declaration of Faith or Shahada (الشهادة)
The word shahada comes from the same Arabic root as martyr, which is to make a witness of your life in laying it down for God. Thus the witness statement is a declaration of faith that communicates a powerful assurance of self and identity. The Arabic statement is often translated as (لَا إِلَهَ إِلَّا الله مُحَمَّدٌ رَسُولُ الله): "There is no god but God (and) Mohamed is the messenger of God." This is only partially true as it means more than these simple words alone. As stated in the Islam section previously, the unity or oneness of God is critical to the faith and important for all Muslims to understand, accept, and fully embrace. The name Allah emphasizes the God—the one and only God—all holiness in one. The statement includes a powerful assertion of God's existence and the critical role of Mohamed as the Messenger of the God. The Arabic word

rasool (رَسُول) can be translated as messenger or prophet. In this case, the meaning is broader and includes the concept of conveying the divine message instantiated in the form of the word of God as recited by Mohamed and then later recorded as the Quran.

Daily Prayer

Muslims accept that they are to pray five times a day if at all possible. The prayers come at dawn, noon, afternoon (when the sun is midway between noon and the horizon), sunset, and dark (when darkness is complete). Each prayer has set words and actions associated with it. The prayers are said facing the Ka'aba (the central structure in the Grand Mosque) in Mecca. Prayers can be said anywhere though the preferred option is in a mosque. These prayers serve as a reminder of the importance of God.

Charitable Giving or Zakat (زكاة)

One interpretation of *zakat* can be that which purifies. The idea being that caring for the poor and needy draws one closer to God. The generally accepted amount is 2.5 percent of all wealth—not just income, but savings and property as well. This draws on the notion of Arabic generosity—the importance of giving to others less fortunate and not hording wealth. By calling on the saved and propertied money, this encourages people to use their money rather than horde it. There are significant legal discussions on the exact definition of what is included in the 2.5 percent calculation and what the base amount for giving is. Those who have very little are exempt from this requirement, but determining what constitutes "little" is ruled upon differently in the different Islamic legal schools.

Fasting or Sawm (صوم)

Most people are aware of the Muslim practice of fasting during the month of Ramadan. There are three kinds of fasting in Islam: ritual, fasting as compensation for repentance, and ascetic fasting. All of these types of fasting include similar practices: abstinence from food, drink, physical sensual pleasures (smoking, sexual relations, chewing gum, etc.), and passionate emotions (anger, lust, greed, profane language, etc.) from dawn to darkness. Several people are exempt from fasting—people with medical conditions, menstruating or nursing women, small children, the elderly, etc. Where possible, exempt persons should make up their fasting once the reason for their exemption has passed. The idea of fasting is to demonstrate control of the body and to purify oneself from sin. Fasting during Ramadan is obligatory for those not exempt, but there are other holy days and even other days of the week when Muslims fast.

Pilgrimage to Mecca or Hajj (حج)

Every able bodied Muslim is expected to make the Hajj at least once in their lifetime. It is considered a great honor to travel to Mecca and participate in this event. As modern transportation has made it possible for more and more Muslims to make this journey, the Hajj has taken on a spectacle with millions of people gathered at the Great Mosque in prayer. The Hajj is only during the Islamic month of Dhu al-Hijjah, the third month after Ramadan. Pilgrimages outside of this month are not considered Hajj though many Muslims consider it an honor to worship at the Great Mosque at any time. The Hajj consists of specific rituals that remind the pilgrim of the faithfulness of Abraham and his wife Hagar and their child Ishmael. The Hajj celebration includes a ritual animal sacrifice (typically a sheep or goat) that coincides with the Islamic holy celebration of the feast of slaughtering or Eid al-Adha celebrated by Muslims globally. This feast commemorates the gift of a ram, which God provided for Abraham in place of his son Ishmael whom he was commanded to sacrifice. It is worth noting that Muslims believe it was Ishmael Abraham who was called on to sacrifice whereas Christians and Jews believe it was Isaac. Arabs claim descent from Abraham through Ishmael.

Why does it matter to ISIS? These pillars are often interwoven into ISIS propaganda, literature, and videos as a means of appealing to the faithful.

Islamic Conquests (Seventh Century)

Dates: 634–661 CE

What is important? For the sake of this entry, the discussion of Islamic expansion is confined to the Rashidun Caliphate. The reason for this limitation is driven by space and by the Salafist ideology of the subjects of this book. As Salafists ISIS subscribes to the importance of the early generations of the prophet and his companions, which coincide with the Rashidun period. As stated elsewhere, when one looks at this period of expansion and what was accomplished by the Islamic armies in just a couple of dozen years it can appear miraculous. The forays beyond the Arabian Peninsula began even before the prophet's death. Mohamed sent an army into what is today Jordan that fought and lost to the Romans. Following the prophet's death in 632, many Arab tribes broke away from Islam believing that their loyalty oath was to Mohamed himself. The first caliph Abu Bakr fought his first wars bringing the Arabs together in unity under the banner of Islam and allegiance to the caliph. Once that was accomplished, then Abu Bakr sent the armies out to the north. The first army was sent against the Sassanid Persian Empire in 633. A year later another army was sent against the Romans with a general focus on the city of Damascus, Syria.

The Muslim (Arab) armies fought mostly on foot though they always had mounted forces as well. They divided their forces into tribal groups often translated as squadrons. The tribal relationships kept the forces loyal. In addition, a loose command structure prevented offense and friction within a force experienced in raiding and not schooled in large protracted campaigns. The missions assigned to subordinate units were based on general purposes that allowed for tremendous freedom in execution. Lengthy battles often ensued. Many of the major fights lasted for days—sometimes nearly a week or more. The warriors fighting in this army were united in their goal of spreading the faith and their belief that they would receive a heavenly reward if they died in battle. Even though the battles often took a long time to reach an ultimate conclusion, the Muslim forces were fast moving and reacted quickly to situations arising in the battle—both opportunities to be exploited and setbacks requiring response or withdrawal. They were counseled to keep the desert to their backs so that, if pressed, they could flee back into the desert, which was essentially their natural habitat as Bedouin warriors. One major fight against the Persians saw a Muslim force put a river to their back with disastrous consequences. This did not happen again in a major battle in this period.

Although the large empires did not crumble at once, they suffered heavy defeats during this period. The Persians were essentially destroyed as an empire by the end of this period, and the Romans pushed north into modern-day Turkey. Once Mesopotamia, the Levant, and Iran were clear, the armies of Islam began flowing west along the North African shore. Egypt fell in 639 and most of the rest of North Africa by 652. Much of the Muslim's success can be attributed to capitalizing on the natural flow of things; they simply kept moving, always fighting the next enemy beyond the one they had just defeated. As the armies advanced, they sometimes were invited to assist in various disputes. Some Roman governors invited Muslim forces in to assert their independence from Constantinople only to lose their independence to the invited Muslim armies. By the end of this period, the Middle East and North Africa had shifted from primarily Christian rule to primarily Muslim rule.

Although the religious allegiance of the leadership in this period changed, the vast majority of the population maintained their personal religious affiliations. There were very few instances of conversion by the sword. Those who submitted to the Muslim invaders were allowed to pay a tax to provide for the protection of the Muslim forces. Most of the Muslim fighters stayed in camps outside the major urban areas in order to keep Islam and the native religions separate. The conversion of the populace happened over time, typically generations.

Why does it matter to ISIS? ISIS characterizes itself as a Muslim force fighting in the style of these early armies. It looks toward the past for historical examples of when and how battles were fought. Alhough it does not seek to fight exactly as the Muslims did anciently, ISIS does follow some of the same general patterns described previously.

Israel

Dates: independence declared May 14, 1948

What is important? It can be said that the modern incarnation of the jihadi movement got its intellectual roots from the Palestinian opposition fighters of the 1960s and 1970s as they used terror to grab the world's attention and explain their desire for self-determination. The very existence of Israel as a predominantly Jewish state that defeated each and every one of their Arab neighbors in war was deemed insulting and humiliating by groups like ISIS. Jews were identified in the Quran and the teachings of the prophet as protected people—those needing the protection of the Muslims to survive within the caliphate. Here were protected people that were now the dominant people. This could not be. There must be some conspiracy that made this situation happen. Of course the conspiracy was that Israel is a modern-day crusader state thrust into the Middle East by European powers and kept in a dominant position by Western technology and weapons. Although ISIS does not mention Israel in all of its articles and broadcasts it is typically there as an undercurrent theme.

What follows is a brief description of the major conflicts in Israel's history. The country was born in conflict; even before it declared itself to be a state it was under attack. What the modern state of Israel refers to as its *War of Independence* was fought in 1947 to 1948. In 1923, the League of Nations instituted the temporary rule of Palestine by Great Britain (known as the British Mandate). Prior to this mandate, Palestine was under Ottoman control. The British Mandate was set to end on May 14, 1948. The United Nations had adopted a partition plan that proposed the establishment of independent Arab and Jewish states with international oversight for the city of Jerusalem, but the plan was uncertain to come into effect before the mandate ended. Zionist leaders (Jews who favored an independent Jewish state) declared their independence and the war was on. Israel defeated armies from Egypt, Jordan, and Syria along with additional forces from other Arab states. This abject failure in conflict by the Arab states led to several political changes including a coup de tat against the King in Egypt and a revolution in Syria. None of the countries were actually ready to fight except Jordan whose military was trained and led primarily by British officers.

The next war is referred to as the *1956 War* or the *Suez Crisis*. This war was based on something out of fiction as the British government was angry with the Egyptian government for nationalizing the Suez Canal and the British and French wanted Israel to attack across the Sinai toward the canal. French and British forces would call for a cease fire and then land paratroopers with the argument that they were there to protect the canal. The entire world knew of the charade very soon after the conflict began. Although the Israelis made it to the canal, they eventually withdrew under international pressure led by the United States.

In 1967 Egypt, acting on warnings given by the Soviet Union of impending Israeli attacks on their Arab neighbors, prepared for war and blocked the exit from the Gulf of Aqaba—Israel's only access to the Red Sea and ultimately the Indian Ocean. This was deemed to be a *casus belli* (or justification for war) by Israel. The United States was fully committed to Vietnam and not interested in sorting out the problem. Israel ultimately decided to go to war to protect its national interests and what it believed to be its national survival in what many call the *Six Day War* or the *1967 War*. Here Israel had stunning victories against Egypt. It destroyed the Egyptian air force on the ground in a surprise attack, and it then marched across the Sinai Peninsula to the Suez Canal. It then turned against Jordanian forces that had fired artillery against Israel in an attempt to show solidarity with Egypt. Israel took the West Bank and captured the city of Jerusalem. Finally Israel went against Syria in the Golan Heights and took the land. When people speak of the "occupied territories," it is the Palestinian lands captured in this war—the Gaza Strip, the West Bank, and the Golan Heights.

There followed an uneasy "peace" for several years. This peaceful period included the first of many terrorist attacks launched by Palestinians from neighboring countries against Israel. In this period, Israel adopted a policy it has used until today. It reacts against the country from which an attack is launched as if that country launched the attack.

In 1973, the Arabs surprised Israel in what many call the *Yom Kippur War* or the *October War*. The Egyptians successfully crossed the Suez Canal and pushed the Israelis away from the canal. The Syrians had initial successes in the Golan Heights, but they were later pushed back. The Israelis also penetrated the Egyptian lines by the canal and made a crossing of their own. By the time the United States and the Soviet Union forced the sides to stop fighting, the Israelis had columns on the roads toward Cairo and Damascus. Despite the response, the ultimate result was a peace deal between Israel and Egypt, called the Camp David Accords, where Israel traded the Sinai for peace with Egypt. For this deal, Anwar Sadat, the Egyptian President, was assassinated.

The *Yom Kippur War* or the *October War* could be argued to be the last war that Israel fought against Arab states. All of its other fighting has been against nonstate and substate actors. In 1982, Israel invaded Lebanon to defeat Palestinian opponents who were attacking northern Israel from there. It continued to fight in southern Lebanon from 1982 to 2000. Israel also dealt with Palestinian uprisings or intifadas within the occupied territories in 1987 and again in 2000. Both of the intifadas lasted longer than a year and challenged the notions of what it means to be Israeli. As mentioned in the entry on Hezbollah, Israel fought a war with it in 2006. It also conducted numerous operations against Hamas in the Gaza Strip from 2005 until the present.

Why does it matter to ISIS? Israel serves several roles for ISIS. It is a unifying enemy for most, if not all, salafi-jihadi groups and a constant source of motivation for ISIS. It is unlikely, however, that ISIS will be launching attacks against Israel anytime soon as the Syrian government forces and Hezbollah currently are in between ISIS and Israel.

Jabhat al-Nusra (جبهة النصرة لأهل الشام "The Support Front for the People of Al-Sham")

What is important? Jabhat al-Nusra (or al-Nusra Front as many in the media refer to it) is a salafi-jihadi organization. It is a break off from ISIS sent to Syria in 2012 with the intent of developing the salafi-jihadi opposition to Bashar al-Assad. The group declared itself as a member of al-Qaeda when ISIS changed its name from the Islamic State of Iraq to the Islamic State of Iraq and al-Sham in 2014. This announcement meant that ISIS was now in Syria full time. Consequently, Jabhat al-Nusra would have to either take orders from ISIS or declare its allegiance elsewhere. It chose the second option in aligning with al-Qaeda.

The internal struggle between Jabhat al-Nusra and ISIS captured a lot of media attention in 2014 and 2015 though few reports properly credited the origin of the groups or recognized the reason for the friction.

Fundamentally, Jabhat al-Nusra has the same ideology as ISIS. It does not emphasize the apocalyptic vision nor does it promote the harshest anti-Shia statements. That said, it operates in Syria where the majority of its opponents—the Syrian regime or Hezbollah—are Shia making this difference moot. Jabhat al-Nusra's membership is generally Syrian, another difference from ISIS, which incorporates more foreigners into its fighting organizations.

In the comparison between ISIS and Jabhat al-Nusra, ISIS often comes off as more extreme and less cooperative. There are multiple Sunni states funneling money to the Syrian opposition, and many of them prefer religiously strict organizations if possible. Jabat al-Nusra has often been characterized in this way. As a result, it has been courted by several of the states to break from al-Qaeda with the offer of money as an enticement. So far it has not taken the enticement.

Jabhat al-Nusra is one of the most effective antiregime organizations in Syria. It has been successful in small and medium operations, and it has effectively defeated other less religious opposition groups on multiple occasions. In this regard, it is one of the most formidable non-ISS forces in Syria.

Why does it matter to ISIS? ISIS and Jabhat al-Nusra have fought each other in a variety of places, the most significant being in and around Deir al-Zour. Jabhat al-Nusra has typically fared poorly given that this is an area where ISIS is dominant. It has moved further west in the country, and ISIS has yet to move into those locations. As the competition in Syria continues to play out it is uncertain how this will resolve itself. Right now ISIS has the upper hand, but Jabhat al-Nusra remains its most significant opponent.

Jihad (جهاد)

What is important? The Arabic language does not have upper- and lower-case letters so there is no way to distinguish the difference between words based solely on a capital letter. For example, in English one can communicate two different things when talking about crusade depending on whether a capital or lower-case letter is used to begin the word. The use of lower case denotes a supreme commitment of effort toward any project that is deemed valuable while the use of a capital letter typically refers to the Crusading period discussed previously (see Crusades). The comparable word in Arabic is jihad or Jihad. As written in English, the lower-case version can mean to strive, to apply oneself, to struggle, to persevere. When begun with an upper-case letter, it takes on a different meaning—holy war for the defense of the faith. Jihad when written with a lower—case first letter can carry the same meaning, but the point is to communicate that the word has multiple meanings. For most Muslims, it means a personal struggle—fasting during the month of Ramadan is typically considered a jihad, for example.

It is a small group of Muslims that thinks of jihad as something to be waged with violence in the defense of the faith. This is true regardless of the circumstances or the period in history. Most people are not inclined to perform acts of violence regardless of the precipitating cause. There are two kinds of jihad in Islamic law—compulsory and voluntary. An example of compulsory jihad would be the invasion of a Muslim country by a non-Muslim country. The Soviet Union's perceived invasion of Afghanistan is one such example. The compulsion for fighting moves in concentric rings from those directly affected outward to a point where it may be a compulsion on all Muslims. If those people most closely affected by the invasion are not capable of stopping the aggressors and driving them back, then those next closest to the area are under the obligation to fight and so on until the aggressors are driven from Muslim lands.

The voluntary form of jihad is more controversial and tends to be preached by jihadi thinkers. It is based on interpretations of jurisprudence given when the borders between Muslim and non-Muslim lands were open and raids and engagements between the parties were common. In this case, the interpretation is that Muslims are free to wage jihad as a means of punishing the nonbelievers. Abdullah Azzam, the intellectual thinker behind al-Qaeda, wrote a legal treatise describing these two forms of jihad. He advocated for the performance of both, though his priority was on driving the Soviets from Afghanistan at the time of writing.

Why does it matter to ISIS? ISIS believes that Muslim lands have been invaded by western nonbelieving countries physically and conceptually through the spread of the ideas of non-believers. All of the countries of the region, other than the Islamic State, are contaminated by the western beliefs, making jihad necessary in order to remove the invaders and their ideas. This is obligatory. The region must be cleansed. In this case, the caliph has also called for a general jihad, making it obligatory for all Muslims everywhere to respond, not simply those who are geographically closest to the Middle East.

Kharajites or Khawarij (خوارج, الخارجية)

What is important? Kharajites are literally those who went out. They are outsiders. The word kharajite is derived from the root for such words as outside, exit, etc. Thus the term refers to those outside the faith or outside the norms and beliefs of the community of believers.

This group dates back to the period of succession following the death of the third caliph of Sunni Islam, Uthman ibn Affan. The Kharajites, then referred to by a different name, argued that the succession should be determined by combat of champions of any Muslim and not just Quraysh or even Arabs. They tended to favor Ali. Some have even suggested that they were responsible for the murder of Uthman. Regardless, they were a dedicated group committed to having a clean succession. Rather than have the competition, there was a negotiated settlement that placed Ali as the caliph after an indecisive battle between the two forces.

The Kharajites took it on themselves to assassinate each of the main participants in the succession struggle though only Ali was actually killed while at prayers in Kufa, Iraq. The group continued for some time as a plague on rulers deemed to be impure, but it has not again shaped the debate of the succession or of the faith as it did at the beginning. The group has moderated over the centuries such that its intellectual and literal descendants are one of the most moderate forms of modern Islam in Oman and in small pockets elsewhere.

Why does it matter to ISIS? Some, including the King of Jordan, have used the word Kharajites or Khawarij to designate ISIS. The historical and contextual baggage associated with the words help emphasize the status of ISIS as being outside the larger Muslim community; many view it as outside the law and the accepted norms of the faith and community of believers. It is unclear how much this has resonated within Islam.

Kobane, Battle of

Dates: September 13, 2014–March 15, 2015

What is important? Kobane is the Turkish name for a village that sits on Syria's northern border with Turkey about a third of the way along the border from west to east. It is along a tributary stream of the Euphrates River. The

Arabic name for the village is Ayn al-Arab (Arab Spring or Spring of the Arab). The city had a population of about 40,000 people. As ISIS advanced toward the city, tens of thousands of residents escaped into Turkey.

In October 2014, ISIS advanced capturing dozens and then hundreds of villages. This is a predominantly Kurdish area, and the Kurds fled in large numbers. Kurdish fighters from the YPG defended the villages and the city of Kobane. The YPG were joined by elements of the free Syrian Army and other opposition groups to the Syrian regime and to ISIS.

ISIS enjoyed initial success; it captured more than 60 percent of the city by the end of 2014. In January 2015, the YPG and others counterattacked and drove back ISIS from Kobane and from most of the villages previously taken. By March 2015, the pre-Kobane lines were generally restored. The counterattack enjoyed significant support from coalition aircraft, but none from the Turkish military that overwatched the battle area.

Why does it matter to ISIS? The Battle of Kobane is held up as the coalition model of success. While the coalition claims to have retaken the city through a combination of coalition airpower and indigenous "boots on the ground" ISIS claims to have accomplished what it intended to achieve in Kobane. The city was destroyed (more than 70 percent of the buildings damaged or destroyed) and no one can live there.

Levant (al-Sham)

What is important? See al-Sham (Levant).

Why does it matter to ISIS? See al-Sham (Levant).

Mahdi (مهدي)

What is important? The Mahdi is a figure that features prominently in both Sunni and Shia Islam though with different specific expressions and expectations. The Arabic root is also used in the words for peaceful, smooth, and calm. Simply stated, a Mahdi is a righteous person. In terms of Islam specifically it means one who smooths the paths before. In general, the Mahdi is a person who will rule before the Day of Judgment or Day of Resurrection as a forerunner to those end times.

The Mahdi is not explicitly referenced in the Quran, but there are several references to the Mahdi in the hadith. In some branches of Shia Islam, it is believed that the Mahdi has already come and is in hiding until the end of times when he will reveal himself. In some interpretations, Jesus is the Mahdi though this is not commonly accepted.

The role and position of the Mahdi are somewhat mystical and it carries with it a great deal of significance. Over time there have been several people who claimed to be the Mahdi and who drew hundreds and thousands of people to it. In these declarations, entire societies have been motivated to follow a leader who offered them an opportunity to bring about the end of days.

Why does it matter to ISIS? While ISIS has not, as yet, made reference to the Mahdi, it is a group focused on Islamic end-of-days prophecies. This makes understanding the Mahdi, who will play a key role in the fulfillment of these prophecies, useful as part of a study of the Islamic State.

Mosul, Iraq

What is important? Mosul is the second largest urban area in modern-day Iraq. It sits astride the Tigris River. Anciently, the Assyrian capital of Nineveh was on the eastern bank of the river where modern-day Mosul sits. Mosul was the capital city of the Ninawa governorate in Iraq until June 2014 when it was captured by ISIS. The city has a population of around one million people though specific numbers vary significantly (between 750,000 and 2,500,000) depending on the source. The largest estimates are no longer true as hundreds of thousands have fled before and during ISIS control. The lowest estimates refer to the urban center only and not the greater metropolitan area. Prior to the invasion of ISIS, the city was predominantly Arab with Kurdish, Turcoman, and Yazidi minorities.

Mosul has consistently been a regionally important city going all the way back to Assyrian times. In historic significance, Salah al-Din (Saladin) ruled from Mosul.

In 2014, ISIS conducted a great deal of engagements with civic and tribal leaders in and around Mosul. Since the fall of Saddam's regime in 2003 the city served as a hotbed for disaffected persons belonging to the Ba'ath party. The groups in opposition to the Shia-dominated government in Baghdad welcomed ISIS and believed that it could control what it perceived to be a backward group. In retrospect, ISIS controlled them as it swept into the city. The initial reports were that ISIS was conducting a prison break in June 2014 and did not have designs on controlling the entire city. The Iraqi security forces responsible for the protection of the city fled at the approach of ISIS, allowing ISIS to take the city as a target of opportunity. There is some question regarding the accuracy of this story, but that was the rumor in June and July 2014 and it deserves some credence. It communicates the opportunistic nature of ISIS and the level of corruption and inherent internal weakness of the Iraqi Security Forces.

It was in Mosul that Abu Bakr al-Baghdadi declared himself caliph and invited all Muslims to come and support the caliphate.

Mosul has been a major source of revenue for ISIS throughout its occupation. The government in Baghdad continued to pay government employees living in Mosul, thus providing a constant source of revenue to ISIS. While these payments have ceased, the taxation of a million or more people provides the single largest source of income to the state coffers. Mosul is also the most urban area controlled by ISIS with all of the amenities to include a major university with medical facilities and chemical laboratories.

North of the city of Mosul lies the Mosul Dam that is an earthen dam built on a geologically unstable foundation of gypsum. The dam has regularly been declared dangerously close to collapse. Should the dam fail, it would risk the lives of hundreds of thousands of people all of the way down the Tigris River valley to Baghdad and beyond.

Why does it matter to ISIS? Mosul is the crown jewel of cities in the caliphate. The coalition's intent was to regain Mosul in 2015, but the fall of Ramadi in May of that year put those plans on hold until early 2016. Although numerous operations with coalition air support (typically conducted by Kurdish fighters) have nibbled away at the villages and road networks around Mosul throughout 2015 the city is still strongly in the hands of ISIS.

Nasheed (نشيد)

What is important? The word in Arabic means chant. A nasheed is a type of music typically performed in acapella as conservative Muslim clergy have issues regarding musical accompaniment. There are several hadith that seem to forbid the use of musical instruments. The famous salafi scholar Ibn Taymiyyah is reported to have said that music was like alcohol to the soul.

Why does it matter to ISIS? Various groups have nasheeds that are available on YouTube or other online media sources. These are like music videos in support of the jihad. ISIS has used nasheeds to promote its message and to link its actions in a heroic narrative. Other groups use these as well. Depending on the group, the video may include music. The most prevalent nasheed for ISIS in 2014 and early 2015 was called the *Islamic State Arises*. The lyrics are as follows. These lyrics give a sense of the narrative being woven by ISIS.

My ummah, dawn has appeared
So await the expected victory
The Islamic State has arisen
By the blood of the righteous

The Islamic State has arisen
By the jihad of the pious
They have offered their souls
In righteousness with constancy and conviction
So that the religion may be established
In which there is the law of the lord of the worlds

My ummah, accept the good news
And don't despair victory is near
The Islamic State has arisen
And the dreaded might has begun

It has arisen tracing out glory
And the period of setting has ended
By faithful men who do not fear warfare
They have created eternal glory
That will not perish or disappear

My ummah, God is our Lord
So grant your blood
For victory will not return
Except by the blood of the martyrs

Who have spent their time hoping for their Lord
In the abode of the prophets
They have offered their souls to God

And for the religion there is self-sacrifice
The people of giving and granting
Are the people of excellence and pride

My ummah, accept the good news
[sword being drawn]
The sun of steadfastness has arisen
Verily we have marched [marching feet]
In masses for the hills the time-honored glory

My ummah, accept the good news [gunshot]
The sun of steadfastness has arisen
Verily we have marched
In masses for the hills the time-honored glory

That we may return the light
Faith and glorious might
By men who have forsaken the dunya
And attained immortality
And have revived the ummah of glory
And the assured victory

My ummah, dawn has appeared
So await the expected victory
The Islamic State has arisen
By the blood of the righteous

Omar, Mohammed

Dates: c. 1950 to 1960–April 23, 2013

Name: Mohammed Omar Mujahid (ملا محمد عمر مجاهد)

Key Events in His Life: Mohammed Omar is also known by many as Mullah Omar. He was an Afghan mujahedeen and the leader of the Taliban. He ruled Afghanistan from September 27, 1996, to November 13, 2001. He lived primarily in Kandahar, and even when he ruled Afghanistan, he rarely left the city. He is enigmatic and few details of his life are known for certain. Only two pictures of him exist, and neither one is certainly him.

He left Afghanistan to study in Pakistan before the Soviet appearance in Afghanistan. He later fought with the mujahedeen and distinguished himself in battle where he lost an eye to shrapnel. Following the Soviet departure, he played almost no role in the fighting of the warlords. Eventually he led a group of students (Talibs or Taliban in the Pashto language) to fight against the injustice of the warlords. One of the myths (or maybe facts) about his command claims that he captured a mosque that supposedly held a cloak worn by the Prophet Mohamed. He placed that cloak on his shoulders and was declared by his followers as amir al-mu'minin (see Amir al-Mu'minin) as foretold of anyone to wear the cloak. He led the Taliban on a series of lightning raids and offensives that captured nearly all of Afghanistan within weeks.

The Taliban are a highly conservative, religiously based organization—it is salafi in some respects—especially with regard to interpretations of the faith and sharia. The rule of the Taliban was deemed harsh and repressive. It took the country backward with respect to treatment of women and education. The Taliban also ended a great deal of the corruption and the abuses of the warlords.

Mohammed Omar died of tuberculosis in 2013, but this fact was kept hidden from the world and his own followers for more than two years. The Taliban finally admitted to his death on July 29, 2015. The fact that such a leader in a well-known struggle involving the United States and other major players could be kept hidden for so long attests to his secretive nature.

Why does it matter? Mohammed Omar listened to and read the writings of Abdullah Azzam. He met with and knew Osama bin Laden before al-Qaeda became known. These intellectual and social connections led bin Laden to have his training bases and his operations run from Afghanistan. It was this connection that led U.S. Forces to Afghanistan in 2001 following the attacks on the United States by al-Qaeda on September 11, 2001.

He was acknowledged by many in the salafi-jihadi community as the amir al-mu'minin. With this title, many declared allegiance to him or at least respected him for the title. The declaration of Abu Bakr al-Baghdadi as the amir al-mu'minin created something of a friction within that community that could not be resolved while he lived.

Operation Desert Storm

Dates: August 2, 1990–February 28, 1991

What is important? In response to the invasion of Kuwait in the summer of 1990, the United States spent nearly six months deploying about 700,000 personnel and thousands of pieces of heavy equipment to the Kingdom of Saudi Arabia as part of a powerful international coalition involving nearly a million personnel and 34 nations.

The objective of the campaign was to expel Iraq from Kuwait. The limited nature of campaign objectives was due in part to UN Security Council resolutions. The multinational nature of the coalition served as a limiting factor as well. Different nations joined the coalition with very different expectations and requirements. In particular, it was feared that the Arab members of the coalition would not go along if the United States required much beyond simply expelling Iraqi forces from Kuwait. Thus there were severe limits.

The military campaign, known as Operation Desert Storm, took place in two parts—an aggressive air campaign that began on January 17, 1991—and a lightning fast ground campaign that began on February 24 and ended on February 28. It is sometimes referred to as the 100-Hour War. Obviously, when combining the air and the ground campaigns together was a lot more than 100 hours. It is certain that without the extensive air campaign, the ground fighting would have been longer with more coalition casualties. As it was, the coalition only suffered about a thousand casualties compared to Iraqi casualties of over 100,000.

President George H. W. Bush called on the Iraqi people to overthrow Saddam Hussein as the President of Iraq. Broadcasts from Arabic language radio stations gave the impression that the coalition would support popular uprisings. This was never the intent of the coalition. Regardless of intent, both the Shias in the south and the Kurds in the north began a popular uprising and enjoyed initial success against regime security forces.

Formal hostilities between the coalition and the Iraqi regime were brought to an end by the U.S. government in coordination with its coalition partners. Coalition and Iraqi military commanders met to discuss the cessation of hostilities and the rules for separating forces. During these discussions, the Iraqi military leaders asked to be able to fly helicopters to allow for logistics functions as the coalition had destroyed all the major bridges over the Tigris and Euphrates Rivers. The coalition leaders agreed to what seemed to be a reasonable request.

The helicopters were instead used to suppress the uprisings and retain government authority throughout Iraq. Following the end of hostilities, a harsh sanctions regime was established that affected Iraqi life at all levels and in every way imaginable. The sanctions were regularly used as a scapegoat by Saddam Hussein for anything bad in Iraq.

Why does it matter to ISIS? The experiences from before, during, and after Operation Desert Storm reverberated both with the U.S. government and the people of Iraq in the initial parts of Operation Iraqi Freedom.

Operation Inherent Resolve

Dates: June 15, 2014–Present

What is important? Operation Inherent Resolve (OIR) is the named operation for the U.S. military in conducting operations against the Islamic State in both Iraq and Syria. Much of this book explains the various parts of this operation, so here it is only given in brief summary. The primary nature of OIR at the time of writing is to advise, assist, and train. It also involves the conduct of air strikes by coalition partner countries in support of the various ground forces resident in Iraq and Syria. Other than limited special operations forces from coalition countries, there have been no deployments of army or Marine combat formations. OIR is separate from the actions of Iran and Russia that have sent combat formations into the conflict zone. The coalition is reported to consist of approximately 65 countries. Early 2016 saw small, but important changes to the coalition commitments as more and more combat elements deployed into Iraq.

Why does it matter to ISIS? As OIR exists under the presidential administration of President Obama, it does not include large U.S. combat formations, nor is it likely to short of a significant attack conducted by ISIS on U.S. soil. It is uncertain how the operation will change when a new president is inaugurated in 2017.

Operation Iraqi Freedom

Dates: Operation Iraqi Freedom (March 20, 2003–August 31, 2010): U.S. military named operation for the invasion of Iraq in order to overthrow the regime of long-time dictator Saddam Hussein and seize purported stockpiles of weapons of mass destruction.

Operation New Dawn (September 1, 2010– December 31, 2011): U.S. military named operation for the advise-and-assist effort in support of the Iraqi security forces and in conjunction with the U.S. withdrawal from Iraq.

What is important? Although technically there were two U.S.-named operations for the conduct of operations in the country of Iraq between 2003 and 2011, they are both typically linked into one named operation: Operation Iraqi Freedom (OIF).

The war began with attacks from the air against key Iraqi leaders—none of which were effective in killing any of the 200 designated senior regime targets. The air campaign was referred to as "Shock and Awe" as it delivered an enormous amount of explosives with precision against the whole of the Iraqi government and infrastructure in a relatively short time. This was designed to paralyze the regime and either cause it to collapse or prevent it from controlling its military forces.

The ground campaign included two main forces advancing side by side from Kuwait-oriented north on Baghdad. On the right (east) was the Marine Expeditionary Force (MEF) that included the U.S. Marine Corps First Division and a United Kingdom division. The Marines attacked all the way to Baghdad whereas the British oriented its efforts on securing the southern city of Basra. On the left (west) was the U.S. Army V Corps (V [(US] Corps) that included the Third Infantry (Mechanized) Division (3 ID) as the main effort with the 101st Air Assault Division (101 ID) in support. It was originally planned for the Fourth Infantry (Mechanized) Division (4 ID) to attack from the north after moving through Turkey, but on March 1, 2003, the Turkish parliament voted against allowing U.S. forces to move through or operate from Turkish territory. The 4 ID was forced to move its equipment from Turkish waters through the Suez Canal and then into and through Kuwait to get into Iraq.

The combat maneuver formations sought to avoid urban areas as much as possible. They moved through them when necessary to cross the Tigris and Euphrates rivers and to move through more difficult terrain like the agricultural areas crisscrossed by irrigation ditches. As V (US) Corps approached Baghdad, the forces were funneled into a narrow geographic area between the Euphrates River and the Razazza Lake. This area is known as the Karbala Gap. In the middle of this area is the city of Karbala. Some of the heaviest fighting happened in this area.

The government of Iraq collapsed rapidly with the primary fighting ending in less than three weeks—one of the fastest conquests of a modern state in history. The defeat of military forces was not the problem, but the governing of a country was for several reasons.

First, the Iraqi governing councils, and later their elected representatives, had little control over the resources and organs of a state. The infrastructure of Iraq was in shambles. Some of the shambles were a result of the combat action in the spring of 2003 and some from the combat actions of 1991. Many others were a result of the economic sanctions imposed on Iraq from 1991 until 2003. The idea that Saddam Hussein would be personally affected by the sanctions or that the organizations and entities essential to his existence as an authority figure in Iraq would be threatened by such sanctions was naïve on the part of western governments. Saddam used what money he obtained to maintain his security and intelligence apparatus and made sure those most essential or loyal to him received the benefits of modernity—electricity, clean water, etc. The rest of the population suffered as the Iraqi infrastructure degraded.

Second, those initially designated to be in the interim governing body were not respected by the Iraqi people. They were either seen as outsiders (exiles given power by the invaders) or as lackeys to the invading forces. To gain credibility, it was almost necessary to be seen as opposing the Coalition Provisional Authority or at least not kowtowing to them in every action. Thus nothing moved as quickly as expected. *Everything in Iraq* is hard, became one of the most often repeated phrases by coalition soldiers and officials. It was said, because it was true.

Third, there were several relatively rapid elections. No one governed for any significant length of time in Iraq until after the period in question. This almost continuous handover of authority from one person to the next—the musical chairs game of Iraqi politics, if you will—fostered a sense of corruption as a means of survival. The Americans were pouring money into the country. If you wanted to get your hands on that money and benefit yourself and your family, then you needed to act while you had the chance. As a result, little was really accomplished with the resources provided because those resources were often squandered or horded and then sent to out of country estates and banks for later use and benefit.

Fourth and most important were the two decisions to unemploy thousands upon thousands of the technically proficient people of Iraq. The orders known as Order One and Order Two put out of work the political leadership and the security leadership. This meant that lots of young, military-trained people and nearly all those who were trained to organize and lead were now without meaningful employment for themselves or their families. Their world was destroyed.

One of the most important objectives to understand is the growing disconnect between how the coalition saw what was happening and what was actually happening. The rise of a sectarian ideological struggle took time to be comprehended by the United States and other members of the coalition. The U.S.-led coalition began to fall apart in 2004 with nine countries withdrawing their forces. The most famous of these was the Spanish contingent that withdrew after the Madrid bombings in 2004 due to the mishandling of blame and a perceived cover-up by the Spanish government regarding who was responsible for the attacks. Another two countries each departed in 2005 and 2006. A new four-star commander named George Casey ran the fighting from a command called Multi-National Forces-Iraq or MNF-I. General Casey believed that limited American participation and visibility within Iraq would both encourage Iraqis to step forward and discourage attacks on U.S. forces. He was sent to Iraq with a mandate to withdraw U.S. forces within 18 months from the time he took command (he commanded from June 4, 2004, until February 10, 2007). This time limit demonstrated more than anything else a lack of understanding of Iraq and what was happening there by senior leaders in Washington, DC. Another example of the disconnect was the fact that many in the Bush Administration and MNF-I hesitated to call what was happening in Iraq a civil war.

The final factor that played a critical role in the war was the improvised explosive device or IED. These devices plagued the United States and coalition military personnel throughout the fighting; more people were wounded or killed by IEDs than any other weapon system in the war.

In 2006, the United States had a midterm election in which the President's party lost control of both the House and the Senate and he entered a period of greater political oversight and scrutiny. This is also when the Surge was decided and Secretary of Defense Donald Rumsfeld resigned. Robert Gates became the new Secretary of Defense.

The final transition of the war came with the inauguration of the Obama Administration that sought to end the war in order to fulfill campaign promises.

Why does it matter to ISIS? The relationship between Operation Iraqi Freedom and ISIS has a great deal to do with the question of genesis. What created ISIS? This question plagued politicians throughout the rise and success of ISIS. Was it the decision to invade, the failed occupation that created chaos and sectarianism in Iraq, the rapid withdrawal that left an unstable and divided Iraq?

Or was it all of the above? The connection between Operation Iraqi Freedom and what has become of the Middle East cannot be undone, but maybe it can be understood.

Ottoman Empire

What is important? The Ottoman Empire ruled modern-day Turkey and most of what is today called the Levant, Mesopotamia, and the Arabian Peninsula from about 1299 to 1924. The empire grew from the earliest periods until the 1500s when it reached its greatest extent; it governed much of the eastern portions of North Africa and a significant portion of southeastern Europe to include all of the Balkan Peninsula. The Ottomans are Turkic people who came into Anatolia as nomadic raiders under the direction of the Abbasid caliphs and remained. They became the Muslim power in Anatolia following the Mongol invasion of Mesopotamia and the collapse of the Abbasids. The group slowly expanded beyond Anatolia with a primary interest toward Europe. It captured Constantinople and effectively ended the Roman (Byzantine) Empire in 1453 CE. It was in this period that it became an empire.

The Ottomans later expanded south to capture the holy cities of Mecca and Medina, and they declared their ruler the successor of the prophet and caliph. The Ottomans fought the Safavids throughout the coexistence of the two empires with the Ottomans generally coming off better and exerting control over Mesopotamia. The Ottomans were Sunni Muslims and under their leadership some of the greatest missionary movements in Islamic history took place. The Ottomans also introduced slave soldiers called Janissaries to the world, and they became one of the first gunpowder empires. They were the last generally accepted caliphate in Islam.

Why does it matter to ISIS? ISIS has declared many other Muslims to be nonbelievers or apostates, and it does not accept the idea that a Turk could be a legitimate successor of the prophet. It tends to reject the Ottoman leadership.

Palmyra, Syria (تدمر)

What is important? Called Tadmoor in Arabic, Palmyra is a city that sits a little more than midway between Damascus and Deir al-Zour on the Euphrates River. It is an ancient city with a history dating back to before the Roman

Empire. One of the most famous leaders of ancient Palmyra was Queen Zenobia who ruled a large and influential empire in the late 200s AD. She is considered a significant figure in Syrian history even today.

Due to its role as a seat of regional leadership and its position anciently on a major caravan route, the city boasted impressive architecture. As it sits on a sort of cross-roads of civilization, the ruins show traces of Roman, Hellenistic, and Mesopotamian influences. Prior to the arrival of ISIS, Palmyra contained some of the most stunning ruins from the Roman and Hellenistic periods. The modern-day city and ruins include a marvelous colonnade and a spectacular temple of Bal. It is this temple and other buildings that were targeted by ISIS when it took the city in the spring of 2015.

Why does it matter to ISIS? ISIS captured the city of Palmyra and the surrounding ruins on May 13, 2015, and entered the world heritage site on May 21, 2015. Since its occupation it has raided and sold artifacts and destroyed structures. The old amphitheater has been used as a place for public executions. Palmyra is a singular example of ISIS as an iconoclastic group and as an opponent of Western civilization and non-Islamic heritage. Palmyra was retaken by Syrian government forces along with Russian fire support on 27 March 2016.

Quran (القُرآن)

What is important? The Holy Quran is considered by Muslims to be the word of God as given to Mohamed by the Angel Gabriel. The Quran was not written by Mohamed nor is it his book. He was commanded by Gabriel to recite and thus each verse (or ayah) and chapter (or sura) of the book was a recitation committed to memory by Mohamed and then recited to his followers, which they in turn memorized and recited. The word Quran means recitation.

The Quran is the unedited and unfiltered word of God. It is more than words and in its written form more than a book. For non-Muslims, it can be difficult to understand the reverence Muslims have for the Quran. A close approximation for Christians could be when the Gospel of John refers to Jesus Christ as the Word. For Muslims, the Quran is the embodiment of the teachings and mind and will of God. In this sense, to desecrate the Quran is to desecrate God himself.

The Quran was not committed to paper until after the death of the prophet. Several of the companions of the prophet worked with scribes to capture all of the words properly. Because the Quran was given in the Arabic language,

Arabic is considered the only authentic language—thus there are no translations of the Quran. All versions of Quran in languages other than Arabic are considered interpretations. The Quran is regarded as the pinnacle of written or spoken Arabic, and indeed any language. In this sense, Arabic is the language of God, and the ideal form of the language is instantiated in the Quran. To hear or read Quranic Arabic is to hear the voice of God.

Quranic scholarship and memorization are worthy of significant respect within the ummah. There are competitions every year for the memorization of the entire book consisting of 114 chapters, or suras. The suras tend to be divided into Meccan or Medinan characterizations depending on the city in which Mohamed resided when the information was received.

Why does it matter to ISIS? The roots of all Islamic arguments for the caliphate begin with Quranic authority. Abu Bakr al-Baghdadi is a graduate of Islamic studies.

Quraysh (قريش)

What is important? The Quraysh tribe was a powerful merchant tribe that ruled the western coasts of Arabia and controlled Mecca and the Ka'aba during the lifetime of the Prophet Mohamed and for many centuries afterward. By tradition, the members of the tribe are descendants of Abraham through his son Ishmael. Mohamed was a member of the Banu Hashim clan of the Quraysh. Generally speaking, the Quraysh were originally hostile to Mohamed and his message of monotheism. This message threatened the importance of the Ka'aba that was then a shrine to polytheism and a source of great profit as tribes made an annual pilgrimage to the site. It was members of the tribe that drove Mohamed to flee Mecca for Medina and members of the tribe who fought against the Muslims in Medina.

When Mohamed united Arabs under the banner of Islam, the Quraysh and members of the various clans and subclans of the Quraysh tribe became the most powerful leaders of the faith both in the conquest of other Arab tribes and in the expansion of Islam beyond the Arabian Peninsula. The Umayyad Caliphate, the Abbasid Caliphate, and the Fatimid Caliphate (Shia) are all based off succession from the Quraysh. The Sunni-Shia split was initially driven by the question of which part of the Quraysh tribe should rule. The Kharajites were driven in their belief that succession and leadership of the ummah should not be linked to lineage, particularly to the Quraysh. In one way or another, much of Islamic history is tied to this tribe and questions about their authority and legitimacy.

Why does it matter to ISIS? ISIS places great significance in the hadith that states that a Quraysh should be the caliph. It emphasizes at every opportunity the fact that caliph Ibrahim is also Abu Bakr al-Qurayshi al-Baghdadi, a descendant of the Quraysh tribe.

Ramadi, Battle of

Dates: November 21, 2014–December 30, 2015 (or present)

What is important? Ramadi is the capital of al-Anbar Province in Iraq. It is a large city of more than 400,000 people, which sits along the Euphrates River about 70 miles from Baghdad and 30 miles from Fallujah. The dates for the battle of Ramadi are interesting in that the battle raged for months. The prime minister of Iraq visited Ramadi on December 30, 2015, but significant portions of the city still remained under ISIS control. The battle began as an insurgency with small groups and small violence that began growing in October 2014 until some reports claimed ISIS controlled about 60 percent of the city.

The fighting in and around the city ebbed and flowed with respect to intensity over the course of a year. ISIS and the Iraqi Army each sent additional forces in support of offensive operations to change the dynamic in the city, but none of them proved decisive until the middle of May 2015 following the loss of Tikrit by ISIS.

Seemingly out of nowhere a major offensive was mounted by ISIS that included more than a dozen powerful truck bombs (each larger than the one used in the Oklahoma City bombing 1995). The cover of a sandstorm was used to capture the last remaining government buildings held by the Iraqi Army. The Iraqi Army fled the city and ISIS took control. It is estimated that ISIS took the city with fewer than 200 fighters against hundreds, if not thousands of Iraqi soldiers. Despite the size of the bombs used and the numbers present in the battle, casualties for both sides were in the hundreds.

The Iraqi government and U.S. senior officials announced an immediate effort to retake the city. That effort began within a matter of days, though it was weak and ineffective. Slow progress occurred over the course of the summer of 2015 with the Iraqi Army isolating the city. On December 8, 2015, the Iraqi Army began a major offensive to retake the city and within three weeks it captured the city center and government buildings, leading to the previously mentioned visit of the prime minister. Pockets of ISIS resistance remained up to the time of writing. Much of the city was destroyed in the recapturing of the city center by the bombs dropped by coalition aircraft and by the IEDs used by ISIS.

Why does it matter to ISIS? Ramadi represents real power. It is a provincial capital, and it is a short distance from Baghdad. It sits on the Euphrates River and controls movement along this major economic artery. Control here gives ISIS credibility.

Raqqa, Syria

What is important? Raqqa is a large modern city sitting on the Euphrates River about two-thirds of the way along the course of the river traveling upstream from Iraq to the Turkish border. The city has more than 200,000 people. The city has an ancient history; it served for a short period as capital of the Abbasid Caliphate under the reign of Caliph Harun al-Rashid during what is often deemed the peak of the Islamic Golden Age. It is this period and this caliph that is featured in some of the stories in *The Book of One Thousand and One Arabian Nights.*

Why does it matter to ISIS? ISIS began battling for the city in 2013 and by January 13, 2014, it gained complete control. The city has become something of the *de facto* capital of the Islamic State. As such, it has been the recipient of several bombing campaigns conducted by coalition and Russian aircraft in 2015 and continuing into 2016, especially following the October 31 downing of a Russian airliner and the November 13, 2015, terrorist attacks in Paris, France.

Safavid Empire

What is important? The Safavid Empire ruled over modern-day Iran, Azerbaijan, Bahrain, and Armenia. It also ruled over portions of Afghanistan, Georgia, Iraq, Kuwait, the North Caucasus, Pakistan, Syria, Turkey, Turkmenistan, and Uzbekistan. The empire expanded and contracted as it competed with other regional powers of the time, which was 1501 to 1722 (also 1729–1736). In general, it was the last Persian Empire. A lot of modern Iranian identity can be traced to the Safavid Empire. Its main regional rival was the Ottoman Empire. Much of the collision between the two happened in modern-day Iraq and eastern Turkey.

Under Safavid leadership, the empire was transformed from a predominantly Sunni populace to a predominantly Shia populace. This was mandatory. In the Safavid period, it was not uncommon for Safavid rulers to use the Sunni-Shia divide as a recruiting tool to inspire those Shias living within Ottoman lands to revolt against their Sunni overlords. This, in part, led to Ottoman expulsion of some Shias living in the border regions and the Anatolian Plateau. Simply put, when the Safavid dynasty began its rule modern-day Iran was generally a Sunni majority place and when it concluded its rule it was a predominantly Shia country. The religious-cultural imperialism and expansionism were unique to the Safavids; no other Shia empire or caliphate had so mandated a change from Sunni to Shia.

Why does it matter to ISIS? ISIS consistently refers to its Iraqi security force opponents as *safawis* that means safavids. It uses this term in the derogatory to emphasize the notion of Shia expansionism.

Sahwa (Sunni Uprising)

What is important? The Sahwa movement was known by many different names during the U.S. occupation of Iraq 2003 to 2011. One of these names was the Sunni Awakening movement (حركة الصحوة السنية) and it is from this group that the term sahwa (meaning *awakening*) is derived.

Organic or emergent are good words to describe what happened in the Sahwa, or awakening, in Anbar province. This movement grew naturally rather than being created by a person or event. The exact beginning of the awakening is nearly impossible to state, but in 2005 and 2006 several tribal leaders in Anbar became frustrated with the death, destruction, and chaos and decided to oppose the foreign fighters. At first, these were not senior tribal leaders, but typically sons or nephews. They gathered small groups of men, and they cooperated with U.S. forces operating in their areas. By the time the Surge began in 2007, the awakening had been going on for more than a year. Sunni tribes were becoming more and more likely to oppose al-Qaeda and other similar groups. Because the local tribes knew who was an Iraqi tribal member and who was a foreigner, it was much easier for them to identify the enemy. The intelligence provided by the awakening was more important than the combat actions conducted by them. In many ways, this is what changed the combat dynamic in Iraq more so than the extra deployment of U.S. soldiers (see The Surge). That said, extra U.S. forces did make engagement with and exploitation of awakening information much more effective.

Sons of Iraq

The Sunni *awakening* that grew in Anbar province became more and more formal over time. By 2007, the U.S. military began paying Sunni "militias" to provide security and intelligence. Over time, these groups of fighters gained the name the *Sons of Iraq*. The idea of U.S. leaders was to integrate these tribal fighters into a formal militia under the authority of the Iraqi government. During 2008, the U.S. exerted pressure on the Nuri al-Maliki led government to bring these fighters into some official status. By the end of the year, tens of thousands of fighters were receiving pay from the Iraqi government. Critics of the program likened this to paying bribe money to people who had American and Iraqi blood on their hands. Those who supported the program expressed the benefits in terms of reduced violence, increased intelligence reporting on foreign fighters and al-Qaeda (and other extremist group's) operatives and operations. Payment of the Sons of Iraq was always problematic. The Iraqi prime minister did not want to pay it; it required consistent U.S. attention and pressure to make this happen. Once that pressure ended, the program rapidly ended as well.

Why does it matter to ISIS? There are many answers to this question.

First, ISIS refers to many Sunnis it perceives to be supporting the enemy (however, it defines that term) as sahwa. So, for ISIS this is a derogative term that connotes collaborator.

Second, the sahwa movement or awakening is seen by the coalition as the way to turn the tides against ISIS. This worked in 2007 to 2010, so it should work now—so the argument goes. For this reason, there is a lot of emphasis placed on working with Sunni tribes to recreate something like the Sons of Iraq.

Third, the rejection of the Sons of Iraq by the Iraqi government started while U.S. forces were in Iraq. The complete abandonment of these tribe members who believed they sacrificed for Iraq as well as their family and tribe was seen as the worst form of abandonment by the government in Baghdad. This created a significant amount of tension between the Shia government and the Sunnis, especially in al-Anbar Province. In this regard, this created a seam into which ISIS could flow in 2014.

Salafist

What is important? Mohamed said, "The best people are those of my generation, and then those who will come after them (the next generation), and then those who will come after them (i.e. the next generation), and then after them, there will come people whose witness will precede their oaths, and whose oaths will precede their witness" (Sahih Bukhari Volume 8. hadith number 437). This quote from the prophet is the simplest explanation of the perspective of salafi believers. The word salaf means ancestors. One who subscribes to Salafist thought seeks to live according to the teachings and example of the most righteous of people—Mohamed (of course) and those designated by Mohamed as the best generations. This is why Salafist thought focuses on the early interpretations of the faith. It is about returning to that period because this original generation had it right. Over the centuries, this type of thinking has experienced a great deal of variation. Modern salafist thinkers today tend to draw their intellectual roots from Mohamed ibn Abd al-Wahab (see Wahhabi) who lived in what would become Saudi Arabia in the 1800s.

Salafists do not necessarily subscribe to violence. In fact, they are a small subset of Salafism that believes in the use of violence to convey their beliefs. They are typically labeled as salafi-jihadis. Salafists, in general, advocate for their interpretation of the faith through peaceful means.

The basic tenets of Salafism include the following. It bases its legal interpretations strictly from the Quran and the hadeeth, or statements of the prophet. As there are multiple versions of the hadeeth Salafists, use the strictest and most limited of these. Understanding the Quran comes from the Quran and from the hadith and not from rational discourse or reasoned discussion. Understanding of God's word then comes from God's word or the words of his prophet. Salafists believe that Mohamed and his companions give an eternal example of the right way to live. Salafists come from all of the various schools of jurisprudence. The belief is a way to live and not simply an issue of legal interpretation. They also follow the sunna, or actions of the prophet, as accurately as possible. This is not simply in prayer, but in all things known concerning how he lived his life.

Why does it matter to ISIS? ISIS subscribes to a Salafist interpretation of Islam. It is stricter than most others of this sect of Islam, and it also adds a component of violence to the general religious interpretation, making ISIS clearly salafi-jihadis.

Sharia (شريعة)

What is important? The word *sharia* is generally translated as Islamic Law. Islamic Law is different from Western law in that it is not necessarily codified in a set of books on a lawyer's shelf. Sharia consists of a several components: the Quran, the statements of the Prophet Mohamed (hadith), the behaviors and actions of the Prophet Mohamed (the sunna), and the interpretations of judges over time (basic jurisprudence or fiqh). There are four major schools of Islamic legal scholarship in Sunni Islam and one primary one in Shia Islam. Each derives its names from the original primary interpreters: Hanafi, Maliki, Shafi'i, Hanbali, and Jafari. All of the components combined are used to make judgments within the law.

The purpose of Sharia is not necessarily individual correction, but societal benefit. This law is accepted as the best way to have the best community. It may be instructive to understand that the root of the word *sharia* is the same as the root for the word street or path in Arabic. In other words, the law could be seen as the right path on which the community needs to travel to be God's people.

The law addresses a wide array of issues including crime, relationships, property, marriage, etc. It is as holistic as any legal code in the world. Sharia also includes rules of evidence and the consideration of witnesses and personal testimony.

There is no question that Sharia has a lot of connotations in the West as being archaic, backward, and unjust. The point here is not to defend or criticize it, but simply to provide a basic understanding. Sharia is an ancient legal system that dates back to the seventh century, which has effectively brought stability to countless societies over the last 1,400 years. That should be considered before criticism is leveled. In its original application, the legal system was extremely progressive relative to other legal systems of the period. It allowed for rights for women with regard to marriage, divorce, and property ownership. It allowed for the participation of witnesses to determine what is just for the participants in a dispute as well as what was best for the community.

Sharia, as understood by Muslims, is God's law and as such it is perceived by some as infallible.

Why does it matter to ISIS? ISIS is often labeled as an extremist group. Its acceptance and view of Sharia is extreme with respect to the vast majority of Muslims. It sees Sharia as a fixed and divine law that needs to be enforced rigidly. In this manner, it delivers what is perceived to be harsh judgments. That said, consider what is practiced by the governments in the countries where ISIS has the greatest influence. There is little law, and where it is practiced, it is arbitrary. Although most in Iraq, Syria, Libya, and elsewhere do not accept ISIS's harsh legal interpretations, they do accept the fact that those interpretations are based on an understandable law rather than being chaotically and capriciously enforced. If, even harsh laws are enforced consistently, this gives stability over those who do not enforce law at all or who do so by whim.

Shia (شيعة)

What is important? Shia is an abbreviation of Shī'atu 'Alī (شيعة علي), which means the followers or the partisans of Ali ibn Abi Talib. Ali was the son-in-law and cousin of the Prophet Mohamed. He is the fourth caliph in Sunni Islam and considered the first imam (one who stands in front as an example and leader of the faith) in Shia Islam and divinely appointed to be so. The divisions between Sunni and Shia start early in Islamic history with the designation of the successors of the prophet. Most Shias believe that Ali was the only legitimate successor to Mohamed. Shias refuse to accept Abu Bakr as a legitimate caliph (successor). For this refusal, some Sunnis refer to Shias as refusers. This is often common in ISIS literature and speech.

Shia Islam comprises about 10 to 15 percent of Muslims. Most of these live in four countries: Iran, Pakistan, Iraq, and India. There are numerous divisions within Shia Islam. These divisions tend to be based off the last Imam that each group considers legitimate. The largest single group is called the Twelvers because it accepts down to the 12th Imam with Ali being the first. The dominant group in Iran is the Twelvers. The other two major groups are Zaidis (common in Yemen) and Ismailis (numerous countries).

Shias believe in the importance of the family of the prophet and those designated to lead the faith—imams. In this regard, Shia Islam tends to be more hierarchical than does Sunni Islam. As no major branch of Shiism currently believes in a living or present imam, it looks toward religious scholars or ayatollahs. These men provide religious guidance and instruction from the Islamic law based off study.

Shias accept that the descendants of the immediate family of the prophet and the imams were infallible and divinely blessed. They also accept the idea that there are hidden leaders who will come back to lead at the end of days.

Why does it matter to ISIS? ISIS believes that the Shias (all of them) refused to accept the first and rightly guided caliphs (see Caliph, Rashidun) and are therefore worse than non-believers. It considers Shia apostate for rejecting those appointed to rule the Islamic community. Shias are more the enemy than the west. In this regard, ISIS is different in its degree of anti-Shia rhetoric and action than almost all other salafi-jihadi groups that may view the Shia as wrong, but not necessarily apostate.

Soleimani, Qasem

Dates: March 1, 1957–Present

Key Events in His Life: Qasem Soleimani is a major general in the Iranian Revolutionary Guards Corps (IRGC). Since 1998 he has served as the commander of the Quds Force of that military organization. The Quds force is primarily tasked with fighting Iran's battles outside of Iran. It is the extra military and clandestine force for the IRGC. Soleimani has worked extensively with Hezbollah in Southern Lebanon and Hamas. Following the U.S. invasion of Iraq, he became the primary architect and orchestrator of the Iranian support to Shia anti-occupation efforts. He coordinated the training and equipping of mostly Iraqi groups that conducted attacks on U.S. forces and Sunni militias. Following the U.S. withdrawal from Iraq and the increasing Syrian civil war, he played a key role in coordinating Iranian assistance to Syria and developing strategy. With the rise of ISIS and its successful attacks in both Syria and later Iraq, he again became the Iranian leader responsible for coordinating the Iranian and Syrian and Iraqi strategy to oppose ISIS as well as support and sustain the Iranian-friendly regimes in Damascus and Baghdad.

Why does it matter? Qasem Soleimani is one of the most influential people in the Middle East and one of the most critical strategists in the fight against ISIS.

Sunni or ahl al-sunna (أهل السنة)

What is important? This is the denomination of Islam that believes that the first successor of the Prophet Mohamed was his father-in-law Abu Bakr. In Arabic, it is called ahl al-sunna wa al-jamā'a (أهل السنة والجماعة), which means people of the tradition of Mohamed and the consensus of the community of believers. Sunna comprises the practices of the Prophet Mohamed, the things he did that were witnessed and later recorded as his behaviors. As he is considered to be the most righteous of men and the last prophet, it is his life that should be emulated by all Muslims.

Sunni Islam is the largest denomination of Islam consisting of about 85 to 90 percent of Muslims. In addition to the five pillars of Islam, which all Muslims practice, the Sunnis have six articles of faith in which they believe:

1. Reality of the one true God
2. Existence of the angels of God
3. Authority of the books of God, which are books of Abraham, the Torah, the Psalms, the Gospel, and the Quran
4. Following the prophets of God
5. Preparation for and belief in the Day of Judgment
6. Supremacy of God's will

Most Sunnis see themselves as the proper form of Islam, and if asked what they are, will simply respond, Muslim. Within Sunni Islam, there are major divisions based off different interpretations of religious law. The groups are typically referred to as schools of law. Each is named for a famous legal scholar (Ẓāhirī, Shafi'i, Maliki, and Hanbali).

Why does it matter to ISIS? All ISIS followers are Sunni. They all accept the articles of faith listed previously, and they all accept the early caliphs. As discussed under then entry for Salafi, they represent a specific interpretation of this broader division of Islam.

The Surge (see also Sahwa [Sunni Uprising])

What is important? The Surge in Iraq of 2007 to 2009 had already become shrouded in myth by the time this book was written. The purpose of the Surge is regularly misunderstood: what it was and what it did. The intent was to send 30,000 additional U.S. ground forces into Iraq to stabilize the security situation, and by so doing, to create an environment wherein the political problems could be solved. This meant that five additional brigade combat teams were sent into Iraq. Many of the currently deployed brigades were extended to 15 months deployments, rather than 12 months; they were originally tasked to serve. General David Petraeus often spoke of a surge of ideas. This was espoused primarily in the new U.S. Army and USMC field manual titled *Counterinsurgency*. General Petraeus' assumption of command of Multi-National Forces-Iraq was also part of this surge. His plan was to get soldiers off the large forward operating bases and have them live among the people to provide security to the populace. The idea being that if the populace believed that the United States would work and fight for Iraqis, then they would be more supportive of coalition ideas. The additional U.S. forces coincided with a growing Sunni Awakening in which tribal leaders rose up in opposition to al-Qaeda and other extreme groups and worked with coalition forces.

The Surge was more than U.S. forces. It included Iraqi events that most observers and commentators did not understand. When the political debates rage about whether or not the Surge was successful it is important to keep in mind all that is included in the years 2006 to 2009. It is much more than additional soldiers.

Due to the political nature of the Iraq war by 2007, General Petraeus' testimony to the U.S. Congress in September of the year was viewed in a partisan way. Many of the members of Congress accused General Petraeus and Ambassador Crocker (then U.S. ambassador to Iraq) of presenting the Bush Administration's perspective rather than an open assessment from their perspectives. This was part of the criticism in a MoveOn.org advertisement in *The New York Times* as well as other sources.

At the time of the testimony, the BBC reported on a poll of the Iraqi people that stated that 70 percent (93 percent among Sunnis and 50 percent among Shia) of the Iraqi people believed that the Surge made security worse in Iraq. Simple statistics on the number of attacks provided data that indicated that by September 2007 the violence was decreasing, but it would require many more months before the violence returned to 2004 levels.

The debate of success in Iraq is linked to the notion of success or lack of success of the Surge. As noted, this became a critical point in the partisan political fighting in Congress once the Democrats took control in the 2006 elections and also in the 2008 presidential campaign. The questions about success or failure in Iraq became more poignant and significant in 2014 and 2015 as the Islamic State gained control of areas of Iraq and U.S. military forces returned to Iraq to coordinate training and air strikes.

Why does it matter to ISIS? Many U.S. military and some foreign policy leaders believe that the Surge was successful and that reaching out to the populace and convincing Sunni tribes to fight alongside the Iraqi government and the coalition is the model to ultimately defeat ISIS in Iraq. Understanding the mechanics of the Surge is informative in understanding U.S. military thought on fighting ISIS.

Sykes-Picot Agreement

Dates: Created 1916

What is important? Mark Sykes, a British diplomat, and François Georges-Picot, a French diplomat, met and discussed over a course of many meetings the nature of a post-Ottoman Empire Middle East. These discussions were taking place in the heat of trench slaughter in World War I and the governments of both countries represented were looking for a success that would validate the costs of the war. The solution was to divide the Ottoman Empire up into spheres of influence that would allow the allies to have various levels of control over terrain deemed advantageous to each of the participants.

The actual terms of the agreement are not as onerous as many commentators make out. It was the interpretation of those terms that generated the long-standing animosity against both France and Britain in the Middle East to the present.

France was allocated control over portions of what is now south-eastern Turkey at the north-eastern corner of the Mediterranean Sea and Great Britain was given control over Mesopotamia and land between the Mediterranean Sea and the Jordan River. Both countries were also given primacy of advice and counsel to governments to be established in what is now Syria for France and Iraq for Great Britain. It was this last designation that most angered Arabs when the agreement became public. They felt the British government had lied to them and promised the same land to multiple people.

The agreement did not actually decide anything as it was not a treaty, but an agreement between government functionaries. Still, it was the lines drawn in these discussions that became the starting point for drawing the lines of the countries in the current Middle East. It is also this perceived double dealing that so angered the Arabs and others in the region against the West.

Why does it matter to ISIS? ISIS has made a point in video productions and its magazine to communicate that it is erasing the lines drawn by the Sykes-Picot Agreement. In fact, in one video a narrator says as much as it shows a bulldozer wiping away the sand berm that marked the boundary between Syria and Iraq that was essentially created by these two European diplomats.

Tikrit, Battle of

Dates: June 2014–April 17, 2015

What is important? Tikrit is the hometown of Saddam Hussein, and it sits on the Tigris River about 90 miles north of Baghdad. This is a large city of more than 250,000 people. It is also the administrative center for the Salah al-Din Province of Iraq. Tikrit fell to ISIS as part of its June 2014 advances into Iraq. The Iraqi government tried to retake the city in short order, but these attacks failed to achieve any real success. The ISIS force inside Tikrit was uncertain, but some numbers report it at between 2,000 and more than 10,000. The larger numbers are probably inaccurate though Tikrit did serve as a location for operations against other targets in the Tigris River valley.

As with other battles, there were numerous clashes between the armed groups and several attempts to retake the city with insufficient force. In late February 2015, the Popular Mobilization Forces (Shia militias) gathered in force and worked with the Iraqi Army to form a large force of more than 20,000 (some say more than 30,000) fighters. This group attacked on March 2, 2015, and began to successfully move into the city. It was stopped on the outskirts from March 13 to 30, but then the Iraqi government coordinated to get coalition air support. Once the attacks came from the air, the Iraqi forces moved into the city and captured the city center and most of the rest of the city by early April with sporadic fighting that lasted until April 17.

A requirement for the coalition to fly in support of the operation was the withdrawal of militias. This was done somewhat; some groups did pull back, but others continued to fight. Regardless, this was the first major offensive by the Iraqi Army, Popular Mobilization Forces, and the U.S.-led coalition.

Why does it matter to ISIS? As stated previously, this was the first serious coordination between all of the then-present anti-ISIS forces. ISIS lost a major city and a symbolic city as the birthplace of Saddam Hussein.

Umayyad Caliphate

Dates: 661–750 CE (continued to rule from Codoba from 756 to 1031 CE)

What is important? The Umayyad Caliphate was the first dynastic caliphate in Islamic history. It followed the death of Ali ibn Abi Talib as the last of the

Rashidun caliphs. The Umayya ruled primarily from Damascus Syria. The Umayya were a clan of the Quraysh tribe, and Uthman ibn Affan, the third Rashidun caliph, was a member of this clan. His murder and Ali's seeming unwillingness to find those responsible and punish them generated the first major crisis within the ummah. The first ruler of the dynasty was Muawiya ibn Abi Sufyan who served as governor of Syria at the time of Uthman's death. He marched his army on Mecca but arrived after Ali was proclaimed caliph. He demanded those who committed the murder be brought to justice, but this did not happen. Muawiya believed he could and should be caliph. It was not until the assassination of Ali under the hands of the Kharajites that Muawiyah declared himself caliph. He ruled from Damascus as he had as governor and this was where the dynasty continued to rule.

The Umayyads extended the span of control of Islam by conquering all the way into the Iberian Peninsula and the island of Sicily as well as numerous other extensions. The Umayyad Caliphate was the largest singularly governed empire in Islamic history. Following their collapse to the Abbasids, the Islamic world was ruled by more and more local or regional leaders and any one person—caliph or otherwise—struggled to establish or maintain control. It is interesting that the Umayyads provided this largest and most grand manifestation of the ummah yet at the same time they have been viewed by Muslims at the time and to the present as corrupt and less than ideally pious.

The fall of the Umayyads should be seen as inevitable. Ruling an empire that stretched from modern-day India to modern-day Portugal with ancient communication means was impossible for a long period of time. Only the expansion of the faith and the tremendous—battlefield success kept the fractious Arab tribal armies focused. In addition, the Umayyads were the first to deal with governance in a real and practical sense. Were conversions desired if by converting a local governor you lost the substantial *jizya* tax from the nonbelievers? How does one govern an empire with uneducated tribesman over a vast majority nonbelieving and generally better educated populace? These rather basic problems challenged how Muslims viewed the Umayyad rule.

The final problem was the ethnically diverse populations who chaffed under foreign control even if they had converted to Islam. Local populations opposed the leadership with a distant caliph and revolts broke out at various places over the course of this empire and those that followed. This brought the added problem of Muslims killing Muslims—something forbidden. The empire was seen as corrupt and challenged from multiple sides and within. There came a call for cleansing the ummah, and the Abbasids took over. The ruling family member who escaped the Abbasids fled to Cordoba, Spain and established a dynastic succession that ruled from there for hundreds of years.

Why does it matter to ISIS? ISIS does not respect the Umayyad dynasty nor the heritage it represents. It has desecrated and destroyed shrines built to honor Umayyad caliphs in territory under its control. The Umayyads represent to ISIS something of the problem of Islam itself—corruption and an accommodation to the world. This is what ISIS is calling the ummah to correct.

Ummah (أمة)

What is important? This word typically means community. The ummah is used as shorthand to reference the community of believers in Islam. Throughout Islamic writings, this word is important in understanding the simple meaning of the faithful.

Why does it matter to ISIS? ISIS regularly refers to the ummah and its responsibility to protect it. Because it sees itself as the only true worshiper of the faith, it is the ummah and only those who join with it are worthy of that title. All others are unbelievers or apostates.

Wahhabi (وهابية)

What is important? Wahhabism is often referred to as a fundamentalist interpretation of Islam and a form of Salafist thinking. The movement takes its name from Muhammad ibn Abd al-Wahhab (1703–1792) who lived in the north of the Arabian Peninsula. He called for a return to a more correct interpretation of the faith. He challenged the practices of traveling to shrines to pray and worship as a form of idolatry, or shirk in Arabic. He also challenged the innovations, or bid'ah, which had, over time, crept into the faith. Innovations to Islam are a sin as the religion was given in its perfected form to Mohamed. For that reason, one only has to live as Mohamed did to live a similarly correct life. Al-Wahhab made alliance with Mohamed bin Saud who formed and ruled the first Saudi State in the Arabian Peninsula in 1744 to 1818.

The relationship between the Wahhabis and the Saudis is critical and essential to the survival and dominance of both. The Wahhabis have not always or generally been violent, but during the rise of Abdul Aziz bin Saud in his efforts to establish the second Saudi state he made alliance with a group of warriors referred to as the Ikhwan or Brotherhood. These were fighters who strictly adhered to a Wahhabi religious interpretation of the faith. Their successful fighting style helped elevate Abdul Aziz to becoming king of what we today call Saudi Arabia. Once he became king of the majority of the peninsula, to include the holy cities of Mecca and Medina, Abdul Aziz was seen by the Ikhwan as becoming less pure in his faith. He worked with foreigners (he always had, but it became more pronounced), and he seemed to make compromises with other Muslims who were not in agreement with the Ikhwan. Abdul Aziz needed to fight the Ikhwan, but to do so he needed the sanction of Wahhabi clerics who pronounced a fatwa (declaration) making it incumbent on the subjects of a kingdom to follow the king. This declaration allowed Abdul Aziz to go against the Ikhwan who opposed him, but it also bound him to the Wahhabi clerics because he could not have maintained his position without them.

The relationship between the Saudi monarchy and the Wahhabi clerics has typically been complex as it was at the beginning. The monarchy empowers their preaching and teaching and has spread schools all over the region through the use of state money. This has made what many consider to be a minority interpretation of Islam, one of the most widely promulgated interpretations in the country and throughout the region.

As a final note, although one can call Wahhabis Salafists they are not necessarily jihadists. The Ikhwan were an early version of salafi-jihadi thought, but most Wahhabis today do not believe it appropriate to promote their faith by the sword—especially not when they can promote it through the school.

Why does it matter to ISIS? ISIS members would not call themselves Wahhabis, but their intellectual roots with respect to cleansing the faith and ruling a kingdom or caliphate through this interpretation have both intellectual and spiritual connections to the teachings of Muhammad ibn Abd al-Wahhab and the military success of the Ikhwan.

Wilayah (ولاية)

What is important? Wilayah means state or province. It comes from a root word that also means to govern. Thus a wilayah is a place that is governed. Groups that have declared their allegiance to ISIS and that control some territory are typically referred to as a wilayah. Examples are as follows in their English versions and geographic locations (given from west to east):

Wilayat Algeria (al-Jiza'ir)	Northern Algeria
Wilayat West Africa (Gharb al-Afriqiya)	Portions of Nigeria, Chad, and Niger
Wilayat Fezzan	Southwestern Libya
Wilayat Tripoli	Northwestern Libya
Wilayat Barqa	Northeastern Libya
Wilayat Sinai	Sinai Peninsula (Northeastern Egypt)
Wilayat Haramayn	Saudi Arabia
Wilayat Yemen	Yemen
Wilayat Najd	Eastern Saudi Arabia
Wilayat al-Khorasan	Afghanistan-Pakistan Border Region

Just because there is an area with a wilayah declared does not mean that ISIS has significant control there. Some of these wilayahs are more powerful and influential than others. Most, if not all, of the wilayahs act like terrorist groups or nonstate actors. Wilayat Sinai took responsibility for the downing of the Russian airliner on October 31, 2015. Wilayat West Africa (formerly Boko Haram) is one of the most active in terms of attacks, kidnappings, and control of territory.

In late 2015, the activity of Wilayat Barqa captured headlines as it attacked an oil storage facility on the Libyan coast and began controlling the surrounding villages. Other reports of this same group mentioned that senior ISIS leaders moved to the area and began to control the actions. Some surmised that Libya might become a fallback area for ISIS should it lose more cities in Iraq and Syria.

It is unclear what the role and purpose of the wilayahs will be. Right now it seems as if the various groups are linking themselves to ISIS to gain notoriety and possible resources from ISIS. ISIS would have readers of *Dabiq* magazine believe that these wilayahs are part of a growing caliphate that will someday merge into one large governed space with each of these smaller groups now governing much larger, but still subordinate parts of the caliphate. Today this is most clearly seen in Libya where the influence of ISIS and ISIS-affiliated groups grows week by week.

Why does it matter to ISIS? ISIS uses the declarations of the various wilayahs as proof that they are remaining and expanding. This further emphasizes that

ISIS is everywhere and by being everywhere it empowers ISIS to be able to lose somewhere.

Yazidi

What is important? The Yazidi community is a distinct ethnic and religious group that is found in significant numbers in northern Iraq and elsewhere in the region though in declining numbers. A great many have migrated, primarily to Germany, and thus the second largest population of Yazidis in the world resides in Germany with the largest living in Iraq. As with so many things in the Middle East understanding the Yazidis can be complex. The intent here is to give a simple explanation of why they have been targeted by ISIS.

Religious scholars call their religion syncretic that means they have adapted beliefs from other faiths. The deep history of their faith can be traced all the way back to Zoroastrianism of the ancient Persian Empire. Zoroastrians were declared to be people of the book and protected under Islamic law. That said, Yazidis are not precisely in line with Zoroastrian beliefs. They are strict monotheists who believe in God as the creator, but they also believe that God gave the care and consideration of the earth to angels, the chief of which is the Peacock Angel. The reason for bringing this up is to understand why many in the region claim the Yazidis to be devil worshippers. The Peacock Angel fell from favor with God until his tears of remorse regained his position and acceptance before God. This idea of a fall from grace has been linked to a Sufi Islamic belief of the Jinn Iblis who bears some resemblance to the Christian Satan. At times, the Arabic word iblis is translated as Satan. This belief in a divine creature who fell from grace has been interpreted by many as devil worship, for which the Yazidis have been persecuted by many groups over the centuries. ISIS is only the most recent incarnation of persecutors.

The Yazidis are often linked with Kurds. They live in the same villages as Kurds, they speak Kurdish, and to an outsider they look and dress like Kurds. They are not Kurds in a cultural sense as they have separate traditions and behaviors.

Why does it matter to ISIS? With the northern advance of ISIS into Iraq many Yazidi dominated villages came under the control of ISIS. The most notable region was the area surrounding Mount Sinjar. This is an east-west running ridgeline that sits just north of a major transportation route between Mosul, Iraq, and the Syrian border. ISIS attacked the city of Sinjar and the surrounding villages (about August 2014). It massacred civilians and enslaved the women. Because Yazidi women were not considered believers, they were legitimate war booty. The mistreatment of thousands of Yazidi women and children drew the world's attention. U.S. special operations forces were sent to make an assessment of the situation and supplies were air dropped onto the mountain to support the sufferers. The women became a focal point of anti-ISIS rhetoric as a means of communicating the ancient barbarity of the Islamic State. Kurdish forces, with the support of significant U.S and coalition airstrikes, recaptured the area around Mount Sinjar in November 2015.

Appendix: Obama Administration Strategy Report, March 24, 2016

Author's Note: This report reflects a response by the Obama Administration to a Congressional requirement for the administration to provide the strategy whereby they intend to defeat the Islamic State or ISIS. Note the broad generalizations throughout. One of the major criticisms leveled against the report by members of Congress was that this report did not answer the requirement. Yet, there are some places where the report provides some specific details. In this response it is possible for a reader to understand many of the challenges that the U.S. government has had in fighting ISIS. It is questionable if the government fully understands the problem it is facing or if it understands what it needs to do to achieve success versus this problem.

Section 1222 Report: Strategy for the Middle East and to Counter Violent Extremism

This report responds to the requirements of section 1222 of the National Defense Authorization Act (NDAA) for Fiscal Year (FY) 2016, which provides that not later than February 15, 2016, the Secretaries of Defense and State shall submit to the appropriate Committees of Congress "a strategy for the Middle East and to counter violent extremism." The strategy required by section 1222 shall include: (1) a description of the objectives and end state for the United States in the Middle East and with respect to violent extremism; (2) a description of the roles and responsibilities of the Department of State in the strategy; (3) a description of roles and responsibilities of the Department of Defense in the strategy; (4) a description of actions to prevent the weakening and failing of states in the Middle East; (5) a description of actions to counter violent extremism; (6) a description of the resources required by the

Department of Defense to counter ISIL's illicit oil revenues; (7) a list of the state and non-state actors that must be engaged to counter violent extremism; (8) a description of the coalition required to carry out the strategy and the expected lines of effort of such a coalition; (9) an assessment of United States efforts to disrupt and prevent foreign fighters traveling to Syria and Iraq and to disrupt foreign fighters in Syria and Iraq traveling to the United States.

Objectives and End States

The United States' objectives in the Middle East are: that all countries of the region meet their international commitments on non-proliferation; that terrorist groups no longer threaten the United States, our allies, and our interests; that our allies and partners enjoy stability, prosperity, and security; that governments in the region have the strength and legitimacy to provide both security and a positive future for their people; that open lines of communication allow critical trade and natural resources to reach the global economy, including freedom of navigation in the Gulf; that governments respect the human rights of their people and address societal violence and discrimination; that women and men are able to live free from violence and participate fully in the political and economic development of their countries; that economies are open and realize their full potential; to implement the Joint Comprehensive Plan of Action (JCPOA) and ensure Iran's nuclear program remains exclusively peaceful, while also continuing to check Iran's malign influence; to address drivers of violent extremist radicalization and recruitment while we continue to work to counter al-Qa'ida and its affiliates; and that Israel and the Palestinians resolve their conflict through the achievement of a two-state solution.

In the present context, one overarching objective is to degrade and ultimately defeat the Islamic State of Iraq and the Levant (ISIL). Working with Coalition partners and local forces, we are taking the fight to ISIL where it holds territory, because ISIL's control of territory enables it to sustain its fight. Addressing ISIL's self-proclaimed "caliphate" in Iraq and Syria is essential to prevent attacks on the U.S. homeland, and on the home territories of our Coalition partners. We have sought to develop capable and motivated local ground forces to lead the ground fight, since only local forces can ensure a lasting victory. Moreover, we seek to set the conditions for a political solution to the civil war in Syria, and to work towards inclusive governance in Iraq, since these are the only durable means to prevent a future terrorist organization like ISIL from re-emerging in the region. Achieving these objectives requires leveraging the full range of U.S. and Coalition security and stabilization resources, including diplomatic, intelligence, law enforcement, economic, and informational resources.

Destroying ISIL in Iraq and Syria

Our first objective in the campaign against ISIL must be to defeat ISIL at its core. To achieve this objective, the United States leads a 60+ member Global Coalition to counter ISIL, which is consistent with the objectives of the September 2014 National Strategy to Counter ISIL,. This coalition provides a template for identifying nations and multilateral organizations that may support broader efforts to counter violent extremism. The members of the Global Counter-ISIL Coalition have committed themselves to eliminating the specific threat posed by ISIL and have already contributed in various capacities to the effort to combat ISIL in Iraq and Syria, the Middle East region, and beyond. The breadth and diversity of partners supporting this Coalition demonstrates the global and unified nature of its endeavor.

Ending ISIL's control over territory it holds in Iraq and Syria represents a necessary, though not sufficient in and of itself, component of the worldwide campaign to defeat the group and counter its radical ideology. Control of territory provides ISIL access to considerable financial resources and manpower, heightens its ideological appeal to potential foreign adherents, and represents ISIL's military and political center of gravity. But the "state-like" attributes ISIL has sought also create opportunities to degrade its organization. In concert with Coalition partners, we have mapped and are attacking vulnerabilities in ISIL's war-fighting machine, including successful attacks on military objectives that have an impact on ISIL-controlled petroleum and financial infrastructure. ISIL has not had a significant battlefield victory since May 2015. Key Sunni-majority cities in Iraq, such as Tikrit, Bayji, and Ramadi, have been liberated, as well as Sinjar, where ISIL first gained global notoriety after murdering hundreds of Yazidis and pressing thousands more into slavery. In Syria, local forces have retaken al-Hawl and al-Shaddada, which straddle the key supply route connecting the ISIL strongholds of Raqqa and Mosul. This strategy pressures ISIL in more places than just on the battlefield. When we attack ISIL on levels beyond merely the geographic, we stress its resources, strain its ability to command its forces, weaken its capacity for effective offensive or defensive operations, challenge its narrative, and eliminate its capability to control a population. These efforts will break ISIL's image as a functioning state as well as the myth of its overwhelming battlefield prowess, thereby reducing its attractiveness to potential recruits.

Our key military efforts in the near-term will focus on completion of operations to secure and stabilize Ramadi, Iraq, and then building on success there to progress toward Hit and Rutbah, before ultimately stabilizing Anbar Province, and then moving to isolate, pressure, and eventually clear Mosul. The Coalition will continue to intensify air strikes and raids against ISIL targets prior to and during the course of clearance operations. The Coalition will also continue to train, advise, and assist Iraqi forces, including Kurdish forces, while exploiting unconventional opportunities to instigate dissension against ISIL governance in Mosul. In addition, the Coalition will increase training of local police and volunteer forces to hold liberated territory. The Coalition is also supporting efforts by the Iraqi government to restore essential services and create conditions that will enable displaced populations to return and revive their communities. Protecting liberated territories from instability or outright recapture is a key medium-term objective; fostering political processes to make liberation sustainable is a central long-term objective, one requiring support from well outside the security sector.

In Syria, our near-term efforts against ISIL in 2016 are focused on expanding relationships and operational opportunities with appropriately-vetted local forces that are motivated to fight ISIL, and on undermining ISIL's control of Raqqa, the capital of ISIL's self-declared caliphate. To that end, our near-term efforts will focus on exploiting recent successes at Al Hawl, the Tishrin Dam, and Shadadi by enabling moderate Syrian opposition elements to move south to isolate ISIL in Raqqa and undermine its control over the city. The Coalition has intensified raids against ISIL targets across the Syrian battlespace and will utilize a full range of military and related options to increase pressure on ISIL, its resources, and its leadership. Further, the Coalition will continue pursuing relationships with moderate Syrian opposition groups where they can be counted on to participate in specific operations against ISIL. In particular, we are pursuing relationships with groups in southern Syria with an eye toward enabling them to mount unconventional operations to improve our visibility and understanding in the area, to deny ISIL operational freedom, to force ISIL to divert remaining combat power from external operations to internal security, and to weaken ISIL's territorial control. Coalition partners will assist in the training, munitions, and equipment supply for these groups.

In both Iraq and Syria, the Coalition continues its campaign to degrade ISIL's ability to fund its activities, including through attacks on military objectives that have an impact on ISIL controlled petroleum and financial infrastructure. Recent Coalition operations in support of these efforts include Operation TIDAL WAVE II, which began in early November 2015, and which has destroyed roughly 400 oil trucks, disrupting ISIL fuel supply lines that the terrorists use across Syria and Iraq. We assess that TIDAL WAVE II has reduced ISIL's revenue by approximately 30%. These strikes included hitting an "ISIL bank" in Mosul, a key site for collection, storage, and distribution of ISIL revenues.

We were assisted in these efforts by successful intelligence exploitation. A raid last spring captured over seven terabytes of data—digital media, flash drives, CDs, and papers—belonging to "Abu Sayyaf," ISIL's "financial emir." This material provided broad insight into ISIL's financial situation and its vulnerabilities, which we have been able to exploit. ISIL maintains a highly-centralized management of its energy program, which is overseen by nearly 100 members. It also vets some 1,600 energy-related personnel, many of whom are foreign fighters, to maintain tight control over revenue and its distribution. At this point, the network is no longer able to operate openly as it once did, and many of these personnel have been killed.

The destruction of ISIL in Iraq and Syria will help create the conditions necessary to promote more durable stability in both nations. Ensuring stability will require a whole of government approach, in which the U.S. will work closely with local governments as well as in close coordination with our coalition partners. Encouraging increased legitimacy of the national and local governments by encouraging them to be accountable to their citizens and respect citizens' basic human rights are the core of durable stability. It will also require competent police and other local forces that can hold liberated terrain. We are working closely with our Coalition partners to prepare a push for institutional and political reform that will begin as soon as the security situation permits. In Iraq, we are pressing the Government of Iraq regularly to institute political reforms that promote reconciliation and inclusive governance. We are also working with the Government of Iraq to assist with stabilization and reconstruction in liberated areas. Finally, we are also leading an effort to organize financial support for Iraq, so that Iraqi Security Forces (ISF) can continue operations against ISIL notwithstanding depressed oil prices.

In Syria, such stability will require completion of the peace process envisioned in the Geneva Communique and currently being led by the International Syrian Support Group (ISSG) and the United Nations. We have led an international effort to address the Syrian civil war, including negotiating international arrangements, such as the Syrian Cessation of Hostilities and the ISSG process to facilitate an agreement between the Syrian parties to transition away from the current Syrian regime. The political transition envisaged moves beyond the al-Assad-led government regime toward a more representative form allows the rebuilding of Syrian state's key institutions.

Beyond Iraq and Syria, we continue to augment our regular diplomatic, economic, development, law enforcement, and intelligence efforts with our partner nations to enable them to combat ISIL.

The United States supports less secure regional partners that are under threat from ISIL, a threat that may be compounded by other pressures such as refugee flows. We generally pursue five broad types of activities with these regional partners: (1) humanitarian assistance to provide immediate assistance for refugees; (2) economic assistance; (3) security assistance reform; (4) military contingency planning; and (5) institutional capacity building. Our humanitarian assistance has helped relieve the tremendous strain placed on regional partners as they provide for refugees and ensures that refugees have basic needs met. Our economic assistance ensures that fragile economies remain resilient and are able to provide needed jobs. Security assistance reform has helped partner nations overcome systemic or structural barriers to procuring defense items that meet their high priority capability requirements. We have also implemented a variety of new mechanisms to improve interaction with partners on security assistance. Key among these is improved long-term planning processes for security assistance intended to align U.S. support with mutually-prioritized partner capacity gaps. We have sought to focus partners' military leadership on the military *capabilities* they seek to create, not merely on military platforms available for purchase. Where appropriate these activities are complemented by joint contingency planning, as well as by support from U.S. special operations training personnel to improve local capabilities. We are also working to help our partners develop complementary law enforcement and criminal justice sector capabilities to handle terrorism in a rule of law framework.

Rolling Back ISIL Expansion in Other Parts of the Globe

To defeat ISIL worldwide, we must counter the extremist ideology that has drawn fighters and affiliates from around the region and the world. The military campaign in 2016 will focus predominantly on destroying ISIL in Iraq and Syria, but the United States will simultaneously work with partners to pursue diplomatic, intelligence and military efforts against ISIL adherents and continue to partner with key regional actors confronting ISIL affiliates— particularly those in Libya, Afghanistan, Yemen, Sinai, and Nigeria—that threaten partner nations or U.S. interests.

To achieve these goals, we will continue and expand efforts to build the security sector capacity of nations where ISIL operates and to strengthen borderstates and other nations committed to confronting ISIL. Where necessary, we will also take unilateral or partnered action to disrupt emerging ISIL nodes directly. We will continue to seek additional contributions from partner nations to these efforts.

Coalition forces play a critical, but far from exclusive, role in countering ISIL's global expansion. Here, as elsewhere, intensive interagency and international participation will be essential. Intelligence, diplomacy and communication, development and law enforcement efforts are all vital to understanding, responding to, and ultimately reversing ISIL's expansion beyond Iraq and Syria. There may be instances in which the Coalition and/or partner nations can undertake operations for which others lack authorities, can contribute key capabilities, or have knowledge relevant to the fight. Countering violent extremism (CVE) is a critical part of preventing new ISIL affiliates and branches from emerging. DOS and the U.S. Agency for International Development (USAID) have developed a forthcoming joint strategy on countering violent extremism (CVE) to guide these efforts. Under this joint strategy, we will seek to focus and expand diplomatic efforts with governmental, multilateral, and non-governmental actors to promote CVE cooperation. We will expand and elevate CVE within our counterterrorism and broader diplomatic engagement with relevant partners in the Middle East. DOS and USAID are also expanding and targeting rule of law, development, and other foreign assistance programs to help partner nations address specific drivers of violent extremism and enhance CVE partnerships.

Defeating the communications network that supports ISIL's narrative is a central element of CVE and our approach to counter ISIL's expansion. With the transition of the Center for Strategic Counterterrorism Communications to the Global Engagement Center, (GEC), we will expand strategic communications efforts to counter violent extremist messaging and promote alternative voices. The GEC will coordinate and synchronize U.S. Government messaging efforts against ISIL, leverage third-party communicators to deliver credible and effective messages at the local level, and integrate advanced data analytics to improve our understanding of the adversary's message. It will also study the effect of the enemy's message on audiences, as well as provide better assessment of our own messaging efforts. We will also work through our public affairs networks to promote CVE strategic communications. We are retargeting certain Foreign Assistance programs to advance CVE, and will expand and target rule of law, development, and other foreign assistance programs to address specific drivers of violent extremism and enhance CVE partnerships, including through the use of the Counterterrorism Partnership Fund. We are working with national and regional hubs, like the Sawab Center in the United Arab Emirates, to counter online and off-line messaging by violent extremist actors, especially ISIL.

These international CVE efforts are being coordinated closely with domestic CVE efforts led by the new CVE Task Force co-led by the Department of Homeland Security (DHS) and the Department of Justice. The CVE Task Force will: (1) synchronize and integrate whole-of-government counter violent extremism (CVE) programs and activities; (2) leverage new CVE efforts, including those of the DHS Office of Community Partnerships; (3) conduct ongoing strategic planning; and (4) assess and evaluate CVE programs and activities.

Protecting the Homeland and Countering Foreign Terrorist Fighters

We are working closely with foreign partners to address the threat posed by foreign terrorist fighters (FTF) through improved information-sharing, better aviation and border security measures, improved counterterrorism legislation and prosecutions, and more effective CVE efforts in known source communities. The United States is providing significant capacity-building assistance to encourage greater action by partner countries in all of these areas and working to expand law enforcement cooperation and information-sharing.

We have begun to deploy "Foreign Fighter Surge Teams" to European countries with critical FTF and Visa Waiver Program vulnerabilities. These teams deepen bilateral cooperation on information sharing, traveler screening, border security, and law enforcement investigations. We continue to monitor networks and travel patterns with information shared among Coalition governments. Thanks to intensive diplomatic outreach, the U.S. now has agreements with 50 governments to share information on terrorist identities to better identify, track and deter their travel. Since the passage of UNSCR 2178 in September 2014, over 45 countries have passed or updated their laws to more effectively identify and prosecute FTFs.

We are also seeking to disrupt FTF networks through military efforts in Iraq and Syria. Multiple high-profile FTFs have been killed during the course of the counter-ISIL campaign, including Muhammad Emwazi (so-called "Jihadi John") and Junaid Hussain. In December, Coalition airstrikes killed 10 ISIL leaders, including Charaffe al-Mouadan, an external plotter with direct links to Abdelhamid Abaoud, the mastermind of the Paris attacks. The external plotting network remains a core priority for our information gathering and targeting. The death of Jihadi John and other ISIL leaders also helped degrade the external plotting cells, and will help deter individuals who are not yet fully radicalized or recruited by ISIL. Ground operations and other activities also often yield valuable information on FTFs, all of which is catalogued and shared among U.S. departments and agencies and with foreign partners (through military, diplomatic, law enforcement, and/or intelligence channels).

We are providing a separate report to Congress detailing these efforts, as required by Section 7073 of the Department of State, Foreign Operations, and Related Programs Appropriations Act of 2016.

Coalition Activities

The President's Special Envoy to the Counter ISIL Coalition leads a whole of government approach coordinating our efforts with our coalition partners. The Secretaries of State and Defense have each helped secure additional contributions from Coalition partners since a wave of ISIL terrorist attacks in 2015. Leading Coalition members increased their already significant contributions. Others announced expansions of their commitments, including several that expand air operations to include Syria, in addition to Iraq. The Coalition's regional partners also have expressed a willingness to deepen cooperation on counter-ISIL activities. More than one-half of the present 66 Coalition partners have made additional contributions since the fall of 2015.

Catalyzing greater Coalition and international support for the campaign will be a matter of priority in 2016 for the Coalition, but it is one that requires concerted efforts from numerous government ministries, departments, and agencies. This includes ensuring that regional partners do more to secure their borders and disrupt the networks that enable foreign fighters and materials to move in and out of Iraq and Syria. Additional nations can join those already striking in Iraq and Syria, can send conventional and SOF to Syria and Iraq, and can provide police trainers—contributions that we are pressing them to make. These nations and others with significant Muslim populations—from Europe, the broader Middle East, and Southeast Asia—can also contribute by denying ISIL any religious legitimacy and advancing a persuasive counter-narrative. We expect more counter-ISIL ministerial meetings to be held in 2016. Finally, countries such as Iran and Russia can contribute by withholding their support for Bashar al-Assad, who is the chief instigator of radicalism and terrorism in Syria.

Beyond the Counter-ISIL Coalition, the United States is also utilizing other mechanisms to promote international cooperation and burden-sharing to counter terrorism and violent extremism, such as the Global Counterterrorism Forum. Effectively preventing and countering the spread of violent extremism requires a broad-based, international coalition of government and non-governmental actors. The White House CVE Summit and its follow-on process, which culminated with the September 2015 Leaders' Summit to Counter ISIL and Counter Violent Extremism, brought together leaders from over 100 countries and more than 300 civil society actors to support CVE efforts. We are continuing to expand partnerships with local government authorities, civil society, and the private sector to enhance our CVE efforts.

Source: White House. *Strategy for the Middle East and to Counter Violent Extremism.* Report to the Armed Services Committee, March 24, 2016. Washington, D.C.: Government Printing Office.

Chronology

1999		Abu Musab al-Zarqawi travels to Afghanistan and receives funding from Osama bin Laden to start a training camp and he begins the organization Jama'at al Tawhid wal Jihad (JTJ) (جماعة التوحيد والجهاد) or Group of Monotheism and Jihad.
2001	September 11	Attacks by al-Qaeda on the World Trade Center and Pentagon. Saddam Hussein immediately declares that Iraq played no part in the attacks.
	October 7	Operation Enduring Freedom begins with attacks on Afghanistan.
	December 6–17	Battle of Tora Bora in Afghanistan to defeat remnants of al-Qaeda.
	December 7	The Taliban lose its last major stronghold in Afghanistan.
2002	March 1–18	Operation Anaconda attempts to destroy last remnants of al-Qaeda and the Taliban in Afghanistan.
	October 2	U.S. Congress passes joint resolution authorizing use of military force against Iraq.
	October 16	President Bush signs authorization for use of force against Iraq.
2003	February 12	Al-Jazeera releases an audio tape purporting to include a statement from Osama bin Laden recounting the Battle of Tora Bra and urges Muslims to overthrow the regime of Saddam Hussein.
	March 17	President Bush gives a final ultimatum to Saddam Hussein for him to leave Iraq with his sons in 48 hours.

		UN Secretary General orders all UN personnel to leave Iraq.
	March 18	Colin Powell announces a 30-nation "Coalition of the Willing."
	March 20	Operation Iraqi Freedom begins.
	April 10	Baghdad is secured by coalition forces.
	May 1	President Bush announces an end to major combat operations.
	May 12	Paul Bremer arrives in Iraq as the head of the newly formed Coalition Provisional Authority (CPA) and replaces General Jay Garner as the civil leader of Iraq.
	May 23	L. Paul Bremer issues CPA Order Number 2 disbanding the Iraqi Army.
	December 13	Saddam Hussein is captured by soldiers from the First Brigade, Fourth Infantry Division. He was hiding in a hole in a barn in al-Dawr, near Tikrit, Iraq. Saddam stated, "I am Saddam Hussein. I am the president of Iraq. I want to negotiate." The U.S. soldier responded, "President Bush sends his regards."
2004	March 11	Madrid bombings killing 191 on commuter trains.
	March 31	Four Blackwater contractors ambushed and killed in Fallujah.
	April 4–May 1	First Battle of Fallujah (Operation Vigilant Resolve).
	April 18	Spain, led by newly elected José Luis Rodríguez Zapatero (Socialist Party), vows to withdraw its troops.
		Beginning of release of Abu Ghraib prisoner abuse images.
	June 28	At 10:26 a.m., the U.S.-led CPA formally transferred sovereignty of Iraqi territory to the Iraqi interim government, two days ahead of schedule. L. Paul Bremer departed the country two hours later.
	October	ISIS changes its name to Tanzim Qaedat al Jihad fi Bilad al Rafidayn aka al-Qaeda in Iraq (AQI) (تنظيم قاعدة الجهاد في بلاد الرافدين) or Organization of Jihad's Base in Mesopotamia.
	November 7–December 23	Second Battle of Fallujah (Operation Phantom Fury).

	December 19	Suicide car bomb in Najaf, close to the Imam Ali shrine, kills 52 and wounds at least 140. On the same day, a car bomb exploded in Karbala, killing 14 and injuring at least 52.
2005	August 20	Rockets are fired toward a U.S. warship docked in Aqaba.
	November 9	Suicide bombers detonate in three hotels in Amman, Jordan, killing 60.
	November 5–22	Operation Steel Curtain. First large deployment of Iraqi Army in support of coalition operation to remove foreign fighters.
2006	January 15	Al-Qaeda in Iraq forms Mujahideen Shura Council with other groups.
	February 22	The al-Askari mosque in Samarra is bombed. No one is killed, but during retaliatory violence more than a thousand die. This is considered the start of the Iraqi Civil War.
	June 7	Abu Musab al-Zarqawi is killed by a U.S. air strike. It was hoped that his death would ease the sectarian killings rampant in Iraq.
	June 14– October 24	Operation Together Forward. Security plan designed to reduce the sectarian violence in Baghdad since the al-Askari mosque bombing. This was deemed a failure.
	September	Anbar Awakening—30 tribes formed an alliance against AQI.
	October 15	ISIS changes its name to the Islamic State of Iraq (ISI).
	November 7	U.S. Congressional midterm elections. Democrat party wins both chambers.
	December 30	Execution of Saddam Hussein.
2007	January 10	The Iraq War troop surge of 2007 is announced.
	June 13	Al-Askari Mosque bombing blows up two of the mosque's minarets.
	November 1	Statistics for October show a significant reduction in violence since the beginning of "the Surge."
2008	March 20	Al-Jazeera releases Osama bin Laden recording where he states that "Iraq is the perfect base to set up the jihad to liberate Palestine."

	March 23	The United States killed in action exceed 4,000.
	May 8	Abu Ayyub al-Masri is arrested in Mosul. He is the suspected leader of al-Qaeda in Iraq.
	October 26	Abu Kemal raid into Syria by U.S. special operations forces.
	November 4	Barack Obama elected President of the United States.
	November 17	U.S.-Iraq Status of Forces Agreement signed by Iraqi Foreign Minister and U.S. Ambassador to Iraq. This agreement requires U.S. forces to be out of cities in 2009 and out of Iraq by the end of 2011.
	December 14	President Bush signs status of forces agreement. This was the president's fourth and final trip to Baghdad. During the press conference, one of the reporters hurled two shoes at the president in protest for the chaos in Iraq.
2009	January 1	The United States formally transfers security responsibility for Green Zone to Iraq.
		The United States opens new embassy in Baghdad.
	January 20	Barack Obama inaugurated as 44th President of the United States.
2010	April 18	A joint U.S.-Iraqi operation near Tikrit, Iraq, kills Abu Ayyub al-Masri and Abu Omar al-Baghdadi.
	May 16	Abu Bakr al-Baghdadi was announced as the leader of ISI.
	August 18	Last U.S. combat brigade departs Iraq. More than 50,000 U.S. military forces remain in Iraq conducting mostly advice and assist missions.
	August 31	Operation Iraqi Freedom formally ends.
	September 1	Operation New Dawn begins.
	October 31	Baghdad church massacre kills 58 at the Our Lady of Salvation Syriac Catholic cathedral of Baghdad, Iraq, during Sunday evening mass.
2011	December 18	Last U.S. troops leave Iraq.
	May 31	Two AQI Iraqi refugees arrested in Kentucky.
	August	Abu Bakr al-Baghdadi authorized the creation of an al-Qaeda branch in Syria to bring down the Assad regime under the direction of Abu Mohammad al-Golani.

	October 4	U.S. Department of State listed Abu Bakr al-Baghdadi as a Specially Designated Global Terrorist.
2012	January 23	Abu Mohammad al-Golani's group was announced as Jabhat al-Nusra l'Ahl al-Sham or The Support Front for the People of Al-Sham.
	July 22	Abu Bakr al-Baghdadi announced a return of ISI to Iraqi strongholds previously under U.S. control.
	December	The United States designated Jabhat al-Nusra as a terrorist organization and an alias of AQI.
2013	April 8	The Islamic State of Iraq changes its name to the Islamic State of Iraq and al-Sham or ISIS.
	July 22	ISIS organizes a prison breakout from Taji and Abu Ghraib, Iraq.
2014	January 3	ISIS proclaims itself to be the Islamic State in Fallujah.
	June 9	Mosul, Iraq, falls to ISIS.
	June 15	Operation Inherent Resolve begins with a purpose of coordinating a regional response to ISIS.
	June 29	ISIS changes its name to the Islamic State and claims to be a caliphate.
2013	April 8	ISIS takes on the name the Islamic State of Iraq and al Sham (ISIS) Abu Mohammed al-Golani disagreed and broke off from ISIS and declared allegiance to al-Qaeda, creating the al-Qaeda affiliate of Jabhat al-Nusra.
	July 22	ISIS organized prison breaks in Iraq's prisons in Taji and Abu Ghraib, freeing more than 500 prisoners.
	August	Menagh Air Base, Syria captured
	December	ISIS began offensive in Anbar, Iraq.
2014	January 2	ISIS claimed responsibility for car bomb attack that killed four people and wounded dozens in the Beirut suburb of Haret Hreik, one of the headquarters of Hezbollah.
	January 4	Fallujah, Iraq, captured by ISIS.
	January 13	Fallujah Dam taken by progovernment tribes. In the previous week, ISIS militants used the dam to flood area around the city and lowered water levels in the southern Iraqi provinces.

2014   January 25   ISIS announced the creation of a Lebanese arm to fight Hezbollah.

January   Haji Bakr, ISIS's then second-in-command, reported assassinated by Syrian militants.

February 3   Al-Qaeda's general command broke off its links with ISIS.

February   Jabhat al-Nusra joined rebel forces to expel ISIS forces from Deir al-Zour province in Syria.

March 8   Iraqi Prime Minister Nuri al-Maliki accused Saudi Arabia and Qatar of openly funding ISIS.

March 16   Iraqi Security Forces recaptured Ramadi and parts of Fallujah.

April 27   Iraqi helicopters reportedly destroyed an ISIS convoy inside Syria. Possibly the first time Iraqi forces struck outside their country since Operation Desert Storm.

May 1   ISIS carried out a total of seven public killings in the city of Raqqa in northern Syria.

June 7   ISIS captured University of Anbar in Ramadi, Iraq, killed guards and held 1,300 students hostage, before being ousted by the Iraqi military.

June 9   Mosul, Iraq, captured by ISIS.

June 10   ISIS killed 670 Shia inmates of Badush prison in Mosul.

June 11   ISIS seized the Turkish consulate in the Iraqi city of Mosul, and kidnapped the head of the diplomatic mission and several staff members.
Tikrit, Iraq, captured by ISIS.

June 14   The Iraqi Army recaptured the town of al-Mutasim near Samarra retrieving the bodies of 128 Iraqi soldiers and policemen who had been killed in the battle of Mosul.

June 15   Tal Afar, Iraq, captured by ISIS.

June 19   Al-Muthanna Chemical Weapons Facility near Lake Tharthar captured by ISIS.

June 21   Bayji oil refinery captured by ISIS.

June 23   Tal Afar airport captured by ISIS.
Al-Waleed border crossing recaptured by Iraqi forces.

2014	June 24	Syrian Air Force bombed ISIS positions in Iraq for the first time.
	June 25	Al-Nusra Front's branch in the Syrian town of al-Bukamal pledged loyalty to ISIS.
	June 26	Iraq launched its first counterattack against ISIS, an airborne assault to seize back control of Tikrit University.
	June 28	Obama administration requested US$500 million from U.S. Congress to use in the training and arming of "moderate" Syrian rebels to counter the growing threat posed by ISIS in Syria and Iraq.
	June 29	ISIS announced the establishment of a new caliphate. Abu Bakr al-Baghdadi was appointed its caliph (Caliph Ibrahim), and the group formally changed its name to the Islamic State (IS).
	July 2	Abu Bakr al-Baghdadi said that Muslims should unite to capture "Rome" in order to "own the world."
	July 3	ISIS captured Syria's largest oilfield, the al-Omar oilfield, from Jabhat al-Nusra.
	July 5	ISIS releases a video showing Abu Bakr al-Baghdad speaking from the Great Mosque of al-Nuri in Mosul, Iraq.
	July 29–30	To mark the Muslim holy festival of Eid al-Fitr, which ends the period of Ramadan, ISIS released a video showing graphic scenes of a large scale killing of captives.
	August 5	An ISIS offensive in the Sinjar area of northern Iraq forced 30,000–50,000 Yazidis to flee into the mountains.
	August 10	The Battle for Tabqa Air base.
	August 12	The parents of kidnapped American journalist James Foley received an e-mail from his captors.
	August 14	Kurdish Pesh Merga forces and U.S. air strikes broke the ISIS siege on Mount Sinjar, thus allowing tens of thousands of Yazidi refugees trapped there to escape.
		Nuri al-Maliki resigned from his position of Prime Minister of Iraq.

2014	August 15	The United Nations Security Council issued Resolution 2170 condemning ISIS and calling on member states to stop financing for ISIS.
	August 19	ISIS released video of the beheading of James Foley.
	August 21	U.S. military admitted to a covert rescue attempt had been made to rescue James Foley and other Americans held captive in Syria by ISIS. The attempt failed to find the captives and one U.S. soldier was injured. First known engagement of U.S. ground forces and ISIS militants.
	September 2	ISIS released video of the beheading of American journalist Steven Sotloff.
	September 17	ISIS began Battle of Kobane/Ayn al-Arab.
	September 20	The hostages from the Turkish consulate in Mosul who had been captured on June 11, 2014, were released.
	September 22	Two weeks after her abduction, Iraqi human rights activist Samira Salih al-Nuaimi was publicly executed by ISIS.
		Iraqi media stated that 300 Iraqi soldiers were killed by an ISIS chlorine gas attack in Saqlawiyah.
	October 3	ISIS released video of the beheading of British aid worker Alan Henning and threatened American aid worker Peter Kassig.
	October 15	The U.S. anti-ISIS operation was named Operation Inherent Resolve.
	October 16	ISIS driven out of most of Kobane.
	October 17	Three MiG-21 or MiG-23 fighters were being flown by ISIS militants who were undergoing training by former Iraqi Ba'ath officers at al-Jarrah air base.
	October 24	Evidence from Kobane suggests ISIS used chemical weapons against defenders.
	October 31	The UN stated that overall 15,000 foreign fighters had joined ISIS in Iraq and Syria.
	November 8	Twenty-seven ISIS fighters were poisoned by Syrian rebels who had infiltrated as cooks into the Fath El-Shahel camp; 12 were killed.
	November 16	ISIS released video of the beheading of Peter Kassig and the beheading of 15 Syrian Army prisoners.

December 10	Man charged on accounts of homosexuality then thrown off a building in northern Iraq by the Islamic State, then he was stoned to death by a crowd.
December 19	U.S. General James Terry announced that the number of U.S. airstrikes to date on ISIS had increased to 1,361.
December 20	ISIS "military police" executed 100 foreign fighters who attempted to quit and flee from the insurgents' de-facto capital of Raqqa in northern Syria as frustration among militants has been growing.
December 21	Sinjar offensive ended with a decisive Kurdish victory and the city of Sinjar momentarily liberated, as ISIS forces retreated to Tell Afar and Mosul.
December 22	Kurdish forces claimed that ISIS control of Kobane reduced to 30 percent.

2015	January 13	Someone claiming to represent ISIS hacked U.S. Military's Twitter account and threatened vengeance on American soldiers for the U.S.'s intervention against ISIS.
	January 20	ISIS threatened to kill two Japanese hostages unless it received a ransom of $200 million.
		Abu Bakr al-Baghdadi reportedly wounded in an airstrike.
	January 25	ISIS published a video declaring the execution of Haruna Yukawa and revised its demands. It no longer seeks the $200 million ransom; instead, it demands the release of Sajida Mubarak Atrous al-Rishawi in exchange for Kenji Goto and Muath al-Kasasbeh, a Jordanian fighter pilot.
		ISIS control of Kobane reduced to 10 percent.
	January 26	YPG regained Kobane with assistance from US airstrikes.
	January 27	Suspected ISIS terrorists in Libya killed eight people, after storming the Corinthia Hotel in Tripoli and detonating a car bomb.
	January 29	ISIS militant claimed that ISIS has smuggled 4,000 militants into the European Union as civilian refugees. ISIS claimed that the fighters were planning retaliatory attacks.

2015	January 31	ISIS claims to have beheaded Japanese hostage journalist Kenji Goto, the second ISIS execution of a Japanese person.
	February 3	ISIS released a video of Jordanian hostage Muath al-Kasasbeh being burned to death while locked in a cage. Protests occurred in Jordan with some Jordanians demanding revenge on ISIS.
	February 4	Jordan executed two of its AQI prisoners, in retaliation against ISIS's burning of the Jordanian pilot.
	February 7	ISIS claimed that American female hostage Kayla Mueller was killed in the Jordanian airstrike on Raqqa on February 5.
	February 8	ISIS reportedly captured Nofaliya, Libya.
	February 10	President Obama confirmed the death of U.S. hostage Kayla Mueller.
	February 14	The Libyan parliament confirmed the deaths of 21 kidnapped Egyptian Coptic Christian workers in Libya, after the ISIS English-language publication *Dabiq* released photos claiming their execution.
	February 16	Egypt retaliated for the beheading of 21 Egyptian Christians by bombing ISIS camps, training sites, and weapons storage depots in Libya.
	February 23	ISIS stormed the central library of Mosul, destroying about 100,000 books, manuscripts, and newspapers. ISIS abducted 150 Assyrian Christians from villages near Tal Tamr in northeastern Syria, after launching a large offensive in the region. It was reported that ISIS had burned around 8,000 rare books and manuscripts after destroying the Library of Mosul in Iraq.
	February 25	Experts believe that three missing British schoolgirls who had gone to Turkey had traveled to Syria and joined ISIS.
	February 26	Media report about the mass destruction of historical artifacts in the Mosul Museum released, including statues of Lamassu. Jihadi John is identified as Mohammed Emwazi, a 27-year-old Kuwaiti-born British man from a middle-class family who grew up in West London

2015

and graduated from the University of Westminster with a computer programming degree.

March 2   The Iraqi government launched a massive military operation to recapture Tikrit with 30,000 Iraqi soldiers, backed by aircraft, besieging the city on three fronts.

March 5   Reported that ISIS destroyed the ancient Assyrian city of Nimrud and its archeological site, claiming that the city and its related antiquities were blasphemous.

March 6   An Iraqi antiquities official confirmed ISIS's bulldozing of the ancient Assyrian city of Nimrud with unconfirmed amounts of damage.

March 7   Boko Haram declared allegiance to ISIS.

March 8   Mohammed Emwazi, also known as "Jihadi John," apologized to his family for the shame and scrutiny he brought on them after his identity was unmasked.

March 10   ISIS has reportedly destroyed the 10th-century Assyrian monastery of St. George and a Chaldean Catholic seminary near Mosul.

March 11   ISIS threatened on loudspeakers to behead any civilian who tried to leave Mosul. The announcement came one day after U.S. planes dropped paper pamphlets into the city, warning of an imminent military confrontation and advising all civilians to evacuate the city.

March 13   A group of militants from the Islamic Movement of Uzbekistan in Northern Afghanistan swore allegiance to ISIS.

March 15   Fighting around the city of Tikrit led to the near-complete destruction of the tomb of Saddam Hussein located in al-Awja. The former President's body had been moved from the mausoleum and taken to an unknown location in 2014 according to the local Sunni population.

March 18   Abu Bakr al-Baghdadi seriously wounded in a coalition airstrike at the al-Baaj District, in the Nineveh Governorate, near the Syrian border. It was reported that his wounds were so serious that the top ISIS

2015	leaders had a meeting to discuss who would replace him if he died.
March 20	ISIS took responsibility for a quadruple suicide bombing, carried out in Sana'a mosque in Yemen, which killed nearly 150 people.
March 31	Iraqi forces recaptured the city center of Tikrit.
April 8	Anbar Offensive.
	ISIS destroyed the 12th-century Bash Tapia Castle in Mosul.
April 12	The Iraqi government declared Tikrit free of ISIS forces, stating that it was safe for residents to return home, although it was later revealed that pockets of resistance continued to persist until April 17.
	Wilayat Sinai pledged allegiance to ISIS in the Sinai Peninsula.
April 17	130 ISIS sleeper agents hiding in Tikrit were found and killed by Iraq security forces finally ending the Battle of Tikrit.
April 19	Video released showing the murder by shooting and decapitation of approximately 30 people, who were identified as Ethiopian Christians.
April 22	Reported that Abu Ala al-Afri, the self-proclaimed deputy caliph and a former Iraqi physics teacher was installed as the stand-in leader while Baghdadi recuperated from his injuries.
April 25	Video released showing ISIS executioners in the Homs province staging a purported display of sympathy wherein they embrace and forgive two gay men for their sins, before bludgeoning them to death with huge rocks.
May 1	The Guardian newspaper in England reported that Abu Bakr al-Baghdadi was recovering from severe spinal injuries and that he may never be able to resume direct control of ISIS again.
May 3	Curtis Culwell Center attack in Garland, Texas— two men killed by police.
May 5	ISIS claimed responsibility for the Garland, Texas, attack.

2015   May 13   Abu Ala al-Afri, ISIS's Deputy Leader, killed in an airstrike in Tel Afar.

May 15   ISIS released taped message from Abu Bakr al-Baghdadi that proves he was still alive.

May 15–16   Abu Sayyaf killed in Deir al-Zour, Syria, during a U.S. Special Operations Forces raid intended to capture him in.

May 17   ISIS captured Ramadi, Iraq.

May 21   ISIS captured Tadmur and Palmyra, Syria.

May 22   ISIS captured the last border crossing between Syria and Iraq.

ISIS carried out first terror attack in Saudi Arabia—suicide bomber killed at least 21 people in a Shiite mosque in the city of Qatif.

May 28   ISIS claims the seizure of Sirte, Libya Airport.

June 1   ISIS begins mandating that male civilians in Mosul wear full beards and imposes harsh punishments for shaving, up to and including beheading.

June 10   President Obama authorized the deployment of 450 additional American advisors to Iraq to help train Iraqi forces in fighting ISIS.

June 24   ISIS attacked Kobane killing at least 146 people.

June 26   ISIS claimed responsibility for the bombing of a Shiite mosque in Kuwait City (killing at least 27) and attacks on tourists in Sousse, Tunisia (killing 38).

June 27   ISIS demolished the ancient statue Lion of al-Lat in Palmyra.

June 30   Alaa Saadeh, a 23-year-old resident of West New York, New Jersey, is arrested at his home on charges of conspiring to provide material support to ISIS. Other co-conspirators were arrested on June 13 and 17 on similar charges.

July 1   A full-scale offensive in Sinai by the Islamic State affiliate began after sunrise with simultaneous assaults on more than a dozen military checkpoints.

July 3   ISIS released a video showing the execution of 25 Syrian regime soldiers on the Palmyra amphitheater stage.

2015	July 11	ISIS claimed responsibility for a car bomb blast at the Italian consulate in Cairo, Egypt.
	July 16	ISIS militants in Sinai attacked an Egyptian Navy ship with a guided antitank missile.
	August 2	Russian security forces killed 8 ISIS fighters in the North Caucasus.
	August 11	The ISIS-linked Sharia Council in Shaddadi city Syria sentenced to death more than 90 of its own militants who withdrew from their fighting positions without a permission from their command, considering their retreat as "an act of treason."
	August 19	ISIS beheaded Dr. Khaled al-Asaad, retired chief of antiquities for Palmyra.
	August 20	ISIS claimed responsibility for an explosion, near the building of the Egyptian national security agency that killed 29 people, including six policemen, in Cairo.
	August 22	Ayoub El Khazzani, a Moroccan who had links to Islamic State, attempted to kill passengers of a French train leaving from Brussels and going to Paris.
	August 23	Kurdish forces of the YPG exchanged hostages with Islamic State group for the first time. Each side released three hostages.
		Suspected Boko Haram militants ambushed a convoy carrying Nigeria's chief of army staff on a tour of towns in troubled Borno state.
	August 24	Junaid Hussain, 21, was killed in air strike by U.S. forces in Raqqa. The Pentagon confirmed that a U.S. drone strike killed Junaid Hussain, an ISIS operative linked to the Garland, Texas, cartoon contest attack.
	August 30	ISIS destroyed the Temple of Bel in Palmyra.
	September 2	ISIS executed 112 of its gunmen, including 18 leaders, who were shot dead in the old prison, located south of Mosul, explaining that the executions came on the background of its attempt to stage a coup against the organization's leader, Abu Bakr al-Baghdadi.

2015	September 3	ISIS has executed more than 40 of its militants in the Musbaq al-Suney district of al-Mayadin, Syria, saying they have refused to join the battles in Aleppo province. Among those executed were several Saudi leading members who refused to leave Deir ez-Zour province.
	September 25	Some 200 members of the Boko Haram Islamist militant group have given themselves up, in the town of Banki, Nigeria, on the border with Cameroon.
	September 29	ISIS claimed responsibility for the shooting death of an Italian aid worker in Dhaka, Bangladesh; if confirmed, this would be its first attack in Bangladesh.
	October 1	ISIS has arrested, in the northern countryside of Deir al-Zour, some eight militants who were trying to desert the group and flee to Turkey. Dozens of ISIS members had deserted the group and crossed into Turkey in the past few months. Most of them were foreign nationals who had lately recognized the brutality of the alleged caliphate toward Muslim citizens in Syrian and Iraq. Russian Air Force attacked ISIS command center, training camp, and field camp in various locations in Syria.
	October 3	ISIS claimed responsibility for shooting and killing a Japanese man in the Rangpur District of Bangladesh.
	October 6	ISIS has executed about 27 of its elements in Hawija district in the province of Kirkuk, Iraq, because of their escape from the battlefield.
	October 22	Joint Kurdish and U.S. special operations raid freed 69 people from ISIS prison. One U.S. soldier is killed—the first U.S. killed in action in Operation Inherent Resolve.
	October 31	Russian airliner flying from Sharm al-Sheikh crashes killing 224 people. ISIS claimed credit through Wilayat Sinai.
	November 12	ISIS claimed responsibility for two suicide bombs in Beirut, Lebanon that killed 43.

2015	November 13	ISIS claimed responsibility for several coordinated attacks in Paris, France, that killed 130.
	December 2	A husband and wife attack a holiday party in San Bernardino, California killing 14 and injuring 22. Later this couple is loosely connected to ISIS though no proof of training or formal indoctrination exists.
	December 28	Iraqi security forces retake government compound in Ramadi, Iraq.
	December 30	Iraqi Prime Minister Haider al-Abadi visits Ramadi, Iraq.
2016	January 8	Philadelphia, Pennsylvania man shot and severely injured a policeman claiming ISIS as motivation.
	January 16	ISIS executed dozens of civilians and pro-Assad fighters in Deir ez-Zour, Syria. Over 400 civilians were reportedly abducted and taken toward Raqqa.
	January 19	ISIS announced 50 percent reductions in pay for Syrian fighters.
	January 31	Two ISIS suicide bombers attacked the Sayyidah Zaynab Mosque in Damascus, one of Shia Islam's holiest sites, killing 60.
	March 22	ISIS-associated persons attacked two locations (Zaventem Airport and Maelbeek metro station) in Brussels, Belgium leaving at least 31 dead and more than 220 injured.
	March 27	Syrian Armed Forces, with support from the Russian Air Force and allied militias, recaptured Palmyra.
	May 3	U.S. Navy SEAL killed in Iraq after ISIS attacked a Pesh Merga base several kilometers behind the front lines. This was part of an ISIS attack that penetrated 3–5 kilometers into Pesh Merga controlled territory.

Bibliography

Books

Al-Ali, Zaid. *The Struggle for Iraq's Future: How Corruption, Incompetence and Sectarianism Have Undermined Democracy.* New Haven, CT: Yale University Press, 2014.

Allawi, Ali A. *The Occupation of Iraq: Winning the War, Losing the Peace.* New Haven, CT: Yale University Press, 2008.

Bolger, Daniel P. *Why We Lost: A General's Inside Account of the Iraq and Afghanistan Wars.* Boston: Houghton Mifflin Harcourt, 2014.

Broadwell, Paula. *All In: The Education of General David Petraeus.* New York: Penguin Press, 2012.

Bush, George W. *Decision Points.* New York: Random House, Inc., 2010.

Clinton, Hillary. *Hard Choices.* New York: Simon & Schuster Inc., 2014.

Cockburn, Patrick. *The Rise of Islamic State: ISIS and the New Sunni Revolution.* New York: Verso Books, 2015.

Gates, Robert M. *Duty: Memoirs of a Secretary at War.* New York: Alfred A. Knopf, Inc., 2014.

Gentile, Gian. *Wrong Turn: America's Deadly Embrace of Counterinsurgency.* New York: The New Press, 2013.

Gordon, Michael R., and Bernard Trainor. *The Endgame: The Inside Story of the Struggle for Iraq from George W. Bush to Barack Obama.* New York: Vintage, 2013.

Johnson, David E., M. Wade Markel, and Brian Shannon. *The 2008 Battle of Sadr City: Reimagining Urban Combat.* Santa Monica, CA: RAND Corporation, 2013.

Kagan, Kimberly. *The Surge: A Military History.* New York: Encounter Books, 2008.

Kaplan, Fred. *The Insurgents: David Petraeus and the Plot to Change the American Way of War.* New York: Simon & Schuster, 2014.

Kilcullen, David. *Counterinsurgency.* Oxford, United Kingdom: Oxford University Press, 2010.

Kilcullen, David. *The Accidental Guerilla: Fighting Small Wars in the Midst of a Big One*. Oxford: Oxford University Press, 2011.

Mansoor, Peter. *Surge: My Journey with General David Petraeus and the Remaking of the Iraq War*. New Haven, CT: Yale University Press, 2013.

McCants, William. *The ISIS Apocalypse: The History, Strategy, and Doomsday Vision of the Islamic State*. New York: St. Martin's Press, 2015.

McChrystal, Stanley. *My Share of the Task: A Memoir*. New York: Penguin Group, 2013

Morrell, Michael. *The Great War of Our Time: The CIA's Fight against Terrorism— From al Qa'ida to ISIS*. New York: Hatchet Book Group, 2015.

Panetta, Leon. *Worthy Fights: A Memoir of Leadership in War and Peace*. New York: Penguin Group, 2014.

Sky, Emma. *The Unraveling: High Hopes and Missed Opportunities in Iraq*. New York: PublicAffairs, 2015.

Steed, Brian L. *Armed Conflict: Lessons of Modern Warfare*. New York: Ballantine Books, 2003.

Steed, Brian L. *Piercing the Fog of War: Recognizing Change on the Battlefield: Lessons from Military History, 216 BC through Today*. Minneapolis: Zenith Press, 2009.

Steed, Brian L. *Bees and Spiders: Applied Cultural Awareness and the Art of Cross-Cultural Influence*. Houston: Strategic Book Publishing & Rights Agency, LLC, 2014.

Stern, Jessica, and J. M. Berger. *ISIS: The State of Terror*. New York: Ecco Press, 2015.

Weiss, Michael, and Hassan Hassan. *ISIS: Inside the Army of Terror*. New York: Regan Arts, 2015.

Zogby, James. *Arab Voices: What They Are Saying to Us, and Why It Matters*. New York: Palgrave MacMillan, 2012.

Articles

al-Dulaimy, Muhammed, and Hannah Allam, "Iraqis Recount Their Lives under the Islamic State: Cheap Food, Endless Rules," *McClatchy DC* [May 29, 2015]. http://www.mcclatchydc.com/news/nation-world/world/middle-east/article24785074.html [accessed June 4, 2015].

Allam, Hannah, "The 'Magic Words:' How a Simple Phrase Enmeshed the U.S. in Syria's Crisis," *McClatchy* [August 13, 2015]. http://www.mcclatchydc.com/news/nation-world/world/article31016274.html [accessed August 14, 2015].

Arango, Tim, "ISIS Transforming into Functioning State That Uses Terror as Tool," *The New York Times* [July 21, 2015]. http://www.nytimes.com/2015/07/22/world/middleeast/isis-transforming-into-functioning-state-that-uses-terror-as-tool.html [accessed November 6, 2015].

Atran, Scott, "The Real Power of ISIS," *The Daily Beast* [October 25, 2015]. http://www.thedailybeast.com/articles/2015/10/25/the-real-power-of-isis.html [accessed October 26, 2015].

Atran, Scott, "Mindless Terrorists? The Truth about ISIS Is Much Worse," *The Guardian* [November 15, 2015]. http://www.theguardian.com/commentisfree/2015/nov/15/terrorists-isis#_= [accessed November 16, 2015].

Azzam, Abdullah, "Defense of the Muslim Lands: The First Obligation after Iman," Translated by Brothers in Ribatt [1979]. https://archive.org/details/Defense_of_the_Muslim_Lands [accessed November 24, 2015].

Barnard, Ann, and Tim Arango, "Using Violence and Persuasion, ISIS Makes Political Gains," *The New York Times* [June 3, 2015]. http://www.nytimes.com/2015/06/04/world/isis-making-political-gains.html?hp&action=click&pgtype=Homepage&module=first-column-region&region=top-news&WT.nav=top-news&_r=3 [accessed June 4, 2015].

Beinart, Peter, "Don't Be Led Astray by the Legend of the Surge," *Defense One* [August 10, 2015]. http://www.defenseone.com/ideas/2015/08/gop-candidates-led-astray-legend-surge/119011/?oref=d-river [accessed August 11, 2015].

Benhold, Katrin, "Jihad and Girl Power: How ISIS Lured 3 London Girls," *The New York Times* [August 17, 2015]. http://www.nytimes.com/2015/08/18/world/europe/jihad-and-girl-power-how-isis-lured-3-london-teenagers.html?ref=world&_r=1 [August 18, 2015].

Berger, J. M., "America Isn't Losing the War of Ideas to ISIS," *Defense One* [November 11, 2015]. http://www.defenseone.com/ideas/2015/11/america-isnt-losing-war-ideas-isis/123604 [accessed November 13, 2015].

Berger, J. M., and Jonathon Morgan, "The ISIS Twitter Census: Defining and Describing the Population of ISIS Supporters on Twitter." *The Brookings Project on U.S. Relations with the Islamic World*, no. 20 [March 2015]. http://brookings.edu/research/papers/2015/03/isis-twitter-census-berger-morgan?utm_source=Sailthru&utm_medium=email&utm_term=%2AMideast%20Brief&utm_campaign=New%20Campaign [accessed June 2, 2015].

Bhalla, Reva, "The Geopolitics of the Syrian Civil War," *Geopolitical Weekly* [January 21, 2014]. https://www.stratfor.com/weekly/geopolitics-syrian-civil-war?utm_source=freelist-f&utm_medium=email&utm_term=Gweekly&utm_campaign=20150804&utm_content=readmoretext&mc_cid=d98770da07&mc_eid=08cc24dfe0 [accessed August 4, 2015].

Bokhari, Kamran, "Why Shiite Expansion Will Be Short-Lived," *Stratfor* [May 12, 2015]. https://www.stratfor.com/analysis/why-shiite-expansion-will-be-short-lived?utm_source=freelist-f&utm_medium=email&utm_term=article&utm_campaign=20150514&mc_cid=0ac147a275&mc_eid=08cc24dfe0 [accessed May 14, 2015].

Booth, William, and Ruth Eglash, "Israelis Are Calling Attacks a 'New Kind of Palestinian Terrorism,'" *The Washington Post* [December 25, 2015]. https://www

.washingtonpost.com/world/middle_east/israelis-are-calling-attacks-a-new-kind
-of-palestinian-terror/2015/12/24/e162e088-0953-4de5-992e-adb2126f1dcc_story
.html [accessed December 28, 2015].

Bourekba, Moussa, "What Is So Attractive about the 'Islamic State'." *Notes Interna-cionals CIDOB* [March 2015]. http://www.cidob.org/en/publications/publication
_series/notes_internacionals/n1_112/what_is_so_attractive_about_the_islamic
_state [accessed March 6, 2016].

Brannen, Kate, "The Company Getting Rich off the ISIS War," *The Daily Beast* [August 2, 2015]. http://www.thedailybeast.com/articles/2015/08/02/the-company-getting
-rich-off-of-the-isis-war.html [accessed August 4, 2015].

Callimachi, Rukmini, "ISIS and the Lonely Young American," *New York Times* [June 27, 2015]. http://www.nytimes.com/2015/06/28/world/americas/isis-online-recruiting
-american.html [accessed December 10, 2015].

Coles, Isabel, "Islamic State Settles into Ramadi, but Lull Unlikely to Last," *Reuters* [May 28, 2015]. http://www.reuters.com/article/2015/05/28/us-mideast-crisis-ram
adi-idUSKBN0OD2OS20150528 [accessed May 29, 2015].

Collard, Rebecca, "Why ISIS Can Still Defeat the Iraqi Army in Spite of U.S. Help," *Time Magazine* [May 18, 2015]. http://time.com/3882745/isis-ramadi-anbar/#38
82745/isis-ramadi-anbar [accessed May 19, 2015].

Crooke, Alastair, "The ISIS' 'Management of Savagery' in Iraq," *The World Post* [June 30, 2014, updated August 30, 2014]. http://www.huffingtonpost.com/alastair
-crooke/iraq-isis-alqaeda_b_5542575.html [accessed April 17, 2015].

Crowley, Michael, "Who Lost Iraq? Did George W. Bush Create the Islamic State? Did Barack Obama? We Asked the Insiders to Tell Us Who's to Blame." *Politico Magazine* [July/August 2015]. http://www.politico.com/magazine/story/2015/06
/iraq-roundtable-george-w-bush-barack-obama-119221#.VZFRl_lVhHx [accessed June 30, 2015].

Cullison, Allan, "Jihadi Trials: The Circuitous Routes Foreigners Take to Syria and Iraq," *The Wall Street Journal* [2015]. http://graphics.wsj.com/jihadi-trails [accessed August 27, 2015].

Dauber, Cori E., "ISIS and the Family Man," *Small Wars Journal* [July 1, 2015]. http://smallwarsjournal.com/jrnl/art/isis-and-the-family-man [accessed November 6, 2015].

DeRosa, John, "Revising the Battle of the Narrative," *Small Wars Journal* [July 16, 2015]. http://smallwarsjournal.com/jrnl/art/revising-the-battle-of-the-narrative [accessed July 17, 2015].

Dettmer, Jamie, and Jacob Siegel, "What Saddam Gave ISIS," *The Daily Beast* [April 21, 2015]. http://www.thedailybeast.com/articles/2015/04/21/what-saddam-gave
-isis.html [accessed April 25, 2015].

DeYoung, Karen, "How the Obama White House Runs Foreign Policy," *The Washing-ton Post* [August 4, 2015]. https://www.washingtonpost.com/world/national-security

/how-the-obama-white-house-runs-foreign-policy/2015/08/04/2befb960-2fd7
-11e5-8353-1215475949f4_story.html?hpid=z1 [accessed August 6, 2015].

Dougherty, Jill, "How the Media Became One of Putin's Most Powerful Weapons," *The Atlantic* [April 21, 2015]. http://www.theatlantic.com/international/archive/2015 /04/how-the-media-became-putins-most-powerful-weapon/391062/?google _editors_picks=true [accessed April 25, 2015].

Dougherty, Michael Brendan, "The GOP Presidential Field's Dangerous Fantasy on Iraq and Syria," *The Week* [August 17, 2015]. http://theweek.com/articles/571880 /gop-presidential-fields-dangerous-fantasy-iraq-syria [August 18, 2015].

The Economist, "The Terrorists' Vicious Message Is Surprisingly Hard to Rebut," *The Economist* [August 15, 2015]. http://www.economist.com/news/middle-east-and -africa/21660989-terrorists-vicious-message-surprisingly-hard-rebut-propaganda -war?fsrc=scn%2Ftw%2Fte%2Fpe%2Fed%2FThePropagandaWar [accessed August 16, 2015].

Eisenstadt, Michael, "The War against ISIL: In Search of a Viable Strategy," *War on the Rocks* [June 15, 2015]. http://warontherocks.com/2015/06/the-war-against-isil -in-search-of-a-viable-strategy/?singlepage=1 [accessed June 22, 2015].

Eisler, David F., "Beyond Finding the Enemy: Embracing Sociocultural Intelligence in Stability Operations," *Small Wars Journal* [July 14, 2015]. http://smallwarsjournal .com/jrnl/art/beyond-finding-the-enemy-embracing-sociocultural-intelligence-in -stability-operations [accessed July 16, 2015].

Erelle, Anna, "Skyping with the Enemy: I Went Undercover as a Jihadi Girlfriend," *The Guardian* [May 26, 2015]. http://www.theguardian.com/world/2015/may/26 /french-journalist-poses-muslim-convert-isis-anna-erelle [accessed June 3, 2015].

Friedman, Uri, "There's Far More to the Saudi-Iran Feud Than Sunnis-Vs.-Shia," *Defense One* [January 7, 2016]. http://www.defenseone.com/ideas/2016/01/theres -far-more-saudi-iran-feud-sunnis-vs-shia/124944/?oref=d-river [accessed January 8, 2016].

Gartenstein-Ross, Daveed, and Nathaniel Barr, "Fixing How We Fight the Islamic State's Narrative," *War on the Rocks* [January 4, 2016]. http://warontherocks.com /2016/01/fixing-how-we-fight-the-islamic-states-narrative [accessed January 4, 2016].

Gebauer, Matthias, and Holger Stark, "Ex-US Intelligence Chief on Islamic State's Rise: 'We Were Too Dumb,'" *Spiegel Online International* [November 29, 2015]. http://www.spiegel.de/international/world/former-us-intelligence-chief-discusses -development-of-is-a-1065131.html [accessed January 1, 2016].

Ghattas, Kim, "Departing Washington, Next Stop: Reality," Foreign Policy [July 2, 2015]. http://foreignpolicy.com/2015/07/02/departing-washington-next-stop-reality -beirut-syria/?utm_source=Sailthru&utm_medium=email&utm_term =%2AEditors%20Picks&utm_campaign=2015_EditorsPicks_Promo_Russia _Direct_Jun29%20through%207%2F3%2072SO&wp_login_redirect=0 [accessed July 4, 2015].

Ghosh, Bobby, "Yemen's War Is Nearly Lost in the Din of Surrounding Conflicts," *Defense One* [January 5, 2016]. http://www.defenseone.com/threats/2016/01/yemens -war-nearly-lost-din-surrounding-conflicts/124872 [accessed January 6, 2016].

Gould, Joe, "US-ISIS Rumors Hard to Counter, General Says," *Defense News* [May 21, 2015]. http://www.defensenews.com/story/defense/show-daily/sofic/2015/05/19/us -isis-rumors-hard-to-counter-general-says/27616311 [accessed May 21, 2015].

Gould, John, "Was Syrian Train-and-Equip Effort Always a 'Mission Impossible'?," *Defense News* [September 21, 2015]. http://www.defensenews.com/story/defense /policy-budget/warfare/2015/09/21/syrian-train-equip-program-mission -impossible-start/72376560 [accessed September 22, 2015].

Habeck, Mary R., "Jihadist Strategies in the War on Terrorism," *Heritage Lectures: Published by the Heritage Foundation*, no. 855 [November 8, 2015]. http://www .heritage.org/research/lecture/jihadist-strategies-in-the-war-on-terrorism [accessed March 6, 2016].

Hamid, Shadi, "Sisi's Regime is a Gift to the Islamic State," *Brookings* [August 7, 2015]. http://www.brookings.edu/blogs/markaz/posts/2015/08/07-sisi-gift-to-islamic -state-hamid?utm_source=Sailthru&utm_medium=email&utm_term =%2AMideast%20Brief&utm_campaign=New%20Campaign [accessed August 11, 2015].

Hamid, Shadi, "Is There a Method to ISIS's Madness?," *The Atlantic* [November 23, 2015]. http://www.theatlantic.com/international/archive/2015/11/isis-rational-actor -paris-attacks/417312 [accessed November 24, 2015].

Harrison, Ross, "Newsflash: Time Is Running Out to Defeat ISIS," *The National Interest* [August 21, 2015]. http://nationalinterest.org/feature/newsflash-time-running -out-defeat-isis-13650 [accessed August 2015].

Hay, John, "The Deciders: The Disastrous Iraq Policies That Led to ISIS Were Not President Bush's," *The American Conservative.com* [October 27, 2015]. http:// TheAmericanConservative.com [accessed October 29, 2015].

Hegghammerdec, Thomas, "The Soft Power of Militant Jihad," *New York Times* [December 18, 2015]. http://www.nytimes.com/2015/12/20/opinion/sunday/militant -jihads-softer-side.html?_r=0 [accessed December 21, 2015].

Heller, Sam, "Ahrar al-Sham's Revisionist Jihadism," *War on the Rocks* [September 30, 2015]. http://warontherocks.com/2015/09/ahrar-al-shams-revisionist-jihadism/?utm _source=Sailthru&utm_medium=email&utm_campaign=New%20Campaign &utm_term=%2AMideast%20Brief [accessed October 6, 2015].

Hendawi, Hamza, "In Europe, Iraqis and Syrians Escape Islamists' Harsh Rule," *Associated Press* [September 20, 2015]. http://bigstory.ap.org/urn:publicid:ap.org:a262 3767bfb943bc98d65eb97427d791 [accessed September 21, 2015].

Hendawi, Hamza, and Qasim Abdul-Zahra, "IS Top Command Dominated by Ex-Officers in Saddam's Army," *Associated Press* [August 8, 2015]. http://bigstory.ap

.org/urn:publicid:ap.org:75a48c16404c4418938b5f5170140dd4 [accessed August 10, 2015].

Hersh, Seymour M., "The Killing of Osama Bin Laden," *London Review of Books* 37, no.10 [May 21, 2015]. http://www.lrb.co.uk/v37/n10/seymour-m-hersh/the-killing -of-osama-bin-laden [accessed May 21, 2015].

Hoffman, Bruce, "ISIL Is Winning," *Politico* [September 10, 2015]. http://www.politico .com/magazine/story/2015/09/isil-is-winning-213136 [accessed September 14, 2015].

Hubbard, Ben, "In Syria, Potential Ally's Islamist Ties Challenge U.S.," *The New York Times* [August 25, 2015]. http://www.nytimes.com/2015/08/26/world/middleeast /ahrar-al-sham-rebel-force-in-syrias-gray-zone-poses-challenge-to-us.html [accessed August 26, 2015].

Hussain, Ghaffar, "A Brief History of Islamism," *Quilliam* [January 2010]. http://www .quilliamfoundation.org/wp/wp-content/uploads/publications/free/brief-history -of-islamism.pdf [accessed November 6, 2015].

Ignatius, David, "How ISIS Spread in the Middle East," *The Atlantic* [November 1, 2015]. http://www.defenseone.com/ideas/2015/11/how-isis-spread-middle-east /123312 [accessed November 2, 2015].

Jenkins, Simon, "Bombing Is Immoral, Stupid and Never Wins Wars. Syria Is the Latest Victim," *The Guardian* [September 18, 2015]. http://www.theguardian.com /commentisfree/2015/sep/18/bombing-immoral-stupid-syria-victim-deaths-drones [accessed September 19, 2015].

Johnson, David E., "Fighting the 'Islamic State': The Case for U.S. Ground Forces," *Parameters* 45 [April 22, 2015]. https://www.strategicstudiesinstitute.army.mil/pubs /parameters/Issues/Spring_2015/4_Special-Commentary_Johnson.pdf [accessed March 6, 2016].

Kaplan, Jeffrey, and Christopher P. Costa, "The Islamic State and the New Tribalism," *Terrorism and Political Violence*, no. 27 [November 2015], pp. 926–969.

Khaddour, Kheder. *The Assad Regime's Hold on the Syrian State*. Beirut, Lebanon: The Carnegie Middle East Center, 2015.

Kilcullen, David, "We're Losing the War," *The National Interest* [September 15, 2015]. http://nationalinterest.org/blog/the-buzz/we%E2%80%99re-losing-the-war -against-isis-iraq-13848 [accessed September 16, 2015].

Kirkpatrick, David D., Ben Hubbard, and Eric Schmittnov, "ISIS' Grip on Libyan City Gives It a Fallback Option," *New York Times* [November 28, 2015]. http://www .nytimes.com/2015/11/29/world/middleeast/isis-grip-on-libyan-city-gives-it-a -fallback-option.html?_r=0 [accessed December 1, 2015].

Koppell, Carla, "To Fight Extremism, the World Needs to Learn How to Talk to Women," *Foreign Policy* [August 12, 2015]. http://foreignpolicy.com/2015/08/12/to

-fight-extremism-the-world-needs-to-learn-how-to-talk-to-women-boko-haram -isis [accessed August 14, 2015].

Lister, Charles, "Syrian Islamists Reach Out to the U.S., but Serious Issues Remain," *Brookings* [July 14, 2015]. http://www.brookings.edu/blogs/markaz/posts/2015/07 /14-syrian-islamists-us-issues-lister [November 6, 2015].

Maan, Ajit, "ISIS Is Not a Terrorist Organization," *Small Wars Journal* [December 29, 2015]. http://smallwarsjournal.com/jrnl/art/isis-is-not-a-terrorist-organization [accessed December 30, 2015].

Matisek, Jahara, "Drones and Airpower: A Lack of Deterrence in Unconventional Warfare?," *Small Wars Journal* [September 2, 2015]. http://smallwarsjournal.com/jrnl /art/drones-and-airpower-a-lack-of-deterrence-in-unconventional-warfare [accessed September 4, 2015].

Matisek, Jahara, "Let's Make ISIS a State," *Cicero Magazine* [September 30, 2015]. http://ciceromagazine.com/opinion/lets-make-isis-a-state [accessed September 30, 2015].

McCants, William, "The Believer: How an Introvert with a Passion for Religion and Soccer Became Abu Bakr Al-Baghdadi Leader of the Islamic State," *Brookings* [September 1, 2015]. http://www.brookings.edu/research/essays/2015/thebeliever ?utm_source=Sailthru&utm_medium=email&utm_campaign=New%20Cam paign&utm_term=%2AMideast%20Brief [accessed September 4, 2015].

McLeary, Paul, "Why Are the Islamic State's Commanders So Much Better Than the Iraqi Army?," *Foreign Policy* [May 26, 2015]. http://foreignpolicy.com/2015/05/26 /why-are-the-islamic-states-commanders-so-much-better-than-the-iraqi-army [May 27, 2015].

Miller, Greg, "U.S. Launches Secret Drone Campaign to Hunt Islamic State Leaders in Syria," *The Washington Post* [September 1, 2015]. https://www.washingtonpost .com/world/national-security/us-launches-secret-drone-campaign-to-hunt-islamic -state-leaders-in-syria/2015/09/01/723b3e04-5033-11e5-933e-7d06c647a395 _story.html [accessed September 2, 2015].

Miller, Greg, and Scott Higham, "In a Propaganda War against the ISIS, the U.S. Tried to Play by the Enemy's Rules," *The Washington Post* [May 8, 2015]. https://www .washingtonpost.com/world/national-security/in-a-propaganda-war-us-tried-to -play-by-the-enemys-rules/2015/05/08/6eb6b732-e52f-11e4-81ea-0649268f729e _story.html [accessed May 12, 2015].

Miller, Greg, and Souad Mekhennet, "Inside the Surreal World of the Islamic State's Propaganda Machine," *Washington Post* [November 20, 2015]. https://www.washing tonpost.com/world/national-security/inside-the-islamic-states-propaganda -machine/2015/11/20/051e997a-8ce6-11e5-acff-673ae92ddd2b_story.html?hpid =hp_hp-top-table-high_isisprop-115pm%3Ahomepage%2Fstory [accessed November 23, 2015].

Moaveni, Azadeh, "ISIS Women and Enforcers in Syria Recount Collaboration, Anguish and Escape," *New York Times* [November 21, 2015]. http://www.nytimes

.com/2015/11/22/world/middleeast/isis-wives-and-enforcers-in-syria-recount
-collaboration-anguish-and-escape.html?_r=0 [accessed November 23, 2015].

Moghul, Haroon, "The Secret to Defeating the ISIS 'Caliphate' Might Just Be in Islam
Itself," *Defense One* [November 11, 2015]. http://www.defenseone.com/ideas/2015
/11/secret-defeating-isis-caliphate-might-just-be-islam-itself/123608 [accessed
November 13, 2015].

Morris, Loveday, "Mosul Commander Was on Vacation Despite Warnings of Attack,
Report Says," *The Washington Post* [August 27, 2015]. https://www.washingtonpost
.com/world/middle_east/mosul-commander-was-on-vacation-despite-warnings
-of-attack-report-says/2015/08/27/c6e39a46-4a9d-11e5-9f53-d1e3ddfd0cda_story
.html [accessed August 31, 2015].

Naji, Abu Bakr. *The Management of Savagery: The Most Critical Stage through Which
the Umma Will Pass.* Cambridge, MA: John M. Olin Institute for Strategic Studies,
May 23, 2006.

Nance, Malcom W., "ISIS Forces That Now Control Ramadi Are Ex-Baathist Saddam
Loyalists," *The Intercept* [June 3, 2015]. https://theintercept.com/2015/06/03/isis
-forces-exbaathist-saddam-loyalists/?utm_source=Sailthru&utm_medium=email
&utm_term=%2AMideast%20Brief&utm_campaign=New%20Campaign [accessed
June 5, 2015].

Natali, Denise, "Islamic State Infiltrates Iraqi Kurdistan," *Al-Monitor* [June 4, 2015].
http://www.al-monitor.com/pulse/originals/2015/06/is-infiltration-iraqi-kurdistan
.html# [accessed June 6, 2015].

Nawaz, Maajid, and Sam Harris, "We Need to Talk about Islam's Jihadism Problem,"
The Daily Beast [September 15, 2015]. http://www.thedailybeast.com/articles/2015
/09/15/we-need-to-talk-about-islam-s-jihad-problem.html [accessed September 15,
2015].

Nerguizian, Aram. *The Military Balance in a Shattered Levant: Conventional Forces,
Asymmetric Warfare & the Struggle for Syria.* Washington, DC: Center for Strategic & International Studies, 2015.

Nomani, Asra Q., "How the Saudis Churn Out 'Jihad Inc.,' " *The Daily Beast* [January
5, 2016]. http://www.thedailybeast.com/articles/2016/01/05/how-the-saudis-churn
-out-jihad-inc.html [January 5, 2016].

Norland, Rod, "Iraq Forces, Pushing ISIS Out of Tikrit, Give Few Thanks for U.S.
Air Strikes." *The New York Times* [April 2, 2015]. http://www.nytimes.com/2015
/04/03/world/middleeast/isis-forces-pushed-out-of-tikrit.html?smid=pl-share&_r
=1 [accessed April 2, 2015].

Olidort, Jacob, "The Right Question about the Islamic State's Ideology," *War on the
Rocks* [December 24, 2015]. http://warontherocks.com/2015/12/the-right-question
-about-the-islamic-states-ideology [accessed January 5, 2016].

Ottaway, David B., "Saudi Arabia's 'Terrorist' Allies in Yemen," *Wilson Center* [August
3, 2015]. https://www.wilsoncenter.org/publication/saudi-arabias-terrorist-allies
-yemen [November 6, 2015].

Owen, John M., IV, "From Calvin to the Caliphate: What Europe's Wars of Religion Tell Us about the Modern Middle East." *Foreign Affairs* (May/June 2015 issue). https://www.foreignaffairs.com/articles/western-europe/2015-04-20/calvin-caliphate [November 6, 2015].

Parker, Ned, "Power Failure in Iraq as Militias Outgun State," *Reuters* [October 21, 2015]. http://www.reuters.com/investigates/special-report/iraq-abadi/?utm_source =twitter [accessed October 22, 2015].

Patin, Nathan. *The Other Foreign Fighters: An Open-Source Investigation into American Volunteers Fighting the Islamic State in Iraq and Syria.* Leicester, United Kingdom: Bellingcat, 2015.

Peritz, Aki, "What Whac-a-Mole Can Teach Us about How to Fight Terrorism," *Foreign Policy* [August 12, 2015]. http://foreignpolicy.com/2015/08/12/what-whac-a -mole-can-teach-us-about-how-to-fight-terrorism [accessed August 14, 2015].

Prothero, Mitchell, "U.S. Training Helped Mold Top Islamic State Military Commander," *McClatchy DC* [September 15, 2015]. http://www.mcclatchydc.com/news /nation-world/world/middle-east/article35322882.html [accessed September 16, 2015].

Quantum, "The White Papers: Understanding Jihadists in Their Own Words," Volume 2, *Quantum* [March 2015]. https://now.mmedia.me/Pages/ImageStreamer/param /DocId__3f9f8a57-06ab-4909-afbc-2db99976bafe/white-paper-2—.pdf [accessed March 6, 2016].

Raghavan, Sudarsan, "One in Five Syrians Say Islamic State Is a Good Thing, Poll Says," *The Washington Post* [September 15, 2015]. https://www.washingtonpost .com/news/worldviews/wp/2015/09/15/one-in-five-syrians-say-islamic-state-is-a -good-thing-poll-says [accessed September 16, 2015].

Rawnsley, Adam, "Meet the Americans Flocking to Iraq and Syria to Fight the Islamic State," *Foreign Policy* [August 26, 2015]. http://foreignpolicy.com/2015/08/26/meet -the-americans-flocking-to-iraq-and-syria-to-fight-the-islamic-state [accessed August 27, 2015].

Reuter, Christoph, "The Terror Strategist: Secret Files Reveal the Structure of Islamic State," *Spiegel Online International* [April 18, 2015]. http://www.spiegel.de /international/world/islamic-state-files-show-structure-of-islamist-terror-group-a -1029274.html [accessed March 6, 2016].

Roggio, Bill, and Caleb Weiss, "Iraqi Army, Shiite Militias Report Success in Baiji," *The Long War Journal* [October 19, 2015]. http://www.longwarjournal.org/archives /2015/10/iraqi-army-shiite-militias-report-success-in-baiji.php [accessed October 20, 2015].

Rohan, Brian, "In Egypt, Disaffected Youth Increasingly Drawn to Extremism," *Yahoo News* [August 4, 2015]. http://news.yahoo.com/egypts-disaffected-youth-increasingly -calling-violence-055924571.html [accessed August 5, 2015].

Rosenfeld, Jesse, "Hezbollah Fighters Are Fed Up with Fighting Syria's War," *The Daily Beast* [December 30, 2015]. http://www.thedailybeast.com/articles/2015/12/30/hezbollah-fighters-are-fed-up-with-fighting-syria-s-war.html [accessed December 30, 2015].

Ross, Alice, "Hundreds of Civilians Killed in US-Led Air Strikes on ISIS Targets—Report," *The Guardian* [August 3, 2015]. http://www.theguardian.com/world/2015/aug/03/us-led-air-strikes-on-isis-targets-killed-more-than-450-civilians-report?utm_source=Sailthru&utm_medium=email&utm_term=%2AMorning%20Brief&utm_campaign=New%20Campaign [accessed August 5, 2015].

Roston, Aram, "Meet the Obscure Company behind America's Syria Fiasco," *Buzz Feed News* [September 17, 2015]. http://www.buzzfeed.com/aramroston/the-secret-arms-deal-behind-americas-syria-fiasco#.lcAR5DaDdp [accessed September 19, 2015].

Runkle, Benjamin, "The Long Fuse of Obama's Anti-ISIS Strategy," *Foreign Policy* [May 18, 2015]. http://foreignpolicy.com/2015/05/18/the-long-fuse-of-obamas-anti-isis-strategy [accessed May 19, 2015].

Ryan, Missy, "Expanding US Role in Iraq Strains Awkward Alliance with Iran," *The Washington Post* [August 8, 2015]. https://www.washingtonpost.com/world/national-security/expanding-us-role-in-iraq-strains-awkward-alliance-with-iran/2015/08/08/15cbfbe6-39da-11e5-b3ac-8a79bc44e5e2_story.html [accessed August 10, 2015].

Salama, Vivian, and Qassim Abdul-Zahra, "Iraqi Militias Train Young Teens to Face the Threat of IS," *Associated Press* [July 28, 2015]. http://bigstory.ap.org/article/41c185b1794c4021b747d3993dfe58c4/summer-camp-iraqi-shiite-boys-training-fight [accessed July 28, 2015].

Samaan, Maher, and Anne Barnard, "For Those Who Remain in Syria, Daily Life Is a Nightmare," *The New York Times* [September 15, 2015]. http://www.nytimes.com/2015/09/16/world/middleeast/for-those-who-remain-in-syria-daily-life-is-a-nightmare.html?ref=middleeast [accessed September 15, 2015].

Schleifer, Abdallah, ed., "The Muslim 500: The World's 500 Most Influential Muslims, 2016," The Royal Islamic Strategic Studies Centre, Amman Jordan [October 1, 2015]. http://themuslim500.com/downloads/151001-TheMuslim500-2016v009(23%7C48)-Web-Low.pdf [accessed January 5, 2016].

Shear, Michael D., "Biden Sites Progress in Iraq's War with ISIS," *The New York Times* [April 9, 2015]. http://www.nytimes.com/2015/04/10/world/middleeast/biden-cites-progress-in-iraqs-war-with-isis.html [November 6, 2015].

Shinkman, Paul D., "Kobani's Lesson for Ramadi: Victory against ISIS Won't End Bloodshed," *US News* [May 27, 2015]. http://www.usnews.com/news/articles/2015/05/27/kobanis-lesson-for-ramadi-victory-against-isis-wont-end-bloodshed [accessed March 6, 2016].

Shinkman, Paul D., "Poll: Syrians, Iraqis Believe U.S. Created ISIS, Don't Support War," *US News* [December 18, 2015]. http://www.usnews.com/news/articles/2015

-12-18/poll-majority-of-syrians-iraqis-dont-support-obamas-anti-isis-war-believe -us-created-extremists [accessed December 21, 2015].

Shroder, Landon, "What If the Islamic State Won?," *Vice News* [September 16, 2015]. https://news.vice.com/article/what-if-the-islamic-state-won [accessed September 19, 2015].

Sky, Emma, "How Obama Abandoned Iraq: Why the Rise of ISIS and the Fall of Iraq Weren't Inevitable," *Slate* [accessed April 17, 2015]. http://www.slate.com/articles /news_and_politics/foreigners/2015/04/emma_sky_on_america_s_failure_in _iraq_the_rise_of_isis_and_the_fall_of_iraq.single.html [April 21, 2015].

Sky, Emma, "The Carcass of a City ISIS Left Behind," *The Daily Beast* [January 12, 2016]. http://www.thedailybeast.com/articles/2016/01/12/the-carcass-of-a-city-isis -left-behind.html [accessed January 12, 2016].

Sly, Liz, "Iraqis Think the U.S. Is in Cahoots with the Islamic State, and It Is Hurting the War," *Washington Post* [December 1, 2015]. https://www.washingtonpost.com /world/middle_east/iraqis-think-the-us-is-in-cahoots-with-isis-and-it-is-hurting -the-war/2015/12/01/d00968ec-9243-11e5-befa-99ceebcbb272_story.html [accessed December 2, 2015].

Smyth, Phillip, "Iran's Losing Major Operatives in Syria," *The Daily Beast* [October 14, 2015]. http://www.thedailybeast.com/articles/2015/10/14/iran-s-losing-major -operatives-in-syria.html [accessed October 14, 2015].

Steed, Brian L., "The 2008 Battle of Sadr City: Lessons and Application," March 2015.

Steed, Brian L., "Changing the Conversation: Conceptualizing the Fight against Non- State and Post-State Actors," April 2015. http://www.narrativespace.net/support -files/changing_the_conversation.pdf [accessed March 6, 2016].

Tarabay, Jamie, "To Its Citizens, ISIS Shows a Softer Side: A Vocative Analysis of the Group's Propaganda Finds It Wants to Be Loved as well as Feared in Its Own Ter- ritory," *Vocative* [March 20, 2015]. http://www.vocativ.com/world/isis-2/to-its -citizens-isis-also-shows-a-softer-side [accessed September 14, 2015].

Tucker, Patrick, "US Helicopter Shot at by Anti-ISIS Forces; Commander Blames Iran," *Defense One* [May 19, 2015]. http://www.defenseone.com/threats/2015/05 /us-helicopter-shot-anti-isis-forcescommander-blames-iran/113242 [accessed May 21, 2015].

Tucker, Patrick, "Why Do People Join ISIS? Here's What They Say When You Ask Them," *Defense One* [December 8, 2015]. http://www.defenseone.com/threats/2015 /12/why-do-people-join-isis-heres-what-they-say-when-you-ask-them/124295 /?oref=d-mostread [accessed December 10, 2015].

Youssef, Nancy A., and Shane Harris, "How ISIS Actually Lost Ramadi," *The Daily Beast* [December 30, 2015]. http://www.thedailybeast.com/articles/2015/12/30/how -isis-actually-lost-ramadi.html [accessed December 30, 2015].

Watts, Clint, "What Paris Taught Us about the Islamic State," *War on the Rocks* [November 16, 2015]. http://warontherocks.com/2015/11/what-paris-taught-us-about -the-islamic-state [accessed November 16, 2015].

Weiss, Michael, "Confessions of an ISIS Spy: Part One: An Appointment in Istanbul," *The Daily Beast* [November 15, 2015]. http://www.thedailybeast.com/articles/2015 /11/15/confessions-of-an-isis-spy.html [accessed November 16, 2015].

Weiss, Michael, "Confessions of an ISIS Spy: Part Two: How ISIS Picks Its Suicide Bombers," *The Daily Beast* [November 16, 2015]. http://www.thedailybeast.com /articles/2015/11/16/how-isis-picks-its-suicide-bombers.html?via=twitter_page [accessed November 17, 2015].

Weiss, Michael, "Confessions of an ISIS Spy: Part Three: Ministries of Fear," *The Daily Beast* [November 17, 2015]. http://www.thedailybeast.com/articles/2015/11 /17/inside-isis-torture-brigades.html [accessed November 22, 2015].

Weiss, Michael, "Confessions of an ISIS Spy: Part Four: Escaping the Islamic State," *The Daily Beast* [November 18, 2015]. http://www.thedailybeast.com/articles/2015 /11/18/how-i-escaped-from-isis.html [accessed November 22, 2015].

Wilgenburg, Wladimir van, "No Guns, No Money, Ready to Hit ISIS HQ," *The Daily Beast* [October 20, 2015]. http://www.thedailybeast.com/articles/2015/10/20/no -guns-no-money-ready-to-hit-isis-hq.html?via=mobile&source=twitter [accessed October 21, 2015].

Williams, Michael J., "ISIS as a Strategic Actor: Strategy and Counter-Strategy," *The Mackenzie Institute* [April 15, 2015]. http://www.mackenzieinstitute.com/isis -strategic-actor-strategy-counter-strategy [accessed November 6, 2015].

Wood, Graeme, "What ISIS Really Wants," *AP/The Atlantic* [March 2015]. http://www .theatlantic.com/features/archive/2015/02/what-isis-really-wants/384980/?utm _source=Sailthru&utm_medium=email&utm_term=%2AMideast%20Brief&utm _campaign=2014_The%20Middle%20East%20Daily [accessed February 18, 2015].

Wright, Lawrence, "The Master Plan: For the New Theorists of Jihad, Al Qaeda Is Just the Beginning," *The New Yorker* [September 11, 2006]. http://www.newyorker .com/magazine/2006/09/11/the-master-plan [accessed November 6, 2015].

Zimmerman, Rebecca, "Training Foreign Military Forces: Quality vs. Quantity," *War on the Rocks* [July 15, 2015]. http://warontherocks.com/2015/07/training-foreign -military-forces-quality-vs-quantity/?singlepage=1 [accessed July 16, 2015].

Dabiq Magazine

"The Return of the Khalifah," Issue 1 (July 5, 2014).

"The Flood," Issue 2 (July 27, 2014).

"A Call to Hijrah," Issue 3 (September 10, 2014).

"The Failed Crusade," Issue 4 (October 11, 2014).

"Remaining and Expanding," Issue 5 (November 21, 2014).

"Al Qa'idah of Waziristan: A Testimony from Within," Issue 6 (December 29, 2014).

"From Hypocrisy to Apostasy: The Extinction of the Grayzone," Issue 7 (February 12, 2015).

"Shari'ah Alone Will Rule Africa," Issue 8 (March 30, 2015).

"They Plot and Allah Plots," Issue 9 (May 21, 2015).

"The Law of Allah or the Laws of Men," Issue 10 (July 13, 2015).

"From the Battles of Al-Ahzāb to the War of Coalitions," Issue 11 (August 9, 2015).

"Just Terror," Issue 12 (November 18, 2015).

"The Rafidah: From Ibn Saba' to the Dajjal," Issue 13 (January 19, 2016).

"The Murtadd Brotherhood," Issue 14 (April 13, 2016).

Index

About the Author

BRIAN L. STEED is currently an assistant professor of military history at the U.S. Army Command and General Staff College and a U.S. Army Middle East Foreign Area Officer. He served eight-and-a-half consecutive years in the Middle East including assignments in the Levant, Mesopotamia, and the Arabian Peninsula. He served briefly in Iraq in 2005, a full year in 2010–2011, and again in December 2014–February 2015. He was a Jordanian Army Officer as part of the Military Personnel Exchange Program for two-and-a-half years, giving him an immersed perspective in Arab culture, and a liaison to the Israel Defense Forces, providing another immersed experience from a different regional perspective. He has written numerous books on military theory and military history and cultural awareness. His most recent books include *Voices of the Iraq War: Contemporary Accounts of Daily Life* and *Bees and Spiders: Applied Cultural Awareness and the Art of Cross-Cultural Influence*. He has given dozens of presentations on ISIS, the Middle East, and Arab culture to groups ranging from high school students to senior military and government leaders.